NO NIGERIAN WILL MAKE HEAVEN?

- TALES FROM AN ASPIRING FAILED NATION-STATE.

By

Peter Aghogho Omuvwie

NO NIGERIAN WILL MAKE HEAVEN?

Author: Peter Aghogho Omuvwie

Copyright © 2024 Peter Aghogho Omuvwie

The right of Peter Aghogho Omuvwie to be identified as author of this work has been asserted by the author in accordance with section 77 and 78 of the Copyright, Designs and Patents Act 1988.

ISBN 978-1-83538-357-5 (Paperback)
978-1-83538-358-2 (E-Book)

Cover design by Dede Israel for Ganowa Books

Illustrations done by Azeez Ozi-Sanni and Mike Asukwo

Book Layout by:
White Magic Studios
www.whitemagicstudios.co.uk

Published by:
Maple Publishers
Fairbourne Drive, Atterbury,
Milton Keynes,
MK10 9RG, UK
www.maplepublishers.com

A CIP catalogue record for this title is available from the British Library.

All rights reserved. No part of this book may be reproduced or translated by any form or by any means, electronic or mechanical, including photocopying, recording or by any information storage and retrieval system without written permission from the author.

This book is a memoir. It reflects the author's recollections of experiences over time. Some names and characteristics have been changed, some events have been compressed, and some dialogues have been recreated, and the Publisher hereby disclaims any responsibility for them.

– PETER AGHOGHO UNUAKPOVWOTOWHUU 'SPARKS' OMUVWIE –

For God and country...

CONTENTS

ACKNOWLEDGEMENTS 7
INCEPTION 10
INTRODUCTION 17
NIGERIA: NAMING 20
NIGERIA: SETTING 25
NIGERIA: THROUGH TIME 31
NIGERIA: BRIDGE 37
NIGERIA: THE BUILD UP 42
HOLD COURT IN THE STREETS!!! 49
THEORIES! THEORIES!! THEORIES!!! 52
PART 1: THE NIGERIAN SOCIETY AS A HOUSE FOR THE MASSES 195
INFRASTRUCTURE 197
INFRASTRUCTURE: TRANSPORTATION. 205
INFRASTRUCTURE: ELECTRICITY (POWER) 215
DRUG ADDICTS AND THEIR INSATIABLE LITTLE BEASTS. 218
INFRASTRUCTURE: COMMUNICATION 230
AGRICULTURE 237
EDUCATION 244
FORMAL EDUCATION: 248
INFORMAL EDUCATION: 253
FINAL THOUGHTS ON EDUCATION IN NIGERIA: 257
HEALTHCARE 260
SPORTS 273
THE ARTS 282

JOURNALISM AND THE NIGERIAN MEDIA 287
NATURAL RESOURCES 295
NIGERIAN ECONOMY 301
WRAP UP ON PART 1 - THE MASSES 310
PART 2: THE POLITICAL RULING CLASS. 313
POLITICAL RULING CLASS: THE RISE AND RISE OF THE NIGERIAN MAFIA. 315
POLITICAL LEADERSHIP: THE GOVERNMENTAL MEMBERS 323
THE EXECUTIVE 327
THE LEGISLATURE: WHISPERS IN THE STREETS ABOUT THE BIG HALLS IN ABUJA. 333
THE JUDICIARY: CRIMINAL LAW AND THE JUSTICE SYSTEM IN NIGERIA. 340
LAW ENFORCEMENT AND THE NIGERIAN PRISON SYSTEM. 351
JUNGLE JUSTICE IN NIGERIA 360
CONCLUSION ON THE GOVERNMENTAL MEMBERS OF THE POLITICAL RULING CLASS 363
THE NIGERIAN CIVIL SERVICE 367
THE ARMED FORCES 376
TOUTS AS NON-STATE ACTORS. 384
THE DYNAMICS OF NIGERIAN POLITICS: GAME OF LIES! 388
INEC AND THE VALUE OF A GOOD SELECTION PROCESS 393
ECONOMIC AND FINANCIAL CRIMES COMMISSION AND INSECTICIDES. 397
NATIONAL YOUTH SERVICE CORP (NYSC) 402
TITLES vs. VALUE 407
REPUTATION AND FOREIGN RELATIONS 410
PART 3: CLOSING SUMMARY: MAD COUNTRY 413
VERDICT 422
ALTAR CALL 429

ACKNOWLEDGEMENTS

First of all I'd like to specially thank my co-author, the Holy Spirit, for inspiration, guidance and direction throughout this project. I'd just like to say Sir, it was quite a ride for me. I dedicate this book to the loves of my life, my triplet babies JJ, PJ and Zee-baby, daddy loves you all. To my father Peter Odawaren, who's no longer with us; you had such high standards as a man that for a large part of my life I always wondered if I'd ever be able to measure up and all I ever wanted was for you to look at me one day not just as your little boy but as a man that you actually approve of, well I hope you're giving me that look from the other side, keep resting sir. I'd like to thank my mum, Felicia Akpomiemie, there are not even enough words in the English language or thousands of the other languages spoken across the globe so I just say 'thanks ma'. I'd like to thank my elder brother Atare 'Money' who, though just two years older than me became my father, thank you for your support, love and care all through my years in the desert. I appreciate you dear brother. I extend my thanks to my siblings Ukay, Nita and Sammy who despite many setbacks have been my biggest cheerleaders over the years, I love you guys and you know it. To the mother of my kids, Naomi Sethusha, thanks for being a great mother to our children, thank you for all you did and all you do.

Spirituality plays a big part in my life and I am a product of many spiritual guides and teachers over the years of my life's journey. Special recognition and thanks to spiritual fathers Archbishop Godday Iboyi, Rev. Mike Omovudu and my mother, Prophetess Felicia who form my core spiritual support system which I do not take for granted. I'd also like to thank friends who became brothers; Ewoma Vese, who was the sounding board for all my earliest theories for this book and took it upon himself to source whatever materials he could lay his hands on in our very limited Nigerian space at the time to excite my imagination and keep me informed, I thank Nelson Eban for holding my hand and propping me up through my last years in the desert. If I did not make it out of the desert I would not be able to live out my dreams and fulfill my destiny as I'm doing today, so thank you.

I've had many teachers over the years both informal and formal from my primary school, through secondary and the university days, men and women who have all in one way or the other played their part to shape my mind into what it has become today, I thank you all from the bottom of my heart, I love you all and I wish you well. Time is a lackadaisical operator that cares for no one nor stops for anyone, she just keeps going and we're all getting older. We lost so many over the years, too many to list but as that great black poet, 50 Cent, puts it *'joy wouldn't feel so special if it wasn't for pain'*, so keep resting, you're all not forgotten.

I'd like to pay my respects to the late cartoonist, Azeez Ozi-Sanni, who as a cartoonist in one of the biggest national dailies was able to create the time to draw cartoons for a jobless, idealistic writer and dreamer who no one had heard about, listening to my many ideas over the phone and charging next to nothing to encourage me when other cartoonists were too afraid to get involved in a project like this. It's one of my life's greatest regrets that you did not live to see the manifestation of this dream, I feel like I took too long but matters were really out of my control, keep resting sir and thank you once again for adding your talent to my vision, sometimes I feel like Kakashi apologizing at the graves of people he failed. I'd also like to thank cartoonist Mr Mike Asukwo for adding your talent to my vision, I appreciate your professionalism and skill. I acknowledge the work of my publishers on this , the teams at

White Magic publishing and Ganowa Books for an amazing job assisting me to bring this vision to life. Thank you all so much and I appreciate your contributions.

Lastly, I dedicate this book to all Nigerians; past, present and future, and to all the black peoples of this world. There is no need to write an epistle here and you'll read my thoughts when you turn these pages but know that I am one that believes, I believe in your strengths, your greatness and your legend, I see your weaknesses and your limitations also but what is life without imperfections? I call out to all of us, we can do better and we can BE better... seek knowledge, covet wisdom and apply them all for your elevation. Aspire and have a healthy hunger for more, for who can tell you what lies in the unknown just beyond your reach? For better or for worse this is my love letter to you all; my kinsmen, my brothers, my sisters, my enemies, my opposers, lovers and haters, all of you. Drink up my thoughts and make sure to convey to me your immediate taste and your aftertaste of this wine, I would very much like to know and who knows? We might even meet up and have a discussion about it. I'm not a man of many words or many emotions so I'll leave it here, thank you dear reader for purchasing this book and I hope you have a great experience with it. Peace and Love.

Always above,

Peter Aghogho Omuvwie.

INCEPTION

'Dear mother Nigeria,
Why dost thou feed on thine own seeds?'

This was how it started for me sometime in early 2012, exact day unknown... these two lines, repetitive, repetitive, echoing ... and then... <nothing> *blank*. For some reason I could not proceed from these two opening lines neither could I finish, it was essentially an impasse in my mind, stuck. I was a young creative at the time who had mastered the art of writing sixteen bar rap verses in a matter of minutes and I wrote a lot of them on notebooks that I carried everywhere with me. My then ability to write raps in minutes was in stark contrast to a few years before, the early days of my rap dream when I struggled a whole month just to string a couple of lines together that rhymed and made sense but I kept at it because I knew that repetition was the gateway to perfection and if I was to fulfil my then rap dream of becoming the *illest* rapper out of Africa surpassing Modenine and M.I I had to practise hard and master my craft, so for sure I got better at it. Those were good days because hip-hop was still sort of alive even though there was a lot of noise in the global community when Nas predicted its eventual demise and time would show us all that he was right. Now, I have to apologize for digressing, it's a bad little habit of mine that kicks in when I'm talking about things I'm passionate about so you'll see it creep in at different times as you read through this book but know that without such background information about myself I cannot deliver to you, the reader, why those two lines at the beginning that are so important to the creation of this book came to be in the first place, so bear with me.

Being a student in a strict private university, I had no ready access to a studio so I developed a pattern of writing my raps using different imaginary beats playing in my head. The beginning lines of a song or verse broke through my subconscious into my conscious plane and I fashioned an imaginary beat to go with those lines and wrote them down on the back pages of my course notebooks, then I wrote a hook, gave the song a title after which those lines were erased from my mind leaving my consciousness open for more lines to filter in because the previous ones have already been captured in ink; this was how I wrote my songs in those days. But you see, those two opening lines kept coming to me without follow up lines to complete them or even imaginary beats to clothe them with as my other raps would have, it was strange but not too out of the ordinary because not every line that broke through my consciousness from my subconscious became a verse or song. They were either forgotten or broken down and elements of their construct were used for other verses, so problem solved? No, not yet, not in this case. When you look again you'll see that my repeating lines were constructed in old English which was very strange and distracting for me at the time. I tried to mouth them as I would my other raps but they didn't come off my tongue nicely. Where was this influence coming from? I could not place it. Was it because I was an aggressive reader searching ancient and modern writings for hidden wisdoms and secrets? Little matter, I am a creative; providing harmony and continuity is what I was put on the earth for so I decided to look into the light and find the positive in the situation. I figured that these, my repeating lines, in old English were the opening lines of a poem as I unlock new areas of my creativity and delve into poetry which I studied briefly in junior secondary.

Yes! This was a period of brief triumph for me, if I could develop the poetic side of my creativity whilst also delivering super raps then it would give me an advantage in the standings when the books were opened and the greats of the art form were considered because the guys I seek to dethrone wrote and delivered nice raps but if I could do the same and write great poetry on the side that would give me an edge but... of course there was a 'but', as I must have mentioned a million times by now, these two bastard old English poem lines refused to co-operate, they did not multiply themselves into a full poem, neither did they turn into rap lyrics to be captured in ink in my notebook and forgotten for a time to leave my consciousness blank for more lines to filter in. They were instead starting to annoy me with their resilience so it was an impasse like I said earlier but I was not done. I went on the offensive, I wrote these two first lines down on a blank page baiting them, my reasoning being that if I had already captured the first parts in ink then the others would be forced to follow as I looked at them from time to time and I could at least finish this poem and continue to evolve but months passed and nothing changed. In my mind the pattern continued... the lines would break into my consciousness, repeat, repeat and then *blank* they were gone, so at this point you could say my life as a poet was stillborn, it never really took off from these two lines... unsettling.

What this intrusive pattern would accomplish was that it finally forced the light of my consciousness to focus on these lines and to meditate on them, you see, to really pay attention; the older me looking back now would realise that that was a *burning bush* moment for me. So what do we have here? The first line *'Oh! dear Mother Nigeria'* contains the subject, my country Nigeria, and it presents her as a mother, that alone evokes all kinds of emotions within me considering the love and connection I have for my own mother. Not only is she given the role/title of mother she is regarded as *'dear'* which can be interpreted as being cherished or beloved, self- explanatory. And no I did not just add the *'oh'* with the exclamation mark randomly, the *'oh'* appeared in several iterations of the repetitions of the raw thoughts in my conscious mind which I creatively constructed as these lines but became problematic because their inclusion in whatever form they appeared took the nuance of this unfinished poem in a different direction altogether such that I could not reconcile subconsciously or consciously which direction I was to take, it unsettled me internally. This was a distraction within an already distractive line of thought giving you, my dear reader, an insight to layers and elements that compelled me to pay attention and to focus on it. Please stay with me as I attempt to explain further.

As you must know, humans don't think in text but in pictures and ideas that are then transmuted via different vehicles like words, pictures, song, etc. to express the thought so when this disruptive idea kept popping up in my head I tried to capture it as precisely as I could. My first offering for the first line, *'Oh dear Mother Nigeria'* came off bland and disconnected for the gravity of emotions that accompanied this thought so it did not give me rest. I then placed the exclamation after the *'Oh'* to get *'Oh! dear Mother Nigeria'* which made it personal and turned it into a lamentation which was ok but came off just a tad bit too dramatic for me. What kind of creative would I be if I didn't move things around? So I placed it after *'dear'* like so *'Oh dear! Mother Nigeria'* but that gave me the feeling of a face palm moment of embarrassment which while it captured some of the core elements of emotions that accompanied the idea, it did not fully satisfy. The first entry came off as bland, the second one felt like something a Nigerian who cared too deeply for his country would say and the third like something an observing foreigner would say, all contending in my mind; which fork in the road do I take? In the time spent trying to resolve this little quandary alone the idea had taken root hold and started to grow in my mind. How did I resolve this? Well I shall tell it to you a bit later but for now let us look at the second line.

It reads: *'why dost thou feed on thine own seeds?'* and it comes across as a straight forward rhetorical question, we see the subject which was introduced to us as a beloved and cherished mother in the first line being asked an unusual question that goes against the very innate nature of motherhood as nourisher and care giver, what a great contradiction indeed! My creative curiosity was aroused, the artistic part of my subconscious, and I was hit with a brief flash of a picture that has stayed with me till this day. These flashes have happened before in intense moments when I'm drawing from the well of my soul to write the lyrics to my songs so I was not startled, in fact, it has happened so much by this time that I have come to call them 'visions' but I told none of my friends about them lest they see me as weird. This vision was a simple one, there was a big black mother sat astride on the floor with a crown on her head. Her demeanor and countenance was one of sadness and even though she still had a crown on her head and I did not know her from anywhere before this vision, I just knew that she had lost her light and glow at a previous time. She had long arms by her sides and there were lots of babies coming out of her in diapers trying to crawl away from her but she stretched forth her long arms and picked up the babies throwing them in her mouth as they screamed. More babies came out of her and the process repeated itself with only precious few managing to get away from her and escape. It was repulsive with the screams of the babies but what was more disturbing for me was the fact that in this particular vision I had a low line of sight watching it play out like I was one of the babies myself. I had had enough of these visions by this time to know what that means and as obvious and disturbing as it might be for me you should know what it means too.

    Nature continues to show us that mothers are fierce protectors of their young, in some cases we have even seen them sacrifice their lives to ensure the survival of their species and in some other very rare cases we have seen mothers feed on their young for survival after childbirth when they cannot hunt freely... the key word here is for 'survival' and even this is rare not the norm, but here I am faced with a well fed mother gorging on her babies. I was alarmed and intrigued at the same time but sadly I had no ready answers on hand for that great rhetorical question for the ages. Why did I not have the answers? Where could I get the answers? How could I answer this question? A shift, an irreversible shift in my consciousness as I was made aware that I had merely been living in Nigeria like tens of millions of others but have never paid attention, I had merely been existing. Partaking? Yes, but just going through the motions like I was

sleep walking, you know, like a zombie even but suddenly I was awake, I was alive, something had opened up within me that refused to close. I knew it that I would never be the same again, this new opening in my soul made me feel like it was an error on my part not to have the answers to the question posed in my poem, there was sadness for that within me, there was lamentation but in all there was hope also, a light and warmth because I knew within me that I could get the answers if I was willing to search for them, to commit and focus and I would get them. My dear reader, on this day, 'the observer' was born and there was no doubt at this point as to what my quest would be.

As I meditated more on that rich pulsating vein of thought which started off as those flashing lines but had become more than an obsession because it had fully consumed me just like that curious insect tugging at the faint edges of the spider's web. It slowly became clear to me the complexity, scope, the range, the depth of just what I was about to step into. No wonder, this was why the poem could not be finished at the onset no matter how hard I had tried, there was a resistance internally to its continuation and completion because to answer a question like that would require more, a great deal of more. In fact, when I think back I realised that if I had mined a hundred poems from this vein of inspiration I still would not have captured its full essence by way of expression. I had to go deeper, it was an urge but the only logical next step in this quest was to delve deeper into the rabbit hole so yes, I had to go deeper.

What you're about to read is an unfinished poem that metamorphosed into something else, it retains its original first two lines as starters but the continuing lines have been stretched out to form the body of this work. At the time I could sense it was going to be a lot of work but I was hooked and excited to undertake this journey even though I had no title for it nor prior experience writing a book. Scriptures tell us that when great king David, God's beloved, was to go up against the giant of Gath as a young man he gave testimony of how he had killed a lion and a bear in the wilderness and how this giant man, a great soldier would be no different for him. Well I had not written a book before but I always wrote great essays in my literature classes as my teachers would always say, plus I had written my six month final year project in six weeks because I did not want to fail, not to mention the hundreds of songs I had written… what was the worst that could happen? If David had lost that fight with Goliath he would have died a painful death and his countrymen would have become slaves but the consequences for me failing in this was significantly lighter; it would most likely have stayed unfinished and forgotten in my laptop or become lost like so many of my other projects but one thing you will know about me is that I do not like to fail in anything I do. David had his sling and stone, all I had was just a burning desire to properly answer that one question: *'why dost thou feed on thine own seeds?'* it would have to be enough for me.

…come on now, walk with me.

INTRODUCTION

On the day that 'the observer' was born it was like I had awakened from a deep sleep, I looked around me with a new eye for the first time in my life, there was an influx of new information to me like the Nigerian society itself had started talking to me... and I listened. Streets and places that I had passed probably a thousand times without a single thought or concern before now looked different to me, I started to notice the cracks, the puddles and with the puddles came the stench that I had somehow blocked out before, there seemed to be a deliberateness from that time on, a sense of purpose if you will... I also started to take note of the people around me, my people that wore their pains and struggles on their faces like cheap make up, everything that was out of place around me became revealed to me and with them came an influx of emotions that forced me to confront the subject matter of this quest *'mother Nigeria'*; where did I stand with her?

I acknowledged that I loved my country dearly as a patriot but I was also forced to confront the fact that I also hated her in an almost equal measure because as they say familiarity breeds contempt and I was all too familiar with her many shenanigans, after all, I too was one of her many seeds. Having been in contact with her all my life, I have been privileged to study her at close range and my soul has been much influenced by her many beauties and her many imperfections. Thus, the role of the observer was made manifest in that while I went about my daily movements a part of me actively stayed detached but communicated intermittently, ever observing, dispassionately analyzing, greedily assimilating and carefully documenting what would become the contents of this book that I now present to you, my dear reader.

But you see, Nigeria is such a complex country with diverse peoples that if I went ahead and just recorded observations then my perspective, though true, would have been limited and incomplete. Meaning that I might just have found out why mother Nigeria ate five of her kids not knowing the reason or reasons for her eating five hundred others, that would not have been a sufficient outcome of this quest for me. How do I mean? Let me explain with the story of six blind men that came in contact with an elephant that was told long ago. The first blind man touched the elephant's ear and said that the animal felt a little different to the fabrics made by Ejiro the best cloth weaver in the village, he had handled lots of those fabrics and he knew they were sold in the market square. The second touched its smooth, sharp ivory tusks and said that the animal was like the spears of the brave warriors of the king that go to battle to protect the village, the third touched its muscular trunk and said the elephant was like the constrictor that was killed three market days ago when it was caught swallowing eggs from Ochuko's chicken pen, the fourth touched the side of its body and said the elephant was like the mud fence of the king's palace where he sat and begged passersby for alms daily, the fifth touched the elephant's stout legs and said that the animal was built like the trunk of the mango tree he sat under to escape the sun's heat in the noon time and the sixth blind man touched its tail and said it was like the ropes used by the gallant tappers that climbed the palm trees to tap that sweet palm wine that gave him so much joy.

Here are six different individuals who encountered the same animal but have different experiences or opinions if you will; if a discussion were to ensue between them each man would stick to his own story based on his own experiences and find it hard to go with the next man's story but the fact remains that they all encountered the same animal and somewhere in the interaction or conflict of their opinions lay the elephant. That elephant is Nigeria and I am the seventh man with my sight intact attempting to walk around the elephant and capture its form in as much detail as I can to fully understand it. I have to journey deeper and cast my gaze wider so help me God, if I am to do this successfully. I feel at this point we can get into the book proper now.

NIGERIA: NAMING

The name 'Nigeria' as we were taught back when history was still a subject taught to children in Nigerian schools was coined by Flora Shaw, wife of then colonial Governor-General of Nigeria (1914-1919), Frederick Lugard. She was said to be a writer and the colonial editor of *The Times* newspaper in London making her the highest paid female journalist of her time. That little bit was just to tell you that colonialism paid big and took care of everyone involved in it just in case you were wondering, but things could have taken a different turn if the plan to name the country 'Goldesia' after her previous owner Taubman Goldie who sold her to the British government, but that plan did not go through. Now, you cannot imagine what I thought or how I felt writing that but if you're a Nigerian, or an African or just black, I feel like things like this have to be seen because they don't get talked about enough. *'Oh, did he just say the Goldie fellow owned the country?'* Well, you can read it again if you didn't quite catch it the first time. That said, let's continue with our discourse. She was said to have coined the name from the river Niger joining 'Niger' and 'area' hence the name 'Nigeria'. In the past I usually spent a great deal of time pondering the circumstances of this naming because a name, and who does the naming are important, so I did a little digging.

In the times before Flora Shaw, early European maps labelled the sub-Saharan areas of Africa as 'Negritia' or Negroland' meaning 'land of the blacks'. I do not know much about her personal life but as a writer I must assume that she was a reader too, did she perhaps draw inspiration from this? I cannot say for certain but the name of the river 'Niger' had also been in use before her time, it is the Latin word for 'black' and many of the latter European languages draw their word for black from it. I assume that it could not have been a description for the river itself as the river is not a black water river but more for the peoples that occupied the lands around it. This word is found in the first King James translation of the bible published in 1611. Acts 13:1 where a Jew named 'Simon' who was called 'Niger' was in the church at Antioch with other prophets and teachers. Now I do not think they were talking about a river when this character was described here as black. The new testament texts were originally written in some form of Greek and the Greek word translated there was *niyep* (pronounced *neeg'-er*) which was of Latin origin meaning 'black'. Other sources suggest that the word 'Niger' is not even of Latin origin but was formed from the Tuareg name for the river *egereou n-igereouen (gher n-ghren)* meaning 'river among rivers' to emphasize its greatness which was later transformed across time, physical space, different peoples and tongues to 'Niger'.

I can relate to just how ethnic names can change over time because I too faced a similar situation like that in my life and I'll tell you a little story about how I came to be called Peter. My father was entertaining some of his white friends and business partners at his home in Sapele. The legend has it that as they sat and talked, I walked unsteadily into the room in the manner of toddlers who haven't totally mastered the fine art of walking at that age and one of the white men remarked, "Oh look at this beautiful baby," looking at me adoringly then he asked, "What's his name?" This presented a little quandary for my dad not because he didn't want to tell his friends the name of his son but because of the name itself. The native name given to me by my dad is 'Unuakpovwotowhuu' which was shortened to 'Unuakpor' and even just 'Unu' because it was giving the people around problems with pronunciation, how much more a bunch of foreigners? It's not a bad name and I will not lie to you by telling you that I learnt how to spell and pronounce it properly in one day. However, if I try to explain its meaning here it would take us in an entirely different direction. What I will say is that the first full iteration of my name translates differently to the second and the third translates directly from my Okpe dialect to English as 'mouth'. You can read James 3:5 - 10 to get the meaning of my full name. So back to the story, my dad paused because he didn't want his white friends to bite off their tongues trying to pronounce my name so he quickly called me 'Peter' which was his own foreign name of Greek origin meaning 'rock'.

    Now why am I digging deep into the origin and meaning of the name 'Nigeria' like this? It is because in the intangible spiritual realm that birthed this physical realm that we dwell in, names and their meanings have a measure of significance and influence over the things named after them that transcends into the physical... simply put, a name and its meaning works with the destiny of that which is named after it. Africans from ancient times to present times have always known this simple spiritual truth that is why you will seldom find an original African name without a meaning unlike some other parts of the world where cute sounding names without meanings are just given to people. This is not to say that the effect of a name is absolute, no, it differs from case to case. If I were to give an analogy of it I would say that in the spirit realm, a name is like a ray of light and you would need several rays to create a beam depending on the size of the beam. On its own, that ray might not do much or mean much but if you were to create an illuminating beam, that ray was a good thing to have to add to other rays to create that beam. To show you that the effect of names are not absolute I give you two famous examples; a shallow search of the meaning of the name 'Judas' today will give you answers like 'traitor' or 'one who betrays' but that's not the real meaning. The name Judas is from Judah, a Hebrew name which means praise, a good name to have, right? It was even the name of one of the twelve tribes of the old Israel. Now consider 'Adolf' which means 'noble wolf' also a good name. Both names are good names but could not on their own stop their famous bearers from doing what they did, to this end you will not find many people bearing these names today. Oh, at this point I look back longingly at the bush path that was supposed to take me back to the village and see how far I have strayed because of the beautiful ripe fruits of the almond trees in the forest. I must hurry back.

So, why did I dig deep into the naming of the country? Why am I going through so much trouble for it? It is because I want to be as thorough as possible in my quest, to try to see from the very beginning, from scratch if you will, if errors were made in the naming of the country that have manifested as patterns or contributed in some way to the mess that the country is today. From that river two countries in west Africa have gotten their names, a state in Nigeria is named directly after it, another state Kwara which is the ethnic *Nupe* name for the river Niger meaning 'sea' or 'lake' in their dialect bears a semblance in pronunciation to 'Quorra' a foreign name for the river Niger that appeared in early European maps. This semblance in pronunciation and the fact that 'Quorra' is not an indigenous European word leads me to believe that it's a corruption of *'Kwara'* and still her influence continues. Another state Benue ('mother of waters' from *be* 'mother' and *nue* 'water') is named after the longest tributary river that empties into the river Niger. The peoples that inhabit the lands around this river are also called after it so much so that not time, distance or even the cruel salty waters of the Atlantic could wash away that name stamp and identity from them at home or after they were forcefully carted away into the diaspora.

The word 'Niger' did not go away, it is the root word in 'nigger' the most offensive term in the world for the black peoples in the United States because it was used by white slave owners to refer to their black slaves. It came to embody the pain, humiliation, emotional and physical suffering, dehumanization and the loss endured in that period that permeates to this day. Our brothers and sisters across the Atlantic forbade everyone else from using this name on them but in a classic case of black absurdity turned around and then proceeded to call it to themselves from sun up till sun down without limit so, no, that iteration did not go away also. We in the motherland and others scattered across the globe in solidarity picked up that offence for the sake of our shared racial trauma. At a later time I will give my thoughts on this name but this is neither the time nor the place for that discourse lest I digress again from main point.

Slavery was abolished in America in the 1860s after **hundreds** of years and that name was widely used before then, the first record of Flora Shaw using the name 'Nigeria' in her article for *The Times* was in 1897, so as I said earlier I have spent a great deal of time pondering what her true motives were at the moment of its use. Was it scholarly? Derogatory? I do not know for sure because of limited information available but still looking around there seems to be evidence that the name had been used in print by someone before her and if that were so then it must have been used orally too. As the wife of the colonial governor general for that period, it makes sense that official credit was given to her so here we are, 'Niger-area' as it was called would later become the largest populated black territory on the planet.

NIGERIA: SETTING

Geographically, Nigeria is strategically placed. Although zoned as part of West Africa, a look at the map shows that she occupies an almost central position in Africa which speaks to proximity and accessibility to other territories for commerce. On that vein of accessibility she is not landlocked, she has a long oil rich coast line from Lagos in the South West to Cross River in the South East which conjures a plethora of revenue generating activities from ship building, ship maintenance, on shore and off shore drilling to tourism just to name a few for her people and we haven't even scratched the surface yet, we haven't, and this is just the coastal area.

She has enough land space for agriculture and whatever money-making ventures that man engages with the lands at his disposal on this planet, what can I say here? You should know them. The weather I can say, now that I've witnessed just how cruel true winter can be, is nice and relatively warm all year round, meaning production can be done all year with little climatic interference. She is not located along any tectonic fault lines that causes earthquakes nor does she have active volcanoes or lie in the path of destructive tornadoes or any natural disasters that might limit her productivity or wipe out her efforts. The countries that have these disasters have learned to cope and even flourish despite them just to let you know.

Okay maybe the gods played a cruel trick on her and her lands are infertile but you can look at Egypt and the new Israel, countries located in the desert that still manage amazing agricultural outputs but Nigeria with nutrient rich lands naturally irrigated by two great rivers flowing from both her shoulders, joined at her heart before flowing down to her lush crotch cannot feed herself; instead she feeds on her children and her hunger is insatiable. What if I were to add that her fertile lands also house different kinds of mineral resources that are used in manufacturing and other diverse applications? Surely, this should count for something, right? Under normal circumstances it would but this is not so in her case and I want to know why.

What about her human resources? Is it that she's just this big dysfunctional machine with not enough people to run her? That is not the case because it is estimated that over 200 million people occupy this territory. Without a proper census in decades it is difficult to really know but looking at the nationwide 2023 election numbers I would estimate that it is more over 100 million people than over 200 million but that's just me. So, whether 100 million plus or 200 million plus people that's still way more than most successful nations in the world today have and on a micro scale they are some of the most vibrant, intelligent and hardworking people you'll ever meet anywhere in the world but this has somehow surprisingly not reflected in the overall situation of the country. It is for head scratching realities like this one that this quest we are embarked on is seeking to unravel.

There is a Nigerian proverb that says: *'person wey dey stay near river no dey baff with spit'* which in English translates to: a person living near the river does not bath with saliva, another one like it says: *'person wey dey baff inside river no dey complain say soap dey enter him eye'* which translates to: a person taking his bath in the river does not complain that the soap is entering his eyes and causing him irritation, why? Because he is surrounded by water and can easily wash the soap off his eyes to stop the irritation with it. Both parables in their simplicity speak about the contrast of being in lack while surrounded with plenty, it is a highly unusual situation indeed. With the settings and attributes of our subject that I have presented to you thus far, I put it to you that under normal circumstances it is impossible for a country like this to be poor but indeed she is… she is! So we see the man living on the river bank not just being unable to bathe with water from the river but even his own saliva is taken from him.

The people are not stupid, they might not know a lot but they know some things at least. The average Nigerian on the street knows that the country has way more to offer than what we are seeing today hence the cliché for decades now among the people that: Nigeria is blessed. They also call their country a 'great' country, another cliché, but who can blame them? Sweet words can help dull some of the sting but alone they can never fill up an empty stomach. I always say that having the potentials to be great is not the same thing as actually being great, having the potentials to do great things is good but it is not the same as actually doing or having done great things, there are levels to these things.

Nigeria being regarded as the biggest economy in Africa is one of the greatest contradictions in the history of mankind, the true welfare of a country is not measured in lofty numbers posted year in and year out but is rather seen in the welfare of her ordinary citizens and the most vulnerable among them, so with this criteria in mind can I look at Nigeria and call her blessed? I would not call a man blessed because he has a large chunk of gold deposit in his land somewhere, I call him blessed when he has a deposit of gold in his land and he is able to locate it, mine it. Depending on the size of the deposit he can start processing it to add value or if the quantity is not too large he takes it to a dealer, sells it and then uses the proceeds to take care of his home, his wife and his kids. He puts some away for his children to inherit when they are of age and then invests the excesses in something lucrative that would yield substantial returns for him in future. Depending on the trajectory of his life he can use the experience gained to prospect other lands for gold developing a trade in the process that his children can then learn and grow into to teach and pass along to their children after them. With his new standing he is able to build strong, mutually benefitting alliances with other 'blessed' men like himself because no man is an island and also extend a helping hand to those around him of lesser standing… then and only then can I call him blessed because his life is markedly better than what it was before he discovered the gold in his land and his future is secured but having the gold deposit in his land alone just does not cut it for me.

When the wife and children of the 'blessed' man with the gold in his land starve and aimlessly walk the streets bare feet, clothed in rags, devoid of covering, protection, shelter and condemned to be afflicted by those around them it is an anomaly and an aberration, this is not the sign of a blessing but rather a curse. Now, it is important that you understand that I do not write this book lightly, I did not come here to rant or to vent my frustration. Am I sad and angry at the condition of my country? Yes, very much so I am… but am I going to now let my emotions get the better of me and dictate to me what I should write here? No, a great man once said that anger is the wind that blows out the candle of the mind. We must put our emotions aside and logically confront this beast of a problem if we are to slay it. So when I look you in your eyes and say to you with all seriousness that Nigeria, my country, is under a curse you must understand that I'm not veering to hyperbole neither am I referring to superstitions. I know it is my nature to make a lot of jokes but on this I am serious.

In a world that has become ever so carnal and so sense based it is increasingly difficult to discuss the intangible laws, operations and mysteries of the eternal spirit realm and their effects on the physical realm which we dwell in without the usual eye roll or blank stare but truth is truth regardless, and it does not require applause, fanfare or fireworks for it to be truth, it just is. People these days are so plugged into the matrix that they simply cannot entertain the thought of anything existing outside of it. In the over a decade since I started observing Nigeria in the midst of the chaos and distractions one thing is clear to me; it is that this country as with some others even though my focus is on this one for now, the fact remains that there are countries that exist in the midst of riches but are surely being slowly and methodically taken backwards. I say all that to say this, that anybody, and by that I mean anyone at all that is familiar with the operations of the spirit realm that takes a look at the transgenerational consistency in the patterns and operations in the country which, by the way, I must emphasize here are not random, can point to the unmistakable effects of spiritual intelligence, spiritual intention, spiritual intervention, spiritual territorial legality as exercised by principalities. You can also imagine the spiritual power generated, the sacrifice it takes to initiate, maintain, uphold and to further propagate the exchange in this spiritual transaction we are witnessing play out.

In the spiritual sciences it is an irrefutable reality that the spiritual realm controls the physical realm, the physical realm is an offshoot and a child of the spiritual, a projection and you might say a crystallization of the intangible. These realms though clearly defined with their own characteristics and separate from each other are not apart of each other as there are constant interactions between them such that actions in the physical can have implications in the spirit realm and vice versa. The spiritual predates the physical, envelopes it, nourishes and sustains it such that there are similarities between them mirroring this relationship but the laws of the physical are different from those of the spiritual. When I say predate, the spiritual is eternal while the physical is trapped in time, which means that it had a beginning and if it had a beginning there will surely be an end to it and all this though confusing for some or even a little distracting is to give understanding. To this end, if we are to really trace the root cause of the problems of Nigeria, I mean the root to the root causes from which there is no further depth or layer to unravel we will have to go full spiritual but like I told you earlier; this is a carnal world we live in and spiritual things will sound like foolishness to them. Yes, I know that I lost a lot of you there for a second, *'oh so African of him to blame spirits for the predicament of his country rather than to take accountability'* and then yes, I can also hear your thoughts about that. I understand, and I promise you that we will look at the physical aspects of things in great depth too but as a man of the spirit it would be a great disservice to you on my part were I to ignore deep key spiritual truths on this matter and indeed life in general just because they would not make for popular reading. Also to be fair, you did see 'heaven' in the title of the book when you purchased it, what did you think we were going to be talking about the whole time? That said let's keep it moving.

NIGERIA: THROUGH TIME

They say that you do not know where you are going until you know where you have been so to talk about this current territory now named Nigeria we will have to travel through time and look at the peoples that have always occupied these lands even before her boundaries were carved out for her just over a hundred years ago. The interaction of different powerful forces brought about the form of her current territory and other forces can also interact to change that form in the future. What I mean to say is that these territorial forms can change but the peoples have always been hence my interest is more in the peoples. These black peoples that occupied these lands are made up of lots of ethnic groups and tribes which had existed separately and interacted with each other for centuries. It is with respect to this that I have continuously used 'peoples' in its plural form to describe them.

Now when I say a lot of ethnic groups I mean like a lot, lot of them. Nigeria alone has over 250 ethnic groups each with their own customs, language, food, dress etc. and this shows you just the type of diversity we are talking about here presenting a unique situation from which unique problems can arise but they all existed together spread out across these lands from ancient times. Their interactions are not unlike interactions that exist between neighbouring countries today like trade, marriages, cultural exchanges and even conflicts among others. Some of the tribes include Okpe which is my tribe, Igala, Urhobo, Yoruba, Tiv, Nupe, Efik, Bini, Hausa, Itsekiri, Ijaw, Fulani, Esan, Igbo, Ibibio just to name a few. There are lots of books and online articles that cover this subject should you like to know more but we cannot I'm afraid cover it extensively here as it is not the focus of this study.

I usually consider myself to be a man of very little emotions but that has not stopped me from being overwhelmed anytime I look at the history of the black peoples of the African continent and their descendants after them. I can see why it's avoided by all even the people it's about but like I always say we cannot continue to run from these things forever because there are still a lot of unresolved issues that persist to this day. To put it simply, the history of sub-Saharan Africa is one of brutal exploitation, sure there are bright spots scattered here and there across it but it has predominantly been that. I understand that many may not agree with this dour presentation and it's not because I'm a glass half empty kind of guy or anything like that, but it has more to do with my rationale and analysis of things and situations if anything else.

For instance, when we watched 2013's *12 Years a Slave* movie, we were all horrified by it but those I watched it with took some little relief when the main character was reunited with his family in the end. I could not share their sentiments for two reasons I will briefly list here. The first was that I could not stop thinking about the time he had lost with his family and secondly I could not stop thinking about all the other poor souls left behind at that plantation. So when we see Brad Pitt's character forcefully hold and lead the Chiwetel Ejiofor's character away from the evil master to the carriage that would take him back to freedom in the movie, what did you see? And how did it make you feel? I saw one black man picked out from among many black people children included, might I add, and the whole situation looked like a total loss to me. Needless to say I could not derive any joy from that movie. Same way it is when people try to point out the 'bright spots' to me in African history, so you can see that this trip through time would not be an enjoyable one for me but one I must undertake so I can extract some key points that would prove uselful to us as we go about our original quest.

The history of slave trade in Africa spans over 1,000 years counting to this day, now read that, slowly let it sink in. While the sale of humans as slaves is not exactly a novel concept as it existed before this time span nor was it peculiar to sub-Saharan Africa alone, the sheer scale, impact, uninterrupted continuity, brutality and legacy of slave trade on the black race is one that has never been seen before anywhere in human history nor will it ever be repeated again, I think, which makes it peculiar in a not good way. I have to be careful here because I do not want to be pulled into the emotional side of this distasteful matter, it has been covered to some degree by outsiders which offers diverse materials you can consume should you want to go down that path but perhaps when or if a generation of our people should rise to maturity someday they would be able to look at things from the viewpoint of natives to shed more light. My interests for the sake of this work is in the resource aspect of this trade and the dangerous recurring patterns that stemmed from it that are still in effect to this day.

The trade itself is a mechanism of exchange that sees the human, material and natural resources of the sub-Saharan peoples consistently flow to other lands to build, develop and better those lands while in return the providers get loss, pain, suffering and despair bringing to my mind the words of wise king Solomon when he said; *'My mother's children were angry with me; they made me the keeper of the(ir) vineyards; but mine own vineyard have I not kept'* (**Songs of Solomon 1:6**) parenthesis mine. Keeping in mind the fundamental economic principle that most resources are finite while the needs/wants of man are infinite, this mechanism taking different forms but consistent I must add has successfully taken resources out of our hands and given them to outsiders without stopping creating an ever- enlarging pit for the black race for more than a thousand years now and still counting. Who is to blame for this situation? I tell you that the blame for this is large enough to be shared between the buyers and sellers alike but for me I put the higher blame on my people, I will explain later.

In the esoteric spiritual sciences it is known that when a physical phenomenon or pattern like this one we're talking about here keeps recurring with such accuracy and consistency through time in the life of an individual or a nation or a people then it takes spiritual force to sustain it. In this case when I consider the gravity of this influence and the time it has gone on for it leads me to say then that higher spiritual forces are at play here. In the physical, if we are to attribute it to just the deficiencies of my people then I must remind you that they like all other peoples and races of men in the earth even the ones that are prospering today all have their different deficiencies and if so that it's just deficiencies then the law of averages should have kicked in multiple times to balance things out but this vicious intentional cycle like a raging forest fire burning through time continues unabated. Speaking from a purely physical point of view, the subsequent generations should have been able to learn from the mistakes of the fathers, can we now say that their inability to learn, adapt and evolve to change the circumstances is just down to their stupidity and foolishness? Nay I'm afraid, that is not deep enough, it is too simplistic and convenient to be the answer to this problem, plus I must tell you that the black race like all other races is a gathering of people with similar physical features and in every natural gathering of people there are both intelligent and stupid people in that population so that answer will not stand and our quest continues.

The trade in humans can be traced back to the ninth century with the trans-Saharan slave trade where the Arab world using desert Ber-Ber tribes as intermediaries bought slaves among other goods. This trade was not exclusive as the Arabs traded in black slaves from sub-Sahara and white slaves obtained from raids on coastal European lands taken to the Arab world. The men, castrated, were used for manual works while the women were used as concubines and house staff. You can do your detailed reading on this, my focus here is that from the ninth century to the fifteenth century when the Europeans became involved in the trade of black people they had organised and built themselves to the point that they were no longer on the market as products but became traders themselves. The damage and scale that they achieved in this venture in a relatively short period of time relegated the Arabian trans-Saharan trade to the back seat of history whenever slave trade is talked about. The trans-Saharan trade ran from the ninth century till present day while the trans-Atlantic started from the fifteenth century till date, well over a thousand years, and in all this who was the major denominator? It was the blacks, they lost their greatest asset which was their human resources, carted away to build foreign lands while their lands lay in ruins, plundered and pillaged, doomed to be so till this very day. And for those overly religious ones let me just say here that no religion was exempt from this; the Arabs were Muslims, the Europeans were Christians while the Africans who were the sellers practised the traditional religions of their lands.

The numbers involved are mind boggling but its general trajectory is like that of demonic possession for spiritual reference or drug addiction for physical reference. It started out mild and innocently enough until it consumed its host and left it in a far worse state than it met it, and that is if it ever stops at all. The lands and the peoples within were exploited from all directions through every available route by every and anyone capable; nine million slaves for the trans-Saharan trade up north, four million north-west through the Red sea, another four million through the Swahili ports of the Indian ocean east of the motherland and then fifteen million or more depending on the author or source through the big shark of them all, the trans-Atlantic slave trade on the western side! Erm… these are human beings we are talking about by the way; living, breathing humans. To go into the horrors that they encountered on their various journeys and destinations is a can that I cannot open here because it will take us off course, what I will just say to the young black peoples of this world is: ease off on the social media and read, be curious and read then maybe you'll have genuine reasons in your heart to act different and be different. **'They made me the keeper of the(ir) vineyards; but mine own vineyard have I not kept'.**

I know we're supposed to be talking about the history of Nigeria but the history of Nigeria is the history of the black peoples of sub-Saharan Africa and please do not let my narration make you think it just *slaves, slaves, slaves* as there was a rich history of a prosperous and proud people before it and the same can still be crafted after it. There is still much greatness and good intermingled in that history but the thousand plus year old stench and stain of this trade on these peoples is one that no perfume or bleach sold in the market has been able to wipe off. I say all that to show you without contradiction that by the time the weakened continent was finally colonised and occupied it was a broken and defeated people that were later carved up into the territories and the countries of Africa that you see today. These people have lived in this weakened, broken, defeated and subjugated state for hundreds of years with whole generations living and dying in this condition, babies being born and growing into this vicious cycle that permeated every aspect of their existence with no area left untouched which has created a culture, a way of life and basically defined the way of life of these people. At this point I think we can start to break off from the vast lands and narrow down our focus back to our subject matter.

NIGERIA: BRIDGE

The exploitation of these people and their lands continued but took a different dimension, the key here is that it definitely continued. Looking at Nigeria, the tribes in the north participated in the trans-Saharan slave trade while those in the south participated in the trans-Atlantic version of the trade which in crude terms was a continuous leakage from the northern and southern parts of the country. A trade that started simply as a way to get some gain by selling off criminals and other undesirables opened a door of demand that demanded satisfying. Raids on the natives were carried out both by outsiders on the natives to get product, and tribes preyed on other tribes with the losers being sold off as slaves. Those tribes were even aided with weapons and other gifts by the outsiders in those wars and they grew strong feeding off their neighbouring tribes but perhaps it never occurred to them that a person that has seen you sell off your brother that looks just like you but speaks a different language without reservation can never trust you to not do same to him someday.

This is not to say that there was no internal resistance to this trade from the natives, there was much resistance and all that is well documented should you want to look it up but the outcome of things sadly shows that the resistance obviously failed. When those raiding tribes in partnership with their foreign investors had depleted the resources of the land and there was nowhere else to turn to, their partners turned on them and conquered them completing the divide and conquer manoeuvre; so partners they were no more because in conquering they now became masters to those they formerly called friends, brothers and partners, alas colonialism was born in the land. Now why, you might ask, did they just not kill off the natives and take over their lands? That would have been a bad business move on their part. Because they had utilized the products they had earlier acquired in plantations on distant lands reaping great profits in the process so killing off the remaining products would have been a huge business loss for them as there would be no continuity; who would have done the hard labour?

Colonialism marked a strategic shift in the business strategy of the foreign investors in Africa where they could then replicate the successful business model that they had developed and perfected in faraway lands while keeping a weakened and malleable native population in place to fuel production for them among other things. All this, I must add here was not without much pain and bloodshed on the part of the natives but what was still consistent is the unbroken pattern I spoke of before where the human, material and natural resources of the motherland by some method or mechanism is taken away to develop and better foreign lands while the original owners and providers of these resources continue to live in pain, lack and poverty such that even during colonialism while they were still producing they were now producing for their colonial masters with their own lands benefitting little to nothing in exchange. The interaction between the parties was no longer a trade in terms of exchange but was now an extortion with vital resources flowing from the colonised to coloniser.

So here we have an easy target; a people that refused to evolve and band together to fight off their many adversaries. Tales have spread about her endless riches bringing interested parties from Europe to her shores. The land was vast, the tribes plenty, all speaking different languages, the European powers carved her up with the Brutish... oops! Sorry, my mistake... I should have said British, yes, the British controlling the territory that is to be called Nigeria while the French and other collectors controlled other parts of the continent. They exported agricultural produces and mineral exports for their factories but to administrate effectively they partitioned the lands creating the Northern and Southern protectorates which were amalgamated to form Nigeria in 1914 and then independence in 1960. I feel like running through it all but a part of me feels a responsibility to shed more light as all this is not common knowledge in Nigeria so here might be only where some people might get to see information like this.

In the 1900s, the vast and relatively barren Northern protectorate was not making any money for the British compared to the Lagos colony and the southern protectorate of the Niger both of which had access to the sea. See, it is important for you to understand that this was always a business for these people, they had made investments in shipping and soldiers to these lands and so like every entrepreneur they expected returns for their investment. So the Northern protectorate not making them any money was bad business. As a matter of fact, the Northern protectorate was still receiving financial aid from London at the time for its administration and survival while the fertile South was a really profitable business venture. Frederick Lugard who was the governor of the Northern protectorate at the time was the one that pushed for amalgamation with the home office because he had this *'genius'* idea to offset the deficit from the North with the surpluses from the South, a marriage of convenience, one which in his own words he described as between 'a poor husband and a rich wife'. As a Southerner I can only but hold my head. I wish I was able to travel through time and get to him at this time when this was still all just an idea in his head because he killed us. Anyways, his offer was initially rejected because the home office was more interested in the merger between the Lagos colony and the Southern protectorate which were separate at the time. This would later happen in his absence in 1906 and both were now called the Southern protectorate.

Now Lugard who couldn't get his wish to see the South and the North joined resigned from his office and went to be governor of Hong Kong. I always wonder what his personal motivation and interest in the matter was and why he felt so strongly about joining the Northern and Southern protectorates that he would even go as far as to resign from his post for not getting that wish granted. What were the true driving forces behind his obsession? The forefathers say that sometimes when a strong child is to be born into the world it forces the father and mother to come together because he/she still has to obey the natural laws of procreation to be granted legal entrance into this plane. Anyways, he was called back 6 years later to oversee the amalgamation process, 6 years fr the colonisers to see that they were losing money in the North and had to push that burden onto someone else. On January 1st 1914 the amalgamation was announced with integration being a transient process spanning before and after that date.

On paper, it does not look so bad, I mean, looking at it on the macro level but on the micro level, taking into account the diversity of the components in terms of the tribes and peoples that make up the individual protectorates being merged you can start to see how future problems could arise. In all of this playing out you can see for sure that it was powerful external forces at play once again shaping the lives of these people, the natives, and charting the course of their destiny not an expression of their own collective will. There was no referendum or consensus, many of them were not even consulted before this was implemented as they were already colonised and deemed the property of their colonisers. With this arrangement, tribes that originally would have thrived on their own were roped into this business that is Nigeria, and don't forget, it was a business for profit done with the backing of colonial might. Sadly there was not much that could have been done by way of resistance. I mean try to imagine, put yourself in the shoes of the average tribesman of the time, imagine sitting down in your hut in the village after a hard day in the farm working to contribute your quota to the colonial levy, drinking freshly tapped palm wine and waiting for one of your wives to bring you your dinner and the town crier goes round saying that your village or community has been zoned as part of a country, what will you do? Probably nothing because the implication of that announcement will not register immediately, neither will the effects too, those things take time or, not so much time as experienced in the Nigerian case.

People, their children, their lands, their belongings and their livestock were drawn into a binding union of different components with the whole greater than the individual parts such that if any of those tribes was engaging in activities that threatened the whole union then the whole union suffers for it without accountability from this erring component. It is upon this factitious foundation that the country Nigeria was amalgamated and created, not shared values or free will; a recipe for disaster if I ever saw one.

NIGERIA: THE BUILD UP

There is a saying that history will repeat itself if it is not studied, and when science takes on a problem the cause of that problem has to first be determined to help with a solution. I strongly believe that to understand the present Nigeria we have to look at the past Nigeria. To me the Nigerian union is one that was jinxed from the very beginning because of the foundation of ethnicity, religion and nepotism, all with roots that run very deep into the psyche of the populace that it was built on. The country that was formed and named on October 1st 1960 when she got her independence from British colonial rule was advertised as a democracy but was in fact an ethnocracy. An ethnocracy is the rule or leadership of a multi-ethnic society based on ethnicity rather than merit, where the dominant ethnic groups tussle among themselves for control and power; and the minority ethnic groups are just expected to sit still and take it all in. You can see that this was never going to be an effective way to govern a country, so even though the name of the territory had been changed and the system of government in force had been changed it was still the same people. The same infighting between ethnic groups that allowed a few people to come in ships and take over a vast and numerically superior continent was still very much in play and we shall take a brief look before we move on.

The prominent political figures of the time that spearheaded the movement and push for independence are Ahmadu Bello, Tafawa Balewa, Nnamdi Azikiwe and Obafemi Awolowo. The political parties of the first republic were:

1. NPC - Northern People's Congress:- Headed by Ahmadu Bello and representing the Hausa/Fulani in the North.
2. AG – Action Group:- Headed by Chief Obafemi Awolowo and representing the Yoruba in the West.
3. NCNC – National Council of Nigeria and the Camerouns:- Headed by Dr. Nnamdi Azikiwe and representing the Igbo in the East.

These parties were just merely political vehicles for the three prominent tribes in Nigeria, they were not borne out of some political ideology to move the country forward even though that might have been said and, repeatedly so, for effect. The truth is that at the heart of it all was that same age old tussle for superiority. Now, some might disagree with this statement but having observed how operations are carried out in this part of the world I most assure you that if you check you'll see that a mission statement, vision, constitution and whatever else is needed to form political parties anywhere else in the world was prepared by these political parties and communicated to the Nigerian public life has taught me to always look at what people do not what they say. The patterns observed for the past hundreds of years support this.

Now I have tried to navigate through these times all the while trying to avoid ethnic sentiments that are so integral to the lives of these peoples and their story but a complete story cannot be told without it. The very nature of the union that created this country was problematic to look at then, and looks problematic to me even today. You had a large Northern protectorate which couldn't meet her budgetary requirements and got financial support from London, the possibility alone of which connotes some type of existing relationship or bond versus a smaller in land mass Southern protectorate that always had budgetary surpluses both of which the British hastily tacked together like a bad tailor job handing the power over this new creation to the North, a power which sees the North suddenly in control of the resources of the South directly from the hands of the Colonisers themselves. This is what some call 'creation of a country' in post-colonial Africa, but this is where I make my *'I-smell-a-rat'* face and call 'political fraud', now, how did I arrive at this?

We all know about paternity fraud where a woman in a union with a man goes out to other men outside of her home and secretly brings back the seed from these other men to the man she is in a union with, and presents the seed(s) to him as his own after which he then works for the rest of his life to provide and care for the seed(s) and their bearer as his own in ignorance of the fact. This is where I draw my inspiration from for this case. A coloniser has two colonies living side by side as a business enterprise, he has to spend money out of pocket for one while the other gives him some profit; what would you do if you wanted to make a clean break and just walk away without having to be responsible for both in the future seeing as you have already benefitted immensely in the past? You tell me. I want to say here that I do not count myself among those Nigerians that like to blame the British for everything wrong with Nigeria in 2024, but if we are going to be thorough in this quest then no stone will be left unturned. So who was the victim of political fraud in this scenario? It was most definitely the people of the Southern protectorate.

The events in Nigeria after 1960 plays out like a bad movie, there was widespread corruption in the political stratosphere indicating a change in the direction of the flow of the resources of the land from the hands of the former colonisers into the hands of the political class of the newly created country. Chief Obafemi Awolowo was arrested in 1963 on charges of treason and corruption, and was sentenced to ten years in prison, there was a very corrupt election held in 1964 that saw ballot boxes openly stuffed to inflate election figures essentially boycotting the people power of the electorates, taking away their voice and right to choose in the matter. The election was basically a North vs South affair showing the continuous internal ethnic divide and tussle; with all these different forces at play it took just six years for the first military coup to take place in the country in 1966.

These poor people just can't catch a break, it is easy to always make excuses for them as the broken and defeated but their docility is nothing short of repulsive at this point. The handover from the British was a missed opportunity, while they cowered in the corner and allowed themselves to be manipulated and used a new evil was on the rise right in front of their eyes but they did not take decisive action. I know, just coming off colonialism there must have been after effects, the new power structure in the newly created country saw resources of the land flowing not into the territory and her peoples but into the hands of the political class and they openly abused their power and the resources that power got them over the people. The politicians lived flamboyant lifestyles off the scarce resources of a land that had suffered centuries of exploitation, extraction and deprivation and badly needed a boost. The military stepped in and took over power in what should have be seen as a straightforward attempt to restore order but in a multi-ethnic society like ours every move like that was always going to first be scrutinized with ethnic lens.

I do not want to dwell much on this but I'll leave some comments. The Nigerian history books will tell you that the coup was a failure because the multi-ethnic coup plotters did not succeed in their attempt to seize power in Lagos the then capital of the country but were pushed back up north. When you present the facts like that you can see why the historians called it an unsuccessful coup but when you put on ethnic lens and take a second look you cannot help but ask questions. The young predominantly south-Eastern plotters stormed Lagos from the North killing the prime minister along with other top political and military figures from other ethnic groups, then a senior south-eastern military officer survives this attack and mounts the resistance that pushes the plotters back up north. The president of South-eastern descent just happened to be conveniently out of the country during this attack so he was spared. The plotters went back up north to resume their command while a senior south-eastern military officer took power off the hands of a depleted political class and the coup plotters were not punished at all looking like a win-win situation for the south-east. You see? The ethnic lens do give it all a sinister spin from the viewpoint of the other ethnic groups.

I will ask the question which I think you are asking in your mind: well what did the Nigerian masses do after their prime minister was killed in that manner and their democracy turned into military rule overnight? The answer is – nothing; they did nothing building upon their time earned reputation as a people that do nothing when real action is required, to their very own detriment I might add. The other ethnic groups were watching; the prime-minister who was killed was of northern descent, it took just seven months for a counter-coup when Northern officers in the military started killing South-eastern officers stationed in the South-west. This killing of South-easterners soon spread to other parts of the country and into the killing of civilians which led to the first civil war in Nigeria because the South-easterners then tried to leave the marriage (secession) but were not allowed to. This war would last for three years ending with the surrender of the South-east in 1970 but not before claiming millions of black lives including lots of black children in the process.

Now, we can get into the dynamics of who drew first blood and all that bickering back and forth but my focus all this while has always been on the resources of the land and the direction they flow to; I don't want to lose sight of that so I present my questions to you. It took seven years for this war to happen in the newly mapped out territory. The British having been in this area for hundreds of years were well aware of the internal ethnic friction in these parts and still held considerable power over the newly created nation-state; my question now is, why did they not suggest the dissolution of the union for the sake of peace? Why did they insist on its continuation and even supplied military support to keep the nation together? What did they stand to gain from all this? Well, when a fisherman has cast his drag net in a wide area across the river, will you now tell him to cut that net up and allow some fishes to escape thereby impacting his bountiful harvest? No, that would be a bad business move on his part. It has taken me over a decade to write this book so when I say political fraud you must know that I did not write it lightly, if you are a Nigerian you must stop and turn this slowly in your mind and ponder deeply on these things and their consequences.

To help with the war efforts volunteers were drafted into the army from all over the country, 'patriots' who wanted to do their bit and fight for their fatherland to either keep it together as one or crush the secessionists fully if they had to. I commend their valour and patriotism but you see I am a quester, and sometimes I just cannot help myself so I must ask my question, oh great dead patriots; if I had a potion that could bring back to life all the Nigerians who fought and died in this war both on the side of the nation-state and that of the secessionists, seeing everything that has happened in Nigeria to their children, grandchildren and other common people of the land these past fifty-four years since the war ended how many of them will still fight for the side that they fought for during the Nigeria-Biafra civil war? I pray you do tell, they say dead men tell no tales but what I would give to hear the answers from those poor souls!

The war ended in 1970 with death toll estimated to be three million and that's human beings, in case you were wondering. It took just five years for there to be another coup and from this point on a pattern emerges where there is a coup, the military takes over power from the politicians to 'save' the country from the corruption and embezzling of the politicians, they too are corrupt and embezzle and after some years pass they hand over power back to the civilians only for the cycle to repeat itself but in all this we can see the constant here; it was that the resources of the land even though abundant was never properly reinvested into the land to develop her and her peoples, you can see that those resources consistently flowed into foreign hands and lands over the centuries past. In the case of the young created country, the rising political class-military power structure which some societal observers that came before me rightly called Neo-colonialists now extract these resources from the land and her peoples using and abusing the political structure created to achieve this flawlessly. My understanding of the whole situation is that the change of power between the politicians and the military after that war, creation of states and whatever other moves were made have all been distractions to throw a lackadaisical and passive people off their scent. The one constant thing in it all is that the resources of the land have steadily not made their way into the hands of the common people to better their lives, that is the one take away I want for you through this time shuffle, if in doubt look at the Nigerian people.

To wrap it up and tie it to the present, the military last handed power over to the politicians in 1999 and there have been four-year cycles of corrupt elections held till present but that thousand year plus cycle has not changed regardless of the circumstances and scenarios. At least the colonisers put infrastructures in place to make their exploitation work run smoothly but since the hand over to the natives in 1960 the country and most especially her peoples have been tied in an inescapable choke-hold of slow, steady, meticulously guided and controlled regression; the unbroken pattern continues.

HOLD COURT IN THE STREETS!!!

Welcome to my court, look for a place where you can stand and observe the proceedings; and no noise please, lest I send you off, I don't want any distractions... this is serious business. This is one of the earliest visions I had when the whole idea for this book was still taking shape. The visions came randomly to me, each different from the other but when they came they gave me deeper insight into the complex problem before me because there were not many books I could consult and I was at a crossroads

as to how I could proceed. In this one we're holding court in the streets, mother Nigeria stands in the dock, the readers are the jury, while Nigerians are the witnesses, the wronged, the guilty, the court officials, the audience in court and even reporters covering proceedings. There is a soft but firm call, leave the comfort of your homes, your offices, your shops or whatever you're doing and come to court Nigerians, you stand accused here this day and the society you have created for yourselves stands as evidence against you, so what say you? how do you plead; guilty or not guilty? Somehow it does not matter what you plead here because judgement has been passed already, but we go through it anyways.

Who's the judge here? Well it's me, on whose authority you might ask? Erm... I don't really know, this was no regular courtroom but there I was in a robe, standing in the street and heading proceedings. Well, not just in the street but more specifically on a heap of bones in the street, a heap made up of the skulls and bones of millions of dead Nigerians, Nigerians who have died long before this geographical location came to be called Nigeria. Men, women and children, those who died due to injustice done to them by their own country and I'll tell you a secret here my friend, the bones do speak. In this particular vision I am standing on a heap of the bones of our ancestors while they watch from the other side in dismay and yes they are witnesses too in this court and have a special interest in this special case. They silently watch proceedings, pained expressions on their faces, pained by the mess their seeds have become in the world today. I am surrounded by the masses, the Nigerian people of all ages and class as witnesses. They surround me in a circle and in the middle of that circle the leaders of this country, past and present are facing me. They are the condemned and they have come to answer to me for their numerous crimes against my people.

As the judge I had promised that my verdict will not be based on emotions but on logic, evidence and sound reasoning. The issues I will discuss with you all, will be looked at from all angles so as to create perspective and in some cases I'll let you, the reader, give your own verdict but just like law systems the world over today, it also means that my court is not perfect. As such, sometimes I might punish or condemn the innocent or set the guilty free; that is a part and parcel of life.

So once again I welcome you to the court in the streets, we're close to the equator so the sun is out and hot, if I stay out here for too long I might get darker and turn into a Ghanaian *tongue out* so for that reason I want to try as much as I can to run through the issues we have to discuss but I must tell you they are very plenty. Out here in this court there will be no respect for ill-gotten wealth or false might or even political office for that matter, just right and wrong. There will be no roof to protect us from the scorching sun or the drenching rain (maybe I snuck in an umbrella for myself *wink*) because in this moment we are all equal and in this equality I will discuss my pain and what I believe to be the pain of millions of Nigerians living, dead and unborn, without fear. So due to the gravity of the matters to be discussed I ask for your undivided attention and before the session is over I will pass judgement. All that said let's get down to business; court rise!! Oops! almost forgot we are all standing already.

THEORIES! THEORIES!! THEORIES!!!

One of the beauties of this life, this very precious plane that we are currently trapped in and even when you consider the other planes shut off to us is interaction. I had once laid back and pondered the earth, the materials and the creatures within, for hours and the only conclusion I could come to was that they were all made for interaction. Without interaction the very existence of existence itself is pointless. It is for this reason that I placed a premium on observing the various interactions of the Nigerian peoples in my quest to get to the very root cause of the problems of Nigeria, my country, my aim being to detect the effects of the interactions between people in the country, to discern the identity of the groups interacting and if possible to reverse engineer their different motives for different interactions. My experience in this is that in the journey to dig down to the root cause of the problems of Nigeria there are many false bottoms and distractions to throw you off the trail making that root very elusive. There were times over the years where I felt like I had finally gotten it and completed my work but a restlessness persisted in my spirit that compelled me to look deeper... *look deeper, there is still more.*

Of course it did not also help that there were precious few materials for research on this topic written by Nigerians themselves which makes it all the more shocking considering the amount of academics and intellectuals this country has produced. If anything this void should give you an insight into the very nature of the people we're looking at; everything has a voice even silence, you just need to know how to listen. I did stumble upon a little book by the patriarch himself Chinua Achebe of blessed memory called *'The Trouble with Nigeria'* published in 1983. Brothers and sisters, when I read the book I could as well have re-printed it under this my current title and I would not be far from the mark showing you the long enduring patterns in the country. In the book, he presented differing perspectives from general school history on the prominent politicians as at the time of British hand over whom the history books refer to as the 'founding fathers' of Nigeria and from background information on Achebe we know that he must not have written lightly as far as objectivity goes. Not to say he was not given to ethnic inclinations as we all are even today but it is good for perspective's sake to see his views from his time. This book, while it gave me some boost and put some wind in my sails, did not satisfy my appetite so I had to keep digging.

It was during my observations and the analysis of them filtering out the many distractions that I started to draw out my own theories to explain the trouble with Nigeria. Due to the complex, multi-layered and multi-dimensional nature of the problems with the Nigerian society taking into account the population and multiple ethnic groups co-existing in such a relatively small land space I will present to you major and minor theories to try to unpack it all. The major theories cut across all or most levels of the problem and the minor ones whilst dealing with certain dimensions or levels of the problem become obsolete as we move to other dimensions. This does not make them useless though, as you cannot get the complete picture of a puzzle if you do not include the little pieces. There are also sub theories within larger theories they share similarities with but they also contain some distinct features worth mentioning that adds clarity to the picture. I will now apply these theories using the present Nigerian societal reality as evidence to test the validity of my theories to see if they hold weight or not.

1. ACUTE SOCIAL FISSION.

'And if a kingdom be divided against itself, that kingdom cannot stand. And if a house be divided against itself, that house cannot stand.'

- Mark 3: 24-25 (kjv)

Fission means a splitting or breaking up into parts. When I look at Nigeria as the subject here representing black societies and communities worldwide this is one of the first things I notice, simply put; it's a lack of unity but to put it like that doesn't fully capture what is happening. This is because blacks live side by side relatively peacefully in communities worldwide, so upon casual observation one can make the assumption that they are united, right? The answer is no, a state of quiet does not automatically equate to peace, unity itself is not the destination but a vital stop along the right pathway to the destination and that destination is the fruits of unity herself.

Acute Social Fission (ASF) is the term that I coined to explain the blanket phenomenon in black communities where the larger black body or mass is constantly being broken down into smaller parts by internal and external forces all the way down to the individual in that community, and these smaller parts within the larger mass are constantly at conflict with each other leaving the black body or mass in a state of constant instability to varying degrees, in effect leaving it weakened. The result of this is that even though the blacks have some numbers on their side, their numbers never amount to much so we see that in the congregation of races on the world stage where all the races of this world come to contend for advantages and visibility the black race is never able to generate enough power to properly contend because whatever energy they create that should have been concentrated in a direction for maximum effect is dissipated internally in acute social fission (**'Unstable as water, thou shall not excel' - Gen 49:4a**). The internal and external forces that lead to this break down vary; they could be ethnicity covering customs and traditions, could be religion, language differences, politics, ideals or even country territories drawn up by foreign interests among other things.

Jesus speaking in Mark 3 teaches us a fundamental truth in political science when he said that a house and a kingdom divided against itself cannot stand and the black house is surely divided against itself. Now, you could be tempted to point out that these differences exist in other races and communities and you would not be far from the truth but I tell you that we are dealing with a peculiar case indeed when you consider the peoples and their history, one where these differences have been amplified over centuries to weaken them for exploitation. I ask you for a moment; in which other race can you find such conditions in a widespread manner? None! This is why blacks generally today are still sleeping, ignoring their history and everything else but I tell you that you cannot go to sleep early when all your neighbors in the neighbourhood are still fully dressed, moving about, looking like they still have something special to do that night. If you go to sleep too early you might miss the passing of a shooting star or the special sighting of a lunar eclipse which occurs once in a blue moon or even beautiful fireworks later lighting up the night skies. You might miss all that or you might just be naked and snoring in your bed when all your neighbours finally band together and break into your house later that night to loot the place.

Human populations are diverse and differences will always exist, a healthy blending and interaction of these differences is the ideal but that is not always the case. ASF being a blanket theory will not help us much on its own so now I have to narrow it down to our subject to give flesh to the bones and capture its form properly.

1a) POLITICAL REPRESSION: RULING CLASS vs. THE MASSES

'The state is a relation of men dominating men, a relation supported by means of legitimate violence'

– Max Weber

Repression is the act of holding back or holding down. Political repression for me from my observation of Nigeria over the years is the act or process of the political class keeping the masses repressed so that they can exploit them with little or no resistance from them or consequences for the exploitative actions of the political class. Please keep this in mind, it is at the heart and soul of everything we will discuss from here on and I do not want to repeat myself as we still have so much to talk about. This already presents to you that we have two social classes in Nigeria according to wealth, power and influence; they are the small political ruling class and the large masses; the middle class no longer exist here or if it still exists it is so minute that its effects are simply negligible to the general Nigerian equation making it an endangered species.

In the new beginning was the Nigerian masses, the already subjugated disjointed masses made up of members of differing ethnic groups, interests and religions, all pulling this great big mass in different directions but conscripted by external forces into a union. Out of this chaos a smaller group made up of elements from all over within this union starts to form and then begins to crystallize. This smaller core group is of the larger mass but does not behave like the larger mass even though it still retains some of its qualities. While the larger mass is without direction, docile, unsure and riddled with internal strife this nucleus group is focused, united and quick, its objectives and interests are clear before it, and it pursues them with ruthless efficiency whilst the larger mass is splintered and pulled apart to different directions by its internal components. The nucleus group is self- aware, self-governing, self-correcting and has intelligence, with the passage of time it quickly moves to consolidate its power and in so doing elevates itself above the larger mass from whence it was formed but it does not separate itself from the larger fully or cut ties with it to become a fully separate functioning entity without the larger mass. No, this would have made it a parallel state in and of itself but it does not do that. Instead it takes the smart road and disguises itself within the larger mass since they are made up of the same elements in the first place, tricking it to relax, lulling it to sleep with vain expressions of shared and aligned interests but this is all a ruse. The nucleus group's main intention is to gain absolute control over the larger mass and to achieve this it has to keep the larger continuously weak and misdirected, enforcing its splinter lines and ruthlessly extracting vital resources from the larger mass but not to kill it; no, that would be a stupid thing to do and this group has intelligence so it does not do that. Instead in the final stroke of brilliant parasitism if I ever saw one it extracts the vital resources from the larger unfocused mass to an extent leaving just enough for it to survive on which is an overall weakened and confused state making the larger mass easy to control, manipulate and exploit. These objectives put it in direct contradiction with the desires, interests and objectives of the larger masses but alas it is too late, they are too caught up in the environment created for them and too ignorant in themselves to know that they are neck deep in a war they have already lost a long time ago.

    This, my dear reader, shows you the relationship between the two socio-economic classes in Nigeria. I once had a vision about this sometime in 2012 when I was to start writing this book and I'll share it with you. I heard the noise first on that day and I'll never forget it for the rest of my life, it was a heart wrenching mixed noise of crying, wailing and screaming, then the scene opens and the source of that disturbing noise was finally revealed to me. It was a mixed multitude of Nigerians, men, women, children, women with little babies on their backs dressed in rags and tattered clothes, looking dirty and unkempt, arms outstretched, looking up at the windows of a big house begging, screaming and making that noise of anguish which

I have not been able to totally banish from my mind till this day. The desolate mob was desperate, they pushed and shoved among themselves like zombies in an apocalypse movie but this great house stood clean and different from the mob in front of it. In front of this house stood armed guards with guns preventing this great impoverished mob from breaking down the doors and storming this building.

Then there was movement behind the windows of this great house, the inhabitants of this great house started to wake up from their sleep to the noise and then I knew that they were the leaders and elites of the country possessing great wealth and resources which they had extracted from the country and they were actually surrounded by it in this scenario. They wake up from their slumber, crooked smiles on their faces, first they survey the wealth and abundance surrounding them before moving to open their windows and look down at the starving mass below out under the hot sun, in this vision I could barely stand the noise of the mob because it was laced with pain and bitterness, and it brought a heaviness

and sadness to my heart but the men and women standing at the windows did not look even the least bit bothered at the noise, it was like they were immune to it or rather they derived some twisted sort of pleasure and joy from it.

I hung back and studied this scene as it played out and felt very sorry for this desolate mob indeed. The elites at the top looked down from the windows at them with such impunity, I could see the raw disdain and disregard in their eyes as they looked down surveying their marvellous creation spread out before them. At this point, they dip their hands into the huge bags of Naira notes surrounding them in their palace and toss some into the crowd below and this sparks a huge frenzy as the people started fighting among themselves to get their hands on any note as they fluttered in the wind down to them, not paying any attention to the person standing next to them as people were getting trampled on in the scuffle. They were not even paying attention to the people throwing the notes down at them or the fact that they have piles and piles of the good stuff in the house with them. They were desperate and some of them were even trying to climb into the building by all means pulling others before them down that were trying to climb also while the armed uniformed guards were keeping them at bay.

I could not help but shake my head when I saw the look of cruel satisfaction on the faces of the political elites up there in that big house looking down below, before I came to myself. This happened in 2012 and I took this vision literally because if you asked any Nigerian on the street the reason why their country is the way it is they will say 'corruption', so I took this vision just to mean the corruption of the leaders but I was mistaken. It was not until 2017 after revisiting it several times in my mind that the implications and meanings of it fully took form that I had been given the full blueprint to a system and I did not know it. Most of the theories I would later come up with to tackle the Nigerian equation came out from just this one vision alone.

We looked at the history of the peoples that occupy this land and for much of it they were subjugated by external forces that came to plunder, so how did this parasitic cancer of a political ruling class come to infect this body? When the British colonised the land they had only a small administrative staff on ground at the top of the power pyramid to govern the subjugated peoples in the land. They relied on locally sourced talent for the bulk of the administrative and clerical duties to help with their colonization and exploitation work in the land with the threat of military back up from their homeland to enforce their authority and keep the natives in line. They would later draw on local talent too to create an indigenous force to continue this. The result of this is that by the time they 'handed over' power during 'independence' there was already a well-defined indigenous political administrative and military structure in place to carry on the mandate of the colonisers. These structures were formed and operated in times of great repression of the peoples of the land, their existence and operations were shaped and moulded by it from infancy to their maturation at independence. They never functioned under true democratic normalcy but the false colonial normalcy created for the time; in my opinion after the handover they never changed from this but have instead evolved.

There are not many documents to shine a light on the way things were at the time but I can postulate, and before I go on I must say that this is one of the things you'll find out when you start to look into these matters that the history is always conveniently missing. For example it is easier to get detailed information on dinosaurs that lived and died millions of years ago, what they ate and how the weather was on the day they died than to get information and history on colonial and local government activities in Nigeria from under a hundred years ago. That said, we can say that the countenance and feelings of the locals towards the colonisers and oppressors would definitely not have been all warm and fuzzy. History mentions several attempts at rebellion by the locals that were crushed by the British so we cannot say that the locals were all in love with the outsiders. With these conditions in mind, for the British to find local talent to work for them must have taken a special breed of locals with a peculiar disposition, mentality and characteristics and these dubious characters were gathered together and given power over their brothers and sisters under colonial authority until they were given the keys to the kingdom in 1960.

This is how they came to be and since then they have recruited like minds for themselves and consolidated their power. The reason they have been so successful in their agenda and thrived in Nigerian society is because unlike the larger Nigerian masses the members of this group are united, they have put aside normal petty differences like ethnicity and religion and remain united in their goal of self-enrichment at the expense of the masses. Even in that vision I noticed that the masses did not try work together to overpower the few guards at the door holding them back to gain entrance into the building. They did not even attempt to burn the house down, instead they just pathetically stood and stretched their hands out begging for scraps and leftovers; what a pity! Make what you will but the fact remains that the battle line has consciously or unconsciously been drawn from before, hence the **Political ruling class vs. Masses**.

1b) ETHNIC RACE:

> *'One! it's me and my nation against the world,*
> *Two! then me and my clan against the nation,*
> *Three! and me and my fam' against the clan,*
> *Four! And me and my brother with no hesitation,*
> *Uh! Go against the fam' until they cave in,*
> *Five! Now who's left in this deadly equation?*
> *That's right, it's me against my brother,*
> *Then we point a kalashnikov and kill one another'*
>
> - K'naan
Tribal War
Distant Relatives album (2010)

When I listen to lyrics like this I am reminded of why I fell in love with the artistry and lyricism of true hip-hop in the first place and in its ability to convey messages. The artist captures and presents the message of the internal conflict in such a poignant manner. Nigeria is the most culturally diverse country in the world; with over 350 ethnic groups and 500 languages spoken, I dare you to show me another country on earth with this much indigenous diversity. This creates a negative and positive outcome of real and alternate timelines projecting the weakness and possible strength of what currently is and what could have been in Nigeria in terms of cultural diversity. I culled this theory from the arms race where neighbouring countries constantly in conflict with one another try to develop or acquire and accumulate more destructive weapons to use on their neighbours creating and maintaining a state of constant tension and instability. The ethnic race theory states that Nigeria cannot be great as a country since the different ethnic groups which have existed long before the amalgamation of the protectorates and creation of the country keep fighting amongst themselves for superiority and control of the country creating instability and ill will.

In Genesis 11 we are told about the tower of Babel where the people of this world with one mind and one language in unity came together to build something great that even God acknowledged that they could not be stopped in what they had set out to do as long as they were united but there are many ways to kill a rat. He finally defeated them by introducing different languages to them breaking their communication and their unity such that they could no longer understand each other so they went their separate ways abandoning the project in the process. Here in Nigeria government projects are abandoned even when everyone involved speaks the same language and that language could be corruption but I digress, pardon me. That move by God was an external soft strategic attack on a body leading to social fission showing you that there are more ways to destroy communities and in fact whole countries than just dropping bombs on them. History tells us that one of the main reasons Africa fell to outsiders was because of in-fighting among ethnic groups which weakened her. The outsiders studied their victims well, exploiting and manipulating ethnic fissures that had always existed, to their advantage.

In my quest to find out the root cause of Nigeria's problems the ethnic race theory was one of the false bottoms I encountered. In earlier iterations of this book it played a major role in how I saw and described the things happening around me in Nigeria. I thought I had finally gotten it and was ready to publish but I did not know that it was the bias of my tribalism speaking through me as an ordinary Nigerian. The surface area of my gaze and understanding was still too small, I was trapped in the very box I was trying to study and break my people out of, its sides were too close to me for me to properly distinguish its features so I had to ascend, to expand my gaze from an elevated position so I could capture more. It did not also help that politicians and everyday Nigerians always say how incredibly difficult it is to govern a country with many ethnic groups like Nigeria. We grew up hearing things like this that are accepted in society as a general truth but now I can look back and see it for what it really is which is indoctrination and social engineering. I look back now and I bow my head in shame to think that I ever drank such septic tank juice without questioning it in the past.

I sadly cannot recall the exact date along this journey but I can tell you the exact circumstances that shattered this stronghold and changed my mind about the ethnic race theory forever. One day as I was scrolling through social media I stumbled upon a watch making video that I initially scrolled past but something in me prodded me to go back and take a look at it. I had no interest because to me those expensive watches like a lot of other things were just foreign made goods marketed to black people that they had to pay exorbitant prices for until those toys became status symbols in black kingdom. It's always some rapper screaming it out in their lyrics and renting them to show off in their music videos so I really wanted no part of that video but that thing in me calmly insisted I give it a look so I did and for the next 20 minutes I watched a guy with all kinds of little tools fiddle with the little pieces, screws and cogs of the watch engine putting it all together and when the video finished I was speechless. Why was I speechless? Was I suddenly dreaming of a luxurious piece on my arm to show the whole world that I've made it? No, you'd know I had gone off the rails if that were the case, the reason for my speechlessness was infinitely more serious than that.

When I finished that first video it was like scales fell off my eyes, like the veils were ripped apart and light finally pierced into my soul on this issue illuminating it, it hit me like a kick in the nuts and I could not stop thinking. My logic on this was simple, I said to myself that if man could take the time, patience and effort to accurately design, create and assemble all these little moving parts of a watch engine together, moving against each other for years without wear and tear and get them to collectively accurately tell time then there should be no excuse from anyone as to why they could not govern a country with 300 tribes or even a thousand tribes for that matter because man is capable. This realization led to a shift in how I viewed our subject matter and indeed the whole world, it was a shift that would cascade and later change the outcome of this very book.

In the eyes of the distant foreigner looking at Nigerians, he or she may be forgiven if all they see is one people, and one country. This should not be so strange because the African looking at say, Asians, too might mistake them to be one people but just like us they are made of different peoples with different cultures all sharing similar physical attributes. To look at the ethnicity of the Nigerian and by extension the African, goes far beyond just physical expressions like language, food and dressing, these are just outward manifestations of roots that run very deep. To look at the ethnicity of the Nigerian is to strip him down to the very core factor or ingredient from which he derives his very identity and his place on this planet. It is not like a school you are registered to that you can change between sessions or finish from, neither is it like a job you take on and can get fired from, it is not like a country which you take up citizenship after five or ten years and are given a passport to show for it, not like your favourite football team that you've supported all your life and you cry when they lose matches then your son can decide to support some other teams, no, it is not even like a marriage which you can divorce yourself out of by signing some few sheets of paper. Ethnicity is for life, like a family you do not get to choose it, you are born into it and you die in it, it can be said to be the very basic programming language of the African's identity. To this end; you cannot separate the ethnicity and culture from the African, neither can you separate the African from his culture, this is the level of depth we are talking about here.

This is the level of pull that ethnicity has on the average Nigerian and to have over 300 of them of varying sizes in close proximity in the country is like having over 300 small countries within one. As if that is not bad enough we have to now factor in the history of the relationship between these tribes over time and the residual effects that continue till this day. We cannot wish away or just write out the dark parts of our history, they are there for us to learn from. I do not consider Africans to be inherently violent people because if they were then that whole continent should have been up in flames a long time ago but there they are, generations after generations bearing the yokes imposed on them and passing it on to their children to continue from where they stopped without much resistance in this vicious cycle. The tribes existed in relative peace until they didn't; they were exploited, manipulated, forced, coerced and they turned on each other hunting each other to be sold as slaves for profit. We could say it like that and just move on and we will not exactly be wrong, you know. Just blame it all on the white man and absolve yourselves of any wrongdoing but that is just like blaming the outsider you catch your cheating spouse with for seducing and manipulating your spouse to commit adultery without acknowledging that your spouse made the decision at the end of the day to cheat.

The external factors have been widely looked at and documented but we as black people, as Africans have till this day not thoroughly looked inwards at ourselves as to how we moved to commit that great sin that led to our eventual demise as a people and we have still not taken steps to address that weakness to prevent a recurrence. I know about the pain, I share in it too but at some point we must move on. The truth is that the presence of many tribes which was meant to show our diversity and creativity as a people was also a great weakness for us. With the many tribes if one tribe refused something, there were always others to approach which left many openings. They say a chain is only as strong as its weakest link, then in this case think of a very long chain with many weak links in it, all it took was the right type of bastards to exploit this fragile situation by pilling and the chain shattered completely! This, however, is not to absolve the Africans and the role that they played in all this. I do not want to go into detailed accounts but studies exist that shows that relatives, not even just tribes now but a percentage of the slaves by their own accounts were people that were sold off by their own relatives into slavery for whatever reason. Now you can choose to discard this as a mis-translation of the time or lies concocted by outsiders to soothe their troubled conscience dividing us further in the process but the fact remains that there is a void that has to be filled by a proper general looking back at our history in a serious manner by us for ourselves if we are to make any progress as a race in this world. The psychological and physical damage from this period was so great and I understand that our people over the past decades have had to focus on healing but this has left so many stones unturned which is hindering us.

I do not want to be thrown off course, my aim here is to show you that the ethnic race exists, to find its origin and then trace it to present day to see how it is used and how it plays out in the general Nigerian equation. The studies clearly point out the dealings of the slave trade era as the source of the lingering distrust among ethnic groups in Nigeria today. Another reason I might add it in, is the difference in the way of life of these ethnic groups and the conflict it ignites in general human behaviour as we have seen in religion, sports or on a larger scale warring nations in the world. These differences if not properly checked, managed and regulated as we see in this case can lead to serious conflict which in turn hinders development. Remember, this ethnic race theory is not acting in isolation, it is a second level fission that compounds the first one I mentioned (**political ruling class v. masses**) and adds to the conflict and disharmony in the general body. This does not discount the first but plays out differently across both social groups locked in conflict.

The **political ruling class** have learnt to put aside things like ethnic and religious differences that can splinter them and threaten their way of life. They understand that their unity is paramount so they are united in their common interests above all else, for them it is a matter of survival. The ethnic race manifests differently in this group, it is used as a criteria for selecting candidates for choice positions in government using the size of the ethnic groups with their influence rather than true meritocracy; for this, the big three tribes in Nigeria come to mind. Now keep in mind that the government in Nigeria is a subset of this group not an expression of the larger

Nigerian masses; this is how Nigeria is an ethnocracy not a true democracy. Ethnicity within this group is also used to determine who gets the larger portion, and who gets what when they share their booties amongst themselves. These booties are the proceeds from the resources of the land that I should have established in your mind by this point is being exploited and extracted from the people, which are, the larger **masses** and their lands leaving these **masses** with just enough crumbs to survive on.

For the **masses**, they are a people of simple disposition and for them the ethnic race takes a more primal and central place in their lives with strings that penetrate deep into them, deeper than the flesh into their minds shaping their innermost thoughts which are then expressed in their day to day actions and dealings with one another. The existence of these strings that bind them into their different ethnic groups creating beautiful cultural diversity in the process also means that the strings can be traced out, pulled and then used to control and manipulate them in the balancing of this thought because life must be lived and studied in balance. Depending on who is pulling the strings the people can be pulled far apart and then flung at each other creating conflict, instability and further divide within the larger masses. How is it possible for a small group to control and overpower a far larger group? Well if that small group is focused and the larger group is divided then the smaller group can overpower them. Considering this equation then anything which can contribute to the division and splintering of the larger group becomes a valuable arrow in the quiver of the smaller group, this is how the principle of the ethnic race theory takes effect.

On the day to day already scarce job opportunities can go to certain people on the basis of their ethnicity rather than their ability, in the marketplace cheaper prices for goods can be proffered because of it, in business dealings and contracting it also plays a role. In terms of conflict we can look at the 1967 Nigeria-Biafra civil war which was said to have claimed three million lives on both sides, has ethnic differences at the heart of it, the Ijaw-Itsekiri conflicts in Delta state in the 1990s which also claimed lives among others is a testament and it continues to manifest till this day. I always ponder and ask myself: are these people blind? Can't they see what is happening around them? Will this thing ever end? Because the pettiness of it all tests my patience. While the ethnic groups were busy fighting and selling each other off, the rest of the world was developing and these days when the focus should be on development and catching up there is still that ethnic struggle taking place and like the class teacher who has just come out from the classroom to see a bunch of students fighting over petty lunch money and biscuits on the playground, oblivious of the hailstorm that is coming just beyond the school fence. I am telling them, no wait, I am screaming at them to abandon the pettiness and childishness of their conflicts and run for shelter lest they be consumed by the ferocity of the hailstorm that is just beyond the fences. The hailstorm of underdevelopment and poverty brought about by overdue neglect since their attention has been on other things, they should save themselves by running and seeking shelter in the classrooms.

1c) RELIGIOUS MANIPULATION:

'Religion is the opium of the masses.'

- Karl Marx

Religion at the heart of it all is just mind control and mind programming. Nigeria is one of the most religious countries in the world, so Marx saying religion is the opium of the masses makes Nigeria a country of addicts. The existence of over 4,000 religions worldwide is a testament to man's innate desire within his spirit to connect to something more, of the 4,000 only 3 are widely practised in Nigeria and they are Christianity, the African traditional religion and Islam. Of these 3 only the African traditional religion is indigenous to the country. Christianity came through the trans-Atlantic European slave traders while Islam was brought in by the trans-Saharan Arab slave traders; both religions were introduced and established in the land through blood, the indigenous African traditional religion practitioners sold their own to foreigners as slaves, what is my point here? There is religion and there are the actions and dealings of men between men. In Nigeria, Christianity is majorly practised in the general South and the Middle-belt with pockets in the North, the African traditional religion is practised in the general South and Middle-belt but I don't know about the North while Islam is majorly practised in the North, the Middle-belt, the South-West and light pockets in the South. Contrary to popular belief today I do not think religion *is* bad, rather I say it *can be* bad and I liken it to a kitchen knife which is a very helpful tool when you need to slice up some onions and tomatoes but in the wrong hands is a very effective murder weapon that can cause great grief; same utensil.

Religion is like ethnicity in that they both have strings that penetrate deep through the flesh to the core. Where they differ and where religion takes it a step further even though it can be changed by the individual unlike ethnicity because of man being a free moral agent is in the fact that religion caters to man's immortal spirit beyond this realm of space and time into eternity while ethnicity is for this world alone. The contentions between the 3 main religions has certainly added a third layer to the social fission which in turn will have some effect on the general Nigerian equation but that alone is not a strong enough reason as different religions are practised in different parts of the world by different people, it's just how the world works. That said, keep in mind we are talking about one of the most religious countries in the world here so for the fact that like ethnicity the strings run very deep, perhaps even deeper in this case, know that this opens those strings up to be pulled and twisted by certain people, at certain times, for certain reasons and to achieve certain outcomes in the masses. To be able to fully understand this topic of religion in Nigeria, we must separate the people from their spirituality, doing that will give us the dealings of the spiritual and the dealings of man; we do this because the spiritual while being powerful is alien to this physical earth realm of ours so for this reason will cause a distraction for us as we try to understand what is really going on here, on the other hand the laws of the universe give the recreated man the authority to dominate, interact and operate in this physical earth realm that we occupy at this moment in time, so for this reason the spiritual always tries to find expression in this realm through man.

I'm sorry if I lost you there for a second, what I was saying basically is just that we must separate the spiritual aspects from the religion in Nigeria for us to look at its physical effects with as few distractions as possible. On the whole the average believers have gone about their business but the emergence of Islamic terrorist groups like Boko Haram and ISIS in the North over the years coupled with their terrorist operations like shootings, bombings and kidnappings claiming lives of Nigerians and spreading grief have greatly added to insecurity in the country, heightened public panic and great loss of properties. Whole parts of the Northern region have been destabilized leading to people being internally displaced in their own country for a prolonged period of time. There is a thriving kidnapping and ransom industry now with supporting services and a supply chain in the region that is slowly spreading to other parts of the country. To add salt to injury it has wondrously proved impossible for the Nigerian security forces to handle over the years. If we wanted to document it all we would simply run out of space in this book for anything else but I feel I should present a proper background to this issue for proper understanding. There have been church shootings by terrorists on a Sunday during service where lots of lives were lost including entire families wiped out and I could go on, there is a full-blown war currently in the country to fight this terrorism leading to more instability and surely all this has caused great animosity in the minds of the people towards one another fuelling hate, and sadly it goes on and on.

Nigeria in recent times has one of the highest figures in terms of religious persecution. The killings of Christian catholic priests and regular Christians in the North which have become commonplace and I stress this again with the security forces doing absolutely nothing by way of investigation and bringing culprits to justice have not done anything to stem the fission. All of this ties into the century old pattern of African lives and the lives of their descendants being too cheap to the extent that it means nothing, and while all this plays out mother Nigeria continues to chomp down on her seeds with no signs of slowing down. The conflict is not just physical but also psychological, there are practising Muslims who know in their hearts that these things are bad but cannot openly criticize because they would feel like they were going against their religion. I fail to reconcile with it all though, there are too many holes to the logic of it all for me; how does kidnapping hundreds of school girls, taking them away from their parents and loved ones into the forest to be married off to terrorists and defiling them with bastard children help to promote a religion? Those poor Nigerian girls and their poor parents, as a parent myself I cannot explain to you the depths I am willing to go to protect my family but this is Nigeria for you. Like I said it's either there are too many holes to the logic or it's me who lacks understanding of these things but I am a quester; and in this world I do not take things as they are presented to me, I ask questions of and I question everything.

One of my favourite questions on on which I meditate constantly is this; how does a numerically small group within a larger group have the advantage to take absolute control of that larger group? Is it possible? Of course it is and Nigeria is a testament of that. I watched a documentary years ago of how little stoats hunt rabbits 10 times their size and it was really informative especially when you break down their strategy. In one of the videos the little predator performed a dance where it thrashed and flung itself wildly on the ground while the bigger and faster rabbit who was feeding some distance away watched the entertainment in amazement, mesmerized by it all. The showman was not deterred, he had an interest and a goal at heart that he would see to the finish so on and on he went, doing the mad dance and throwing himself on the dirt but as you observe you see that each time he did that he was strategically covering ground, closing the distance between himself and the rabbit who was still too mesmerized by the show to take note of this. When the little hunter was within striking range it pounced on the rabbit who realised only too late what was really happening and was just starting to struggle, a quick bite to the back of the neck ended that contest and the little brave hunter had its prize. In strategy terms that is misdirection with the dance providing a distraction and a cover for the stoat's true intentions. When I watched that video my mind immediately went to the Nigerian situation with the political ruling class and the masses. In another scenario the little hunter just chased down the rabbit showing great stamina, harassing and wearing it down before eventually pouncing on it for the kill, same outcome. Here it showed patience, focus, grit and doggedness, all vital qualities for a warrior to possess if he must be victorious. So can a smaller group take control of larger group? If the smaller group is focused like our stoat here and the larger group is distracted and splintered then yes, a smaller group can overpower and defeat a numerically larger group.

When we talk about Islamic terrorism in Nigeria I always emphasize on separating the religion from the terrorist acts themselves. This is because the religion always evokes strong emotions in the minds of the overly religious masses leading them to start arguing among themselves as they feel that their faith is being attacked. This prevents them from being able to properly hold the acts of terrorism to the light to logically break them down for proper understanding, thus they are susceptible to these kinds of attacks every single time. The Nigerian masses are poor and the Nigeria we know is not a weapons manufacturer by any real standards compared to the ones we have seen used to commit acts of terrorism on home soil; so how can these poor people suddenly afford sophisticated guns and bombs to wreak havoc on themselves but cannot feed themselves and take themselves out of poverty? Who has the resources and possible connections to purchase and transport those weapons in large amounts into the country? When news of container loads of weapons and munitions leaving the ports that were intercepted by the few remaining elements with integrity who could not be bought or compromised in the already compromised and utterly corrupt Nigerian security forces made the headlines years ago and no action was taken by the state until those stories died down and the masses were moved on to the next tragic events in their miserable existence as Nigerians, does it all make sense now what those weapons were for? What happened to the weapons that were supposedly 'confiscated'? Did any of you ever bother to find out what became of them? When high profile Nigerians belonging to the Nigerian political ruling class were internationally implicated as sponsors of terrorism years ago what did you think it was all for? When a bunch of nomadic cattle herders roaming the sunny plains of Northern Nigeria in search of water and vegetation for their cattle who have kept this way of life for centuries suddenly become influencers overnight shooting viral internet videos brandishing big guns with munition belts for raiment how did this transformation take place? What was the driving factor behind this abrupt metamorphosis that could not take them out of poverty too?

With the bombings and killings they certainly are not propagating any religion but spreading terror and fear to hapless citizens so who benefits from all this? You have to wake up Nigeria, you all still seem to be sleeping, are there no men amongst you?

How, I ask once again, does a small group take control of a larger group? In this great battle between the Nigerian political ruling class vs. The masses, I tell you, anything that will destabilize your opponent in terms of public panic and insecurity in the country or anything that can be used as a tool for misdirection because of deep emotional attachments of the masses becomes a weapon, this is the art of war even if the masses are largely ignorant that they are engaged in a war, that is irrelevant. Thus, religious manipulation becomes another vital arrow in the quiver of the political ruling class in the battle to repress, subjugate and exploit the Nigerian masses. The religions have been thrust into the limelight of debates in the public space as to why the African continent was colonised and why the black race is currently the least of all the races in the world. There is a lot of confusion on this topic that I am determined to dispel in public consciousness, it has been going on for a long time and so has been accepted as true but that is not so. It is not out of place to see this thought touted in some form in public discourse, the thought is embodied in this quote:

> **'When the missionaries came to Africa they had the bible and we had the land. They said "let us pray". We closed our eyes. When we opened them we had the bible and they had the land.'**

This is beautiful writing, as a writer myself I cannot help but admire the construct of this quote and the way it was put together; so apt, so poignant but it is wrong making it a beautiful lie. This quote is attributed to Jomo Kenyatta, former president of Kenya, it was used by the late great Chinua Achebe in his magnum opus *'Things fall apart'* and it was further made popular in the continent by the late great Bishop Desmond Tutu of South Africa. Now you know that I love the elders and the ancestors right? Okay, you don't? Well, I'm telling you now I do love the elders and the ancestors but I am a quester, it is my very nature to not just accept things as they are given to me but to question everything. With the beautiful way it was crafted I can see the allure and the seduction of it but let us look objectively at what it is telling us; that missionaries came to Africa, pulled wool over the eyes of the natives with religion and took over the resources of the continent which is not just untrue but also distracting from the real issues because you're putting it like a bunch of guys putting on robes showed up on the African shoreline, started throwing bibles and crucifixes at the natives, and when the natives returned from going to pick up these items they found their lands seized and occupied by outsiders. We know that this is not true, Africa was not conquered by missionaries, to say that would be to ignore the art of war, to ignore centuries of trade prior to between the natives and outsiders where the natives were studied, depleted, manipulated and broken down, where strategic alliances were made with betrayers in the camps of the natives, you will have to ignore the failure to communicate and organize by the natives, religion was somewhere in all of this but to make statements like that quote is misleading.

If you had all these heavy weights and elders from that time repeating it then it speaks to the sentiments of their time, sentiments that have lingered to these present times but that was then for their time, we have to go deeper for ours. We must be clear about what happened here, people did not come to try to spread a religion and just in the process of doing that decided to conquer and exploit along the way. There were the monarchies, the soldiers and the businessmen who had been coming to the lands to trade for hundreds of years, they saw abundance, saw the weaknesses of the peoples who owned the lands and the resources, they saw opportunity and they took it. The missionaries saw opportunity to spread their religion too and took it, religion may have played into the propaganda and for a people that were conquered and abused in the way that our people were, I can understand looking from that point and classifying every one of the outsiders during the time of slavery and colonization regardless of their roles as bad, but the weaknesses that made the colonization of this continent thinkable and possible in the first place exist to this day. It is like the diamond tipped disc cutter used to cut a concrete slab with a water pump attached. The water helps the friction between the blade and reinforced concrete slab and also for dust control. I can see how in the eyes of the slab getting cut and feeling great pain the whole disc cutter and water pump is one unit. Religion was that water but it was not the actual blade doing the cutting. People do not really understand the spirit realm even today and it shows, they do not know that it is a realm with an agenda of its own on the earth that does not necessarily align with the agenda of man in the earth. I do not want to preach a sermon here but when you look at Joshua 5: 13 - 14 and even the life of Jesus Christ, you get a sense of what I am talking about. For Jesus, the Jews of the time thought His coming was to save them from Roman invasion and colonization which was a political and a civil matter on the affairs of the men of that time. Well, he came, spent 33 years accomplishing His original spiritual mission here then He left. There was much anger when the supposed messiah died or left, depending on your inclinations, and the Jews were still under Roman rule, needless to say the oral traditions after that were not so favourable towards Him. They called His mother a whore for having a Child out of wedlock, they called Him fake and all sorts of names but He had fulfilled the agenda from whence He came. The spirit realm has an agenda on the earth, the other races have their own agenda, what is the agenda of the black man? If you're black and you read this, settle down and meditate on this question for a few minutes before moving on.

  It is a lack of understanding really. During the whole slavery debacle the colonisers had their agenda, the missionaries had theirs, what was the agenda of the natives? Can a divided people build a tower that can reach into the heavens? These same sentiments are seen today, the modern day church in Nigeria is blamed for everything wrong in the country and it makes me wonder. The church by design is a system created by the spirit realm to further their interests and agenda on the earth, it has neither the authority or the resources on the affairs of man to be blamed for a lack of train coaches and train tracks in the country or working refineries or enough good roads and bridges. That is the work of your political leadership that you supposedly voted into power to govern your affairs, so you can see that you're barking up the wrong tree. The church if anything, is an indictment of the political ruling class in Nigeria because if they can do the projects they do and have the impact that they have in the country from the offerings and tithes of their members, how much more the political leadership that has been in the control of the resources of the lands all these years? We have to start thinking clearly and not let ourselves be manipulated on the basis of religious sentiments.

There are successful nations of different religions in the world today and through history if you check, there are also successful nations of no religion, success has its own principles that involves reaping and sowing. I also think that the angle of attack on Christianity being a foreign religion to the continent needs to be really studied. I'll use my personal life as an example. My father practised a variant of the African traditional religion (ATR), we were introduced to it as children and he forbade us from going to church in the Christian South. My mother was the Christian in our home, so up until I was 16 years old all I ever heard about Jesus Christ and the bible was from our Christian Religious studies in school and I took it as just another one of my school subjects. Fast forward a few years later our father relaxed his grip on our spirituality so he let us choose. I became born again and accepted Jesus Christ as my Lord and saviour but I was not really a serious Christian. As time went on though I started to get serious and really pay attention so one day my mother who is a prophetess had an encounter in a dream and delivered the message to me in the morning when she woke up. God had spoken to her and told her to tell me that He wanted to have a relationship with me and talk to me, He told her to tell me to read the whole bible from cover to cover. Now that's a thick book, but I was a voracious reader and was jobless at the time so I had the time on my hands. I will not share with you the experiences that came out of that two-week binge because they are personal but I will tell you that when I got to the book of Leviticus it was a huge shocker for me. There written in the bible in black and white were things very, very similar to what we had done with our father in the ATR, sacrifices given as commandments and instructions to the biblical Israelites by God through Moses in the desert. I could not believe my eyes taking into context that these are practices that had been in existence in the continent before any white man ever stepped foot on African soil and passed down through generations surviving even great periods of tribulation. It all got me thinking also about the culture of male and female circumcision which has been going on for thousands of years in Africa and was documented in the bible as a commandment and symbol of covenant given to Abram by God (Gen. 17) and of course I had my questions; how really foreign is this religion to this land? When a people do not know their history, and have other people searching their history for them and then hand-feeding it back to them picking and choosing what to present, then such a people are lost and open to manipulation indeed.

The political ruling class use religion the same way they use ethnicity. When they present candidates from among their group for political consideration they use ethnicity to bait the masses into thinking that they have shared qualities or in this case a shared faith with that candidate and the government but this is still all a ruse. There have been many changes of the religion of the leaders and candidates over the years but only the exploitation agenda has remained constant. Also there are different religions practised around the country but nationwide poverty is the only constant here. This is why emotions have to be put aside and in check if we're to tackle these problems objectively and get long lasting solutions. Anyways, I have presented my case to you for religion as an instrument of division within the general masses in Nigeria, spend some more time to think on it but we have a whole book to get through so let's keep it moving.

1d) DINOSAUR STATUS:

> *'Those [who are] abundant in years may not [always] be wise, Nor may the elders [always] understand justice.*
>
> *- Job 32:9 (Amp.)*

As far back as I can remember I have always been a cinephile, one of my favourite movies from the old days is the Steven Spielberg directed classic *'Jurassic Park'* (1993). As a young boy I remember watching this movie with almost equal levels of extreme terror and fascination at the images flashing across the screen and this is a testament to the power of cinema when it is done right. My favourite scene from this movie that made an impression on my young mind then and stuck with me into adulthood is the scene close to the end of the movie where the revived dinosaurs had escaped their enclosures and were trying to eat the humans who had earlier regenerated them but were now trying to stay alive and avoid being eaten by their creation. In the ensuing commotion, one of the dinosaurs, can't fully remember now, might have been a t-Rex struck down a banner with the words 'MILLIONS OF YEARS AGO DINOSAURS RULED THE EARTH' written on it that had stayed hung all movie long up to that point and in what I can only describe as elite scene blocking by Mr Spielberg and his crew time seemed to freeze for an instant while that banner just floats down slowly off the frame... simply brilliant! That was a symbolic scene for me because for as long as that banner had stayed up the message that it bore was true and generally accepted for that reality, that the time of the reign of the dinosaurs in the earth was long past but when the dinosaur, revived through whatever means ripped down the banner it symbolized that the message on the banner was no longer true because here are the dinosaurs back walking the earth and they were back to take over.

That was a movie but if the real life dinosaurs were to ever come back these ferocious beasts would find a different earth than the free earth they had reigned over millions of years ago, they would find that the far smaller, far smarter and far more ferocious species of bipeds called man is now running things on the earth and he's tailor made it to suit himself. How would the dinosaurs cope in this new world? How would they walk on sidewalks without disrupting pedestrian and even car traffic on the road? How would they go into the shops to get food and other things? How would they fly the skies without colliding into the numerous private jets and commercial planes? How would they attend church service to get saved? Wait... does that mean that there would be saved dinosaur souls with us in heaven? How would they get work and who would even type their CVs for them to get the interviews in the first place? Do you think HR would finally learn to behave when handling dino-employees because they know they'd get eaten if they ever tried half the stuff they did with human employees with the dino-employees? These questions, hilarious as they might seem, present the backdrop for this dinosaur theory which is the fourth level of simultaneous fission in our study and it sheds more light on the political ruling class of the country.

The dinosaur theory states that the power, wealth and influence which are all necessary driving forces for change, growth and development in any society in this world, are in the case of Nigeria held and controlled by a small group of old men and women that make up the political ruling class, born mostly within the years of the late 1920s to the early 1960s pre-independence Nigeria. This is why I call them dinosaurs because not only do they lack the energy needed to push for change in these times but they are also coming from times past making them incapable of fully functioning in these rapidly changing times thereby doing further harm to the entire body that makes up the country and holding her back. To drive my point home, I contend with you again that for this reason among many others Nigeria is not really a true democracy; because it is a country ruled by elder statesmen and women. This makes it a gerontocracy. And because it is ruled by the unsuitable and the incompetent, I put it to you that Nigeria is, and has been, a kakistocracy from the start, hence the underdevelopment, the poverty and undue suffering of her citizens. 'Why dost thou feed on thine seeds?' This alone is deep but not deep enough so I will have to break things down further so that my thoughts on these concepts can be fully articulated to you for better understanding.

The seriousness of these matters we are discussing here must not be lost on us at any moment, respect for one's elders is deeply embedded in the heart of the cornerstone of African culture. I know this deeply just as much as I know my own name. Since I was born my father, my mother and older ones around instilled in me a deep sense of respect for my elders, these cornerstones within the culture have not moved for thousands of years, not even the storm of tribulation that raged and spanned centuries in the continent could move them from their resting place; but I say in light of my observations this past decade and all that has happened not only in Nigeria but in sub-Saharan Africa as a whole these past decades, I say that these stones must at least be excavated around and keenly observed with tests conducted to determine their structural integrity for a knowledgeable assessment on how to build on them moving forward as a people. Young Nigerians say that Nigeria has been independent for over 60 years now and that her problems lie in the present. I understand where they are coming from but they are wrong. I insist that her problems come from the past down to the present and everything in between into tomorrow.

The Nigerians born between the late 1920s and the early 1960s are the ones I have aptly named the **notorious generation**. Why? Because they have been the most wasteful generation of wealth of a nation than any generation that has ever existed in the earth up until now. I dare you to look through the history books at any point in time, for any race on the planet from east to west, north to south, and show me a generation that has been as wasteful as the pre-independence **notorious generation** in Nigeria and I tell you that you will not find any. There have been wars, droughts and natural disasters over time that has caused great loss in different lands throughout the history of man on this planet and I must interject that these peoples and lands bounced back from whatever setback they encountered, but nowhere else and at no other time will you find such wilful waste of a country's wealth by born and sworn citizens of that country as you will see in Nigeria since 1960. Even the colonisers exploited and extracted the wealth of the land to build their own home countries and lands so it served a purpose for them at least, there was a calculation to their actions but alas! look at what we have here. These are the great peculiarities that transfixed me to this problem whereby I swore that I would not give up until I got to the bottom of it one way or the other.

Now when I say the **notorious generation** it doesn't mean that everyone born within the aforementioned time frame was involved but the general population from that time frame supplies the ingredients for the notorious ones which is a kind of mini-fission on its own. A lot of the people from that generation were sidelined, many did not live out their full days due to conditions in the country causing them to die before their time and the ones that were unfortunate to grow into old age in modern Nigeria have suffered just as much as the subsequent generations born after them into the present conditions. The sidelined ones would no doubt have found living conditions harder given their age, with many of them dying in anguish and regret in their old age.

These people are not immortal, they cheat the masses but cannot cheat time so as this **notorious generation** grows old and starts to die off they recruit new members from subsequent generations with like mind to continue their work and soon like a monarchy you will start to see them introduce their children and grandchildren after them to continue this trend of exploitation and repression at the expense of the Nigerian masses. The origin of these dinosaurs should not be a secret to you at this point as it is the origin of the political ruling class, they are one and the same and if you doubt it you can check and verify to see that no one born after 1960 in Nigeria has ever been president. This is not just an emotional fest about giving the youths a chance, no, there is something deeper at play here that I have not been able to fully grasp yet because it is elusive like trying to grab hold of a shadow in a dark room. I have grabbed a part of it but I still need light to see clearly what it is I'm holding. When you observe like me you will see that something more sinister that is bigger than just Nigeria is going on here and that the situation is the same for most of the sub-Saharan countries who were former colonies; they all have stalwarts from the old days before independence who either as despots or a group like in Nigeria hold on to the power and control of these nations for endless decades afterwards all the while working tirelessly and consistently to hold these countries down in the same spot they were in or worse still take them backwards while maintaining their power and control over the people within these territories. You can scream 'lust for power' and 'greed' like others have done for decades up till now but that is all a distraction. One thing I'm good at is fishing out the patterns in situations and I can tell you that the consistency of this phenomenon across the former colonies in Africa and whatever form it is happening tailor-made to the individual nations speaks more to intention and intelligence at play rather than chaos.

Here, we see the African tradition and culture of respect with all its merits corrupted whereby it then becomes a tool for the negative indoctrination of a young population who are then reluctant to confront and criticize the dinosaurs who are currently causing destruction and hardship in the society. These dinosaurs which preceded the young ones but should be long extinct are in control of the crucial veins of the national body from times past to the present, their aim and will is geared towards the continuous control and exploitation of the national body putting them in direct contradiction to the aims and desires of the collective mass. This therefore makes positive change in said society impossible. Like I said before, in African culture a great value and respect is placed on old age, but as the observer I've always had my reservations and my questions. In fact I screamed out the day I came across that verse in the book of Job that became the title text for this topic, a great burden was lifted off me that I had carried because of my resentment for the dinosaurs, a great resentment indeed because I could see that what they were doing to the people in the society was simply wrong, old or young, it was just wrong! I can understand the logic behind respect for elders in African culture but there were also a lot of people who were foolish when they were young that grew up into old age along with the wise, ones that Father Time could neither temper nor condition, they all have the gray hair so how can you distinguish? My own personal experiences would not allow me to just blatantly accept age as the prerequisite for wisdom because in my life I have met 60 year old boys and 25 year old men. For example there are a lot of 'old-boys' and 'old-girls' running around the Nigerian political stratosphere today so I have discerned a system by which I weigh the men and women I come in contact with to know their true value rather than to take them at face value. So, the dinosaurs as a group holding on to power and resources in the land, strategically placed at key control points all over the country to ensure the continuous extraction of vital resources from the masses is one of the major reasons why no Nigerian will make heaven.

1e) NORTHERN NIGERIA vs. SOUTHERN NIGERIA: THE FRUITS OF AMALGAMATION.

There might be some eye rolls and sighs at this stage when I say that we have to go back in time to the formation stage of this country to understand her present predominant predicaments but there is a reason. In the spiritual sciences, when you keep having recurring dreams that take you back to specific times and places in your past life like the primary school you attended as a child and long graduated from then it is a spiritual message of stagnancy in your life. In such a case, that all- encompassing extra-dimensional being of light from which all things proceed and are derived, both the seen and the unseen even down to your immortal spirit, is trying to communicate to you specific coordinates along your active life line which have previously been tampered with by the opposing force, of which you have to direct your spiritual warfare towards those coordinates to spiritually change the trajectory and circumstances of your active life line for the better. I will not speak things to you that I know nothing about, this phenomenon that I describe to you was something I suffered from personally for years until I confronted it and by His grace conquered it. We know that the physical is a crystallized projection of the spiritual, a mirror image of sorts if you will, so if in our quest for the root cause of Nigeria's problems we're tugging on and tracing the different cords relevant to this task and those cords keep taking us back to the formation stage like a damaged CD skipping on a spot in the player then it means that there are unaddressed errors in the foundation and formation of Nigeria.

This Northern Nigeria vs. Southern Nigeria debacle is another level of social fission that figured prominently in earlier iterations of this book playing into my own ethno-religious biases and my susceptibility to propaganda as an ordinary Nigerian born and raised in Nigeria, that is until I found it out to be a false bottom, and I will explain. During the process of the amalgamation of the Northern and Southern protectorates of Nigeria, Frederick Lugard in his own words during communication with the British home office described it as a union between a 'poor husband and a rich wife'. That in itself is self-explanatory in that resource-wise both regions were not evenly yoked together. That, coupled with other key differences in ethnicity and religion provided fertile ground for conflict and friction. After the dancing, singing, eating and drinking at the wedding ceremony, the poor husband quickly moved to secure his standing within the union, he moved for control via majority occupation of the political government structure, the civil service and the military based on alleged population superiority. I insist on saying 'alleged' here because there was no credible census conducted to prove that there were more people in the Northern part of Nigeria than in the Southern part, and wait a minute, just before you rush to pull up a map of the country to show me the difference in size of the Northern and Southern parts of the country I will have you know that there is a difference between land mass and population density. If you still decide to point out some census conducted at some point in the history of the country as your proof then I must tell you that I have witnessed several elections conducted in Nigeria in my lifetime and if they are any indication as to how such things are carried out in the country then I as the quester simply cannot accept whatever results presented as conclusive evidence. That aside I must say that we as a people, as a country must learn to seek out transparent facts and proofs as the basis to run our affairs rather than to rely on assumptions and sweeping statements as truths. So anyways, all key pillars of the country had a higher Northern presence which essentially translated to Northern control and there was no prenuptial agreement for this particular union.

When you look at it as I've presented it, it looks logical but it is not quite definite which doesn't make it wrong, just that it's not entirely accurate and this is why I've called it a false bottom. The margins between truth and mistakes when you study things like this are so slim that it is easy to be thrown off course such that when you observe the affairs of Nigeria with a magnifying glass, you have to hold another magnifying glass to that first magnifying glass to see properly. If we say that there is an ethnic race in the country then the winner has been the North, it is no longer a North v. South but more a North over South as reflected in the political structure, civil service, headship of federal parastatal and the military. This has meant that they have produced most of the civilian and military leadership in the country till date with few outliers from other regions interspersed, the unitary federal system currently practised in Nigeria which gives any ethnic group in control of the federal government absolute power over the other ethnic groups, their territories and their resources is just a veiled form of tyranny.

Going by the sentiments in the minds of ordinary Nigerians about the North over South debacle, if we were to ethnically deconstruct the unitary federalism practised in Nigeria and label it as some masterstroke or master plan by the poor husband to control and exploit the wealth of the rich wife then you will see that upon creation in 1960 Nigeria was first a federation that was divided into different regions with their own leadership. It was the military leadership in the person of Major General Aguiyi Ironsi, a man from the South East, that ditched the Republican Constitution of 1963 and changed Nigeria from a federation to a unitary state unifying the civil service too in the process. This led to widespread riots with casualties at the time but it was he who laid the foundation for the current system we see today. Make of that what you will but it was the foundation he laid that was then built on by successive northern leaders. In this system, the natural resources which is mainly from the sale of crude oil from the South-South goes first to the federal government who then hands out a monthly allocation into the waiting caps, bowls and outstretched hands of the 36 states to manage their affairs.

I say it here again that Nigeria is not a democracy and I will prove it. If we are to go by the provisions of ethnocracy then the dominant ethnic group which in this case is the North, is supposed to take the wealth and resources of the country which in this case is the wealth and resources of the South-South and use said resources to develop and enrich her kinsmen and her lands, right? A quick google search of the top 10 poorest states in the country will show you 9 Northern states and 1 South-Eastern state. The extreme widespread poverty coupled with the lack of education, infrastructures and basic amenities paints the real picture of things on ground. This would make for good points for those in the South to banter and make fun of those in the North but the fact of the matter is that the South is not too far behind if not for anything else for the poverty and this is where I start to ask my questions; if the North won the ethnic race then where did all the wealth from crude sales extracted through the federal unitary system go to? Because It is definitely not in the North, go and look at them, the people are very poor, it is not also in the South as they are poor too so where did all the wealth go to? Where is all that tribal love by those in control of the political government structure towards their ethnic brothers and regions? I just hope the scales are falling off some eyes at least, I cannot say all eyes because you black people are a peculiar people in your reasoning and your actions; if the scales don't fall from yours then I have wasted my life this past decade plus putting this book together for you. Digging deeper, based on the answers to the questions I just asked you can see that Nigeria is not even a true ethnocracy.

Nigeria is not a democracy, she is not a true ethnocracy, she is not even a theocracy because then those in power would have focused on their brothers and sisters of same faith but the whole country made up of Christians, Muslims and traditionalists are poor regardless of the publicly professed religions of those in power. She cannot be an eternal gerontocracy because we are currently trapped in time on this plane so our mortal bodies must grow old and die after the natural order. The true dinosaurs and dragons are no longer walking the earth, likewise the notorious generation cannot live forever but through time you can see that the pattern of extraction, exploitation and poverty in the land despite her many riches has been present in the land in varying degrees; through slavery, down to colonialism, and down to this alleged 'independence' they sold to the continent. I will not say much about that right now as we will come to it later. So if she is not all these then what is she truly? Well, I'll tell you, she is a lie and a mirage, a tricky seductive lady indeed and that's why I call her political fraud committed on an ignorant and naive people. All the components of my theories that I have presented to you up until now are marker points along the way of my journey through the years, depending on the level of my enlightenment at the time I stopped at different points of these markers thinking I had arrived at my destination but my co-author with gentle stirrings in my heart let me know that my work was not yet finished. There is cause and there is effect, my goal was the root cause and as I dug deeper I found out that all these ethnicity, religion and others were just tools to manipulate the masses while they are being exploited by the political ruling class which comprises of a small group of men and women from all ethnicities and religions in the country united in their common goal to exploit the resources of the country and appropriate said resources for themselves. The Nigerian political ruling class is a subset of the Nigerian masses but it is also the superset of the Nigerian political government which itself is a system and a structure of men and women from the political ruling class in federal, state, local government positions including the civil service and other parastatals that have the legal rights and authority to rule the Nigerian territory and the peoples within. The Okpe people of Delta state have a parable which in pidgin English says **'the worm wey dey chop bitter kola, na inside the bitter kola e dey dey o'** which in English means that: the worm that destroys the bitter kola, another species of the kola nut family, by eating it from within is usually within the bitter kola nut itself, get it? Just to say that the cancer that destroys a body eventually killing the person is within that body itself and if we can look at a biblical parallel of sorts we can say that **'a little leaven leaveneth the whole lump'** (Gal 5:9).

The political ruling class exists within the masses even though they are distinct from each other. When a government is to be formed in the country the ruling class reaches within its own basket, a basket of itself, and from there presents candidates of certain ethnicity and religion to market those candidates to the masses depending on the region of the country to create a false temporary bridge and resonance with the masses of that region as if to say to them *'we are one people'* and it works. These candidates eventually occupy the political government leadership structure of the country and the operations of the political ruling class continues unhindered because they have members from their group in positions of power in the country to further their interests, objectives and goals. The individuals that make up the masses on the other hand for a time and a season get to live vicariously through their alleged 'representatives' in that leadership structure created by shared ethnicity and religion among other things, where they can then banter others and even exert some form of oppression temporarily over others in the same group as themselves, just of different ethnicity and religion but as a whole group they have just been robbed; their pockets picked in broad daylight with both their eyes wide open when it happened. They have lost the battle of the political ruling class vs. the masses, they are just sadly too poor and too ignorant to even know it.

The Northern and Southern regions of Nigeria have been joined now as a single territory for over 100 years. When you look beyond the mirage and the many distractions you'll see that great care has been taken for the peoples of these regions to never fully know and understand themselves, the insecurity in the regions, the bad roads that lead to accidents that are just conveniently filled with kidnappers along the way among other things to discourage movement and commerce between the peoples of the regions. All play their part in an effective divide and conquer system. In fact the deeper I go I can say that these black peoples of the masses are living their own real life Truman show and don't even know it! The ethnicity and religion along with other divisionary tactics only exist in the minds of the masses as they know it. The rules of the game have changed and too bad for them they live in a world where individuals from among them, who were and in a sense are still a part of them have cast aside these burdens for personal gains and enrichment. In this artificially created reality for the masses, things like ethnicity and religion become tools of manipulation and control by the ruling class, a camouflage and disguising technique to ensure their dominance in the great unspoken battle despite their numerical disadvantage. As a matter of fact their small numbers becomes an advantage for the ruling class as it presents fewer dissenting voices within their ranks to distract them from their goal so they are able to remain focused and united in the battle. Knowing all this I would like to ask some questions before I leave this topic: oh great Nigerian; in the ethnic race in Nigeria who is the winner? In the never- ending Northern Nigeria vs Southern Nigeria debate who do you now think has been the winner so far?

1f) INDIVIDUALISM vs. COLLECTIVISM:

'In individuals, insanity is rare; but in groups, parties, nations and epochs, it is the rule.'

- Friedrich Nietzche.

Nature abhors a vacuum, in life there are dynamic forces and counter-forces simultaneously balancing each other out, adjusting in varying degrees and amounts through time; this constantly moving multi-dimensional dance always seeking balance is what is called existence. Without the balance provided by the counter-forces in nature it would crash with time; nature is alive, nature is energy, nature is mobile, nature is aware, nature is encompassing and finally nature is intelligence. To exist voluntarily or even involuntarily as an entity within this framework, is to be acted upon by these constantly balancing forces and counter-forces until an equilibrium is reached with you in it. The sciences tell us that for inception there is a swimming race between millions of sperm cells and the winner of that thrashing about gets to fertilize the egg while the others die off. I do not even want to talk about the exertion that takes place to introduce the sperm cells in the first place because that is another kind of struggle that has claimed the lives of many brave soldiers. After that a baby is pushed out in great pain and travail, the lungs of that baby from that moment never cease in their work to draw in and expel air, the heart muscles never stop expanding and contracting as they pump oxygen rich blood around the body, the neurons in the brain never stop firing all through the lifetime of that individual, and if the spirit of that individual were to cross over its former house, the shell is not left alone, nature's forces immediately go to work breaking it down and eventually reclaiming it in a continuous process and from this you can see that to live is to struggle, life is a constant battle.

The constant fission for whatever myriad of reasons within the Nigeria peoples and by extension the black populations around the world means that there is a failure for blacks to properly congregate and aggregate themselves. Divisions within human populations are normal, this is what is called human diversity but when these differences are not properly managed it can lead to serious problems within the population. In the case of the black race, the most diverse people in the world, their differences have historically been exploited and magnified for effect. That is the past and we cannot do anything about it now but we can try to handle the lingering consequences of that within the race. When individuals of other races aggregate themselves into nations, they are combining the sum total of their wills and their collective interests into a single entity. When all of this is backed by whatever resources they are able to come up with depending on the ability of that nation, they generate considerable energy and this exerts force to all directions in the world around them. When the nations of this world deal with one another it is these great accumulated forces and energies that interact, and since nations are collections of humans it is also a business between great spiritual energies of the accumulated human spirits and the spiritual cities within that national territory. It is also an interaction between great soul energies from the great minds of the individuals within the nations and finally it is interaction between the aggregated men and women themselves representing both the collective interests as a canopy and the individual wills of their people.

These great forces and energies generated cocooning collective interests and wills are currently colliding against each other in the world and balancing each other out. They may be subtle, they may be visible, overt or covert, their effects may or may not even be readily discernible but make no mistakes they are there. So if you as an individual, no matter how great you think you are, no matter how fast you can run or how high you can jump or how well you can sing or dance, no matter how gifted or talented you might be; all the world is in competition with itself, if you step into this world of great forces and energies on your own you will not be able to generate enough by yourself to adequately compete, thus you just cannot and will not prevail!

> *'And if one prevail against him, two shall withstand him; and a threefold cord is not quickly broken.'*
>
> *Ecclesiastes 4:12 (KJV)*

At the heart of it all, the black problem is a problem of organisation, the lack of organic organisation. Theoretical physicists and astrologers tell us about the existence of black holes, regions in outer space with great gravitational pull that nothing escapes from them not even light rays as fast as they are, the force of the black hole sucks them in. That may be well and good but in the earth today there does not exist a single black nation, a black dense nucleus made up of the concentrated collective wills of black people with enough centripetal force to hold its best human and material resources in place around this black nucleus and fully dedicated to protecting, projecting and upholding the interests of its black citizens and by extension the black peoples of this planet in the midst of the other projected collective interests and wills from other races; there is none. Now you can point out the great nations of this world that have black people living in them and have given them a piece of paper that says they are citizens and I will tell you that while it is good to have good neighbours and to spend time in their houses, no matter how comfortable they make you feel, it is not the same as having your own and being in your own home. Besides, these nations were not primarily planned for black interests from the start. They were not planned for black interests but accommodate black interests to varying degrees and that makes a significant difference in the grand scheme of things. You might also ask me, *"Oh what about all the big black countries in Africa?"* and to that I'll reply that I have begun to show you from the start of this book up to this point and will continue to do so until the end that these countries are held and controlled by a small group of blacks within the general population that hold different interests from that of the larger population. The fact that the controlling group and the oppressed group are all blacks does not mean they are set up and cater to the interests of blacks on the planet, as a matter of fact it's quite the opposite which makes them anti-black. We're not going to throw this on anybody else; this is why black men have to stand up and start tackling black problems in the world.

With this situation in mind you can see that there is a void, a deficit, a black void which is more appropriate for my use in this instance as opposed to the word 'vacuum' used above, such that when the collective forces of others come to bear on a planetary scale there is no force emanating from the blacks to counter-balance the incoming forces so they cannot properly contend for themselves or prevail because they do not have covering, they do not have a voice and they do not have the stature to resist as individuals; this now manifests through different channels and avenues in the world. Nigeria is the most populous black nation with an estimated 200 million people but in global affairs you will see countries with less than 20% of her population either by their own sheer existence or by their alliance with other powerful nations wield more force, voice and stature than her. This is the altar of the continuous racism in the world today, let the spiritual ones use 'altar' in that sentence while the rest of you, fine intellectuals, can substitute the word 'foundation' for 'altar' and you get the meaning; knowing this truth you realise that a white person calling a black person the word 'nigger' is not the true racism, it's an insult at best, school yard name-calling and should have been treated as such but we see grown and mature men and women standing in broad daylight with their eyes wide open looking at the birds flying past while their pockets are being not so subtly picked, right there!

I use Nigeria as an example and I tell you that the black countries of Africa are not real countries, rather they are just territories to define the area and limit of control within the continent and in her case the control is by the political ruling class. The citizens within these divided territories co-exist with one another side by side in the conditions that they find themselves, and this gives the illusion both to themselves and to the outside world that they are a united functioning country but in terms of real congregation, aggregation and organisation to unite their collective wills and forces, and then to channel these forces to bear they are non-existent. For this reason and others I do not look at them as real countries. This is again a black problem and black men worldwide need to stand up and step up as men to tackle the problems of their communities because no one else will do it for you.

So what the acute social fission has accomplished, both the ones I listed and the ones I didn't list, is that if you take the African as an individual, scale up to the family level, then to the state or province which he comes from or which he resides in, and then up to the country level you will see that though physically close to each other they are all in isolation of one another within the land space that makes up the continent. It's like there is a repelling force emanating concentrically from the individuals all the way up their groupings to the continental level. The controlling powers of the different territories on the continent have done a stellar job to keep their isolation going because it benefits their interests; they speak different languages, use different currencies which stifles trade between them, the borders are a hassle to get through from one country to the other, all this means that there is generally little interaction between the citizens of the countries in Africa. The individuals have more knowledge about other far away continents where their focus is firmly fixated on through sports and entertainment than they do with their brothers next to them. It is easier for individuals within the continent to bond with people from other far away continents than other Africans. For example, in present times, with the channels and processes in place it is easier for me as a Nigerian to emigrate to Britain in Europe and settle down than to go to South Africa, another predominantly black country in the same continent. All these factors push the black man in the continent and the others in communities around the world towards individualism, a kind of each-man-for-himself mentality rather than to proper bonding as a collective.

Have you ever come in contact with the average Nigerian before? Many of them are intelligent, hardworking and possess other good mental and physical attributes such that you'll find yourself asking questions about how a people like this came to be in the situation they are in today. This is not to say that they are all perfect because every population of every race in the world has its own share of fools and idiots. The mystery here is that when you stack together many of these brilliant Nigerian individuals together into a country, you do not get a super group of intelligent individuals, instead we see that the attributes of the collective is very different from the attributes of the individuals gathered to form it. So in a way you can say that Nigeria and by extension Africa today is not a projection of the larger percentage of the wills of the individuals that make up the population but rather a sum total of the wills of the general population. For this reason among others I will explain as we move on in this book, many have opted for the individual route but as I pointed earlier, no matter how physically strong an individual is, how genetically gifted they may be or how intelligent they are, they will not be able to on their own generate the required energy to contend with other powerful aggregated energies that have shaped the world and its operations today. It does not matter if the individuals that aggregated themselves to form these powerful collectives are not as physically dominant or mentally intelligent as this one individual; what matters is that they have bonded into these powerful collectives that covers the flaws of the individuals within it. So when the interaction takes place between the forces of this world these intelligent individual black energies get absorbed by the existing powerful collectives making the already powerful stronger in the process, this presents a continuous loss for the black race.

Let us see what we can learn from nature pertaining to this topic. When you consider the 4 big cats of the world which are the lion, leopard, tiger and cheetah, all with their different attributes, the lion is considered as the king of the jungle, why is that? Because the lion is not the fastest. That award goes to the cheetah which is the fastest land animal; the lion is not the strongest, pound for pound in a 1v1, that is the tiger, and in terms of versatility and smarts, of the big 4 the leopard, my personal favourite takes the cake on that so why is the lion regarded as king? The golden reason is because of the lion's complex social characteristics that make them consolidate in groups called prides. You see out of all these big cats the lion is the only true social one among them, the other three are solitary cats who only come together with others of their species in chance encounters that almost always lead to a fight and during mating seasons where they are pushed by nature via hard to resist hormonal urges to ensure the continuity of their species. Alliances can be observed in young cheetah males who band together for varying amounts of time in twos and threes to increase their chances of survival (collectivism) but lion prides take this banding together to a whole different level with pride members numbering from 15 up to as many as 30 cats in some instances comprising of some cubs with females who are the hunters and workers of the group making up the bulk of the population and then one or two dominant males occupying a large territory. Say what you will but either by evolution or just plain traits the lion's collectivism has made it the undisputed king of the jungle. When I think about it if tigers or leopards ever got together to form prides of their own they would be terrifying, thinking about their personal attributes especially the tigers, just try to imagine a pride of tigers! but they do not socialise like that so the lion remains king of them all.

In conclusion I just want to say that animals herd together in the wild for many benefits chief of which is protection from predators because there is safety in numbers. The acute social fission is one of my key theories on why Nigeria is the way she is; what this theory teaches is that no matter the amazing individual, spiritual, physical and mental attributes of blacks, their failure to effectively manage and tone down the divisions among them has broken their numbers down into individuals preventing them from building proper communities and countries as a collective to protect the interest and wills of the individual members that make up the collective. This has made them vulnerable to attacks like exploitation and continuous losers in the great battle of the political ruling class vs the masses because their default existence in Nigeria and anywhere else they find themselves is always one of individualism vs. collectivism.

2. THE WEAPONIZATION OF POVERTY:

> *"The people in the culture of poverty have a strong feeling of marginality, of helplessness, of dependency, of not belonging. They are like aliens in their own country, convinced that the existing institutions do not serve their interests and needs. Along with this feeling of powerlessness is a widespread feeling of inferiority, of personal unworthiness, and discrimination. People with a culture of poverty have very little sense of history. They are a marginal people who know only their own troubles, their own local conditions, their own neighbourhood, [and] their own way of life. Usually, they have neither the knowledge, the vision nor the ideology to see the similarities between their problems and those of others like themselves elsewhere in the world although they are very sensitive indeed to status distinctions."*
>
> - Oscar Lewis
>
> *Five Families: Mexican Case Studies in the Culture of Poverty (1959)*

Listen to me dear Nigerian, you are at war and in this war there is no middle ground, there is no sitting on the fence, no dilly dallying and ignorance here does not give you exemption or protection from this war. First you are a human on planet earth, then you have the disadvantage of being melanated, and then not just black but you're in Africa, what location in Africa? Nigeria! So you see? You are a warrior on the battle field plains, a gladiator in the cruel arena of life, a commodity in a brutal marketplace, yes... you're an antelope caught in the dangerous wild, in the territory of a vicious pride of lions and the only way to survive this is to become a lion yourself. *Oh but I didn't sign up for this* you might say, *I did not choose this life* you might add and you might be partly right but understand that even though you did not choose this life it chose you. You were somewhere in the vastness of eternity then the hands of time had reached out and plucked you like the hands of a valiant boy on the mango tree, so even before you climbed out of your mother and drew in your first breath you were already conscripted, you, poor black baby, unless, just unless, you were lucky enough to be born into the other group but if you're not and you're of the people then you must fight. So quit complaining and fight, you must fight with everything you have if you want to live. This is war and there is no middle ground, the battle horns were sounded a long time ago even before you were born but if you listen intently you will hear them echo across the waves of time to your ears intermingled with the cries of your forebears, it gives a sweet and painful sensation at the same time like when you offer a very dear sacrifice. If you close your eyes and stand still for a brief moment you will feel the earth beneath you tremble to the rhythms of the beating of the war drums with the stompings of over a billion black souls worldwide rushing to battle but this one you find yourself in right now is your post and you must take up for your race. The dead and the dying lie around you but you have no time to weep, you have no time even to consider what's around you, only to fight. This is your time and you must contend for your post until your time is up then you must pass this cursed baton to your children and the doomed generation coming after to continue from where you stopped. All the while this uncaring great war between the political ruling class vs. the Nigerian masses rages on like an unchecked forest fire, taking and giving as it moves on and as they say, all is fair in love and war.

Nigeria is regarded as one of the poorest countries in the world and it has taken a lot of concentrated effort to get her there. All things considered, if she had been allowed to aimlessly stumble about her trajectory or even if she had just been ruled and governed by clueless idiots since the time of her inception she definitely would not be in the position that she is in today. I guess what I'm trying to say is that in the case of the Nigerian barrel, if it had just been leakages from mismanagement and casual theft there would have still been enough left in the barrel to make something out of the country but that is not the case. Instead the barrel is continually systemically emptied of its contents and the container is continually damaged to ensure that it is never able to retain anything of value and that is where I'd like to focus my attention for this theory. You have to keenly and closely observe the operations in Nigeria to see what is really happening in the country because there are many distractions deliberately put there to throw hound dogs like myself off the scent trail but I am committed already, and every time I was thrown off trail I did not simply give up and call off my search, rather I wandered about tirelessly in the spirit and soul realm until I got reconnected, then I proceeded with my work. This is why I insist that to do a thing like we see happening in Nigeria is not random but requires careful planning, intention, execution and perseverance to accomplish. So I make sure to remind myself always that anything can be done in this life, for if a country like Nigeria that is supposed to be high and above could be made poor and pulled to the ground, dragged into poverty and then consistently kept in that state of poverty, ably and adequately maintained in it over these decades, then trust, anything can be done indeed.

When I first started theorizing about poverty in Nigeria I focused on its consequences and effects on the people and the society because that was my outtake from my then limited perspective and experience as a citizen in the country. Like other ordinary Nigerians around me I lamented our daily struggles due to the prevalent poverty that surrounded us, my thoughts and analysis on the matter were clouded by my emotions as I mourned the slow and inevitable demise of my dear country which we were horrifically living out in real time. She had been forced to put on a garment that was neither befitting nor meant for her in the first place. It took some time but I realised that this too was a false bottom as it did not have any impact in the general Nigerian equation that I was formulating at the time and this led me to ask more questions as usual. We, as Nigerians, all know that Nigeria is not a poor country by any means, we knew it like the hand knows the way to the mouth even in a dark room. We also knew that the politicians through corruption were embezzling the money in the country and telling the people that there was no money. Every Nigerian you ask on the street down to the little ones will tell you this without hesitation if you bother to ask so if that was just the answer to the problem then there was no need to write a whole book about what is common knowledge, but of course there's more to it. Besides I never trust anything that everybody believes to be true in the first place. So there is cause and there is effect, we knew the effects of the poverty in the country because we could feel it everyday then the cause we attributed to corruption which was due to the greed of the politicians and this is where I started to have doubts. I questioned that if it was just greed then these people should have been satisfied at some point, and this is where the emotions, the religious teachings, the morals and other mental indoctrination start to play with your mind; like millions of Nigerians do even till this day I naively questioned that surely they must have a conscience for the sufferings of the masses in the country, surely they must feel in their hearts the hunger in the land and see with their eyes the poverty of their people and while I asked these questions the pictures from my earlier vision popped up in my mind and started replaying. Then I recalled that the elites in that building in the vision had been emotionless to the suffering and screaming of the struggling masses beneath them. In fact I could say there was veiled pleasure on their faces, faint smiles like they enjoyed it even and just like that I had a eureka moment!

The problem, you see, was the approach. I had approached it wrongly thinking like everybody else that the poverty in Nigeria was just a consequence of the greed of the political class but when I looked at the bags of cash they had stashed for themselves in the vision and how it correlated to real life I realised that greed could not just be the main reason here so the equation could not be balanced out totally with just greed there as the main active factor. Because I now had this vision etched in my mind and could return to it at will, it became like a CCTV footage of a crime scene that detectives play back over and over again searching for clues because you see Nigeria is a real life crime scene so I returned to that vision and looked repeatedly back and forth from the elites in the building to the struggling screaming masses below and asked myself, what am I missing here? The bags of money are with the elites in the building and lots of bags they were, they had the armed forces in front of the building to protect them from the horde outside so they are safe and settled which means that greed cannot just be the main motivating factor here, so why do these masses still need to be poor and be kept in poverty? This little change in the why opened up a blockade in my mind like a dam breaking and a whole new perspective of thoughts and reasoning were flooded into my consciousness, so why do these people need to be poor and kept in poverty? If you recall in the vision I told you that the elites threw in a small wad of cash into the crowd and watched the frenzy that ensued, right? For as long as they scrambled among themselves for scraps they could never unite to fight and overthrow the elites in the building. That made the money a tool for control, with that tool they were able to sprinkle some in the pocket of the police and armed forces to ensure their protection from the horde. What I drew from this is that if they were ever going to keep their stolen loot away from the very people they stole it from in the first place and not get punished for all they have done in the country then the masses have to remain poor and impoverished because if they ever get money they would challenge the elites and that would be end to the way of life for the elites. This was a high stakes battle and they knew it but the masses do not seem to know that these political elites in this war are fighting for their very own survival; the thoughts kept pouring in.

    Adding all this to what I already knew in terms of the war between the political ruling class vs. the masses it became clear to me that the money or lack of it was not only just a tool for control but it was also a weapon. In war, if you can keep your enemy weak by keeping them constantly poor, uneducated and hungry then they will never be able to rise up to fight against you and even if they did try they'll never be able to win against you because you have resources to sustain you through the battle and they do not. So in my Nigerian equation there was a shift, poverty was no longer just a consequence of greed by the elites but a military strategy employed by the political ruling class against the masses and it works like a charm. Think of a boa constrictor, it is a patient killer. As an ambush predator It hunts by lying in wait motionless for its prey and when the prey comes close it bites and wraps itself around it then starts to squeeze. Every time the prey exhales the boa tightens its grip a little bit more such that the pressure it exerts on its prey's rib cage and the lungs within is slowly, constantly being increased. What this does is that it's depriving the prey of the life giving resources, in this case oxygen, while it's free to draw in as much air as it likes or needs in this case so the prey gets inevitably weakened in that battle and cannot fight back while the boa is sustained and refreshed. This happens until the prey eventually dies and even when the prey is getting swallowed the boa has an extendable trachea among other tricks that allows it to continue to breathe while swallowing large prey. 50 cent used this strategy to great effect in his battle against Ja Rule and Irv Gotti in the 2000s. The political elites like a boa constrictor have their hands or for the sake of continuation of this analogy their folds strategically wrapped tightly around the vital arteries of Nigeria as a country and this is how they exert their control over significantly numerically larger masses, for this is war and the goal is to win, there is no middle ground in it.

So what is this poverty as a weapon deployed by the political elites against the poor masses expected to achieve? Because every weapon has an effect; when you shoot a bullet at a man you expect him to die, when you cut with a knife you expect him to bleed, when you hit with a stick you expect him to hurt, what does poverty achieve? Poverty is a key arrow in the quiver of the elites because it creates the environment for and keeps the people in a state of survival such that they are constantly under stress so cannot think properly and they are so busy trying to survive from day to day that they have no time for anything else or are simply powerless to do anything else even if they have the time. Oscar Lewis captures this concept beautifully in my lead text and this is one of the reasons why I stopped following the day to day news in Nigeria. If we take the economy of Nigeria as an example, the government has been putting out all sorts of figures for all the years that the professional analysts and economists have tried to analyse and present to the people as the reasons for the state of the economy. These men and women spent their entire lives analysing these numbers generated from an artificial scenario created for the country, because of that they could never discover the truth of what is really going on in the country. In my mind the people like that and those that followed them were hooked to the matrix, they were still yet to awaken because for me I found that the more I awakened the less I desired to fit into my environment. So these people tried to apply the economic laws and principles of this world to explain what was fashioned by political will so for that reason the things that happened economically in the country left them confounded and bewildered, and none of their projections ever came to pass for them and those that followed them. 1 Cor 2:11a *'for who among men knows the thoughts of a man except the man's spirit within him?'*

There are different levels of living for man no matter where he finds himself in life, they always take these listed forms of progression or growth and they also apply to nations too because a man is a nation, a woman is a nation, a man and a woman together is a nation and a seed is a forest. The forms of living are the survival mode, comfort zone, leisure and extravagance listed in their progressive order. There is nothing to be too technical about here, at the survival mode the man is in his base state, he is lacking in knowledge and since knowledge is power he is lacking power. A man in survival mode is lacking resources, he is limited, constantly under physical and mental stress, constantly at the mercy of his environment and his inability to change his circumstances, always in lack and everything he has at hand, I mean everything in his possession is geared towards his survival as the name implies. In this sub-human state the man's capabilities are limited but it's only meant to be a temporary state for him to climb higher to the next state and the next and so on. As his resources increase along with his knowledge, his power and his influence he is finally able to exert himself on his environment such that the earth herself and all of eternity would bear record of his time here when he showcases his god-like essence spiritually, mentally and physically to the highest he can attain as his creator originally intended. But this process as with many, many others with enough knowledge can be hacked, and when this happens and the man is kept perpetually in survival mode then instead of him attaining his highest form the opposite occurs and he shrinks in his totality to a sub-human form; spiritually because his connection to the divine will be impeded and affected by his current state, mentally as he cannot think straight being under constant stress and physically as his nourishment is minimal and his ability for proper healthcare is limited. So you see that poverty affects the totality of a man's being, in that survival mode the god-like light of man's essence is dimmed or worse even drained, he is a reproach and a burden to the earth so much so that my conclusion of the whole matter is that a man or a nation in continuously prolonged survival mode is in bondage.

Since the days when the first of the new soul plus spirit man was created and he roamed the plains of Africa, even before genetic material was extracted from him to create the female of his species, after a period of observation where it was determined that this new prototype was the best of the lot yet and could be mass produced, he had been equipped with all he would ever need to subdue the earth, and to grow to become the man on the earth you saw yesterday to the man you see today and the one that will be in the earth tomorrow until the end of this current earth. He did not possess sharp teeth and claws like other biological beings created in the earth or the ability to run very fast and not tire easily. The greatest gifts he was given were sealed up within him and they made him the greatest out of all the created biological beings and rightfully so. As a biological machine he had a brain with which he could access and navigate the vastness of the unsearchable soul realm and tap into the creative powers of his Creators bringing that knowledge and power to bear on the earth. As if that was not enough he was also given the ability to house light, you see man was created by beings of light and he was given the ability to carry this light and be one with this light such that he is always connected to his Maker and he never forgets that he came from something more than he sees and that the earth alone is not all of existence, that there is more and he is like an ambassador here.

So the descendants that came after from the first soul plus spirit man and woman grew and developed from how they were created and that growth has continued till this day never stopping and following the natural order as it should be. So anywhere you see this powerful being called man in the earth in a constant and prolonged survival mode just know that it is not natural and that the natural order has been tampered with. It could be through constant wars, could be resource extraction like we see in Africa or a combination of other factors but the fact remains that the natural order has been tampered with and somehow behind the scenes there is intention behind it, I just hope this makes a little bit of sense to you. Even the previous biological humanoid prototypes created before this one showed this natural progression. Even though they were lacking in ability they still showed progression; they made tools, they created art, they lived in social groups and did some form of animal and plant husbandry showing the potential of what could be achieved until they were phased out, how much more this new man? This is why I have a very deep hatred for poverty, I know I said no emotions as we go through this subject matter but I must tell you here that I have a very deep hatred for poverty because I was born and raised in Nigeria and I have seen what poverty has done to the people around me; I have seen them die inside but still go on breathing, walking around for decades like zombies while still trying to perform before their biological shells expire. I have experienced and seen needless loss that caused me great pain, I have seen wasted potential on an industrial scale and my conclusion remains the same, that poverty is a prison of its own kind and those living in continuous poverty are in bondage.

If we could venture for a bit I'll tell you that spiritually what the political ruling class are doing in Nigeria is called destiny exchange. When a nation that is supposed to be well off is brought to a place of ruin and kept there via supernatural assistance then that's destiny exchange, same thing applies to individuals. Let us consider it in the natural sense, let's say we have an individual born with gifts and a destiny to be a great astronaut for his country when he grows up but his country is held in bondage and grossly mis-managed thereby leaving it grossly under-developed. An under-developed country whose citizens are in survival mode and locked in a battle with perpetual poverty will not have the time for leisurely and extravagant pursuits like astronomy and space travels when their problems are right here on earth staring them menacingly in the face so what can a guy do? He joins his family to the farm to do subsistence farming under the hot sun, a back-breaking life of suffering for a man that should be walking on the moon and be celebrated as a national hero. If one day on his way back from the farm he is hit by a rickety car with faulty headlights as he attempts to cross the dark road at night and he dies due to lack of adequate medical care then his destiny was simply exchanged. How, you may ask? Well if the budget for the astronomy centre was a hundred million naira just for illustration's sake and it was budgeted for and the funds provided for it, but as is the case in Nigeria the funds find their way into private pockets of the political ruling class then they have simply exchanged his destiny and those of other astronauts like him who should have risen from the society. To further elucidate, if the money budgeted for a state-of-the-art hospital in his locality was fifty million naira and a monkey or a snake swallowed it in the office of some political big wig then his and others whose lives could have been saved with a good hospital around them have been shortchanged and their destinies exchanged. You can do the same calculation for roads and other infrastructures that makes the lives of citizens better, this is how that detestable system called destiny exchange works.

Another thing that most people don't know is that the pain and suffering endured by this individual in his lifetime and others like him is a kind of currency in the spirit realm. That realm is not a monolithic one, there are beings of light and there are spirit beings of darkness; when something like this happens the spiritual beings of darkness working in conjunction with strategically helped and placed humans that create these wicked conditions to entrap the people and produce such results gain notoriety from it and are rewarded for it, this is also the same for beings of light when they do good deeds. Now this is just for an individual so imagine the kind of loot that is generated spiritually for an entire nation in this manner. I know I am talking to a diverse audience so if you understand spiritual things then you understand it, and if you don't then it's all good, there's plenty of natural physical analysis for you to feast on and not get lost in the conversation so no worries.

I am a humble painter and none of my brush strokes are wasted. With every single one I apply to the canvas a little bit more of my masterpiece is revealed to the world. The last brush stroke could have been a mistake but it's not wasted because with it I learnt what not to do if I wanted to achieve my aim so the next one goes over it and I tell you I am relentless. I am the humble sculptor and no strike of my mallet on my chisel is wasted on the medium, even if a mistake were to occur I have the creative wit and tricks to mask it and still present my masterpiece. In the general Nigerian equation this theory of poverty is not isolated, in the battle of the political ruling class vs. the masses in Nigeria poverty is a weapon of mass destruction, a nuclear bomb detonated by the political ruling class on the already divided masses plagued by diverse social fission to further weaken them as a body so that the political class can intimidate them, manipulate them and in so doing dominate them. You can tell that in this state the masses are not able to accumulate and generate enough force to contend for their wills and their interests, they are solely in the grasp and absolute control of the political class who can bend them towards any direction at their will and bidding. The goal of this domineering group is the continuous unchallenged and unopposed extraction of the resources of the land while the masses are kept under their control; and poverty helps to achieve this because the masses artificially locked in survival mode will redirect all remaining attention and resources towards surviving thus making them very vulnerable indeed.

3. NIGERIAN MINDSET AND MENTALITY:

> *'Until you have built mental structures, you could not build excellent physical structures. What you see in society is a reflection; it is also a manifestation of the structures of the mind of the people behind whatever you have seen.'*
>
> *- Pastor Chris Oyakhilome.*

Proverbs 23:7a says *'for as he thinketh in his heart, so is he'*, this was then changed to the more popular *'as a man thinks in his heart so is he'* which very aptly captures a psychological truth and fact that shows the relationship between a man, his innate thoughts and how they shape his external conditions. Mindset and mentality have many definitions and mean different things to different people in different fields but in all these different scenarios they retain some core elements. The football manager coaching some of the biggest clubs on the planet requires a kind of mentality from the club, the players and the fans if they are to fight for and win important things. Your supervisor at work tasked with improving productivity requires a type of mentality from the management and working staff to achieve this, the teacher in class trying to get the best out of her students needs them to have the right mentality to grasp the concepts she is teaching, a lover in a relationship seeking fulfilment needs a type of mentality from the other half of that relationship if they are to succeed and many other different scenarios but the common thing in all the cases is that a right mindset and mentality is needed for success.

Mindset simply is self-perception; it refers to an established set of beliefs that a person has about themselves, it is how a person sees themselves and their place or position in this world. Mentality which is closely related to mindset is a pattern of behaviour that characterizes an individual's disposition towards life and since I already told you that to live is to struggle, it refers to how that individual responds to this struggle and other problems that life places in front of them. Now I'm sure that the professional psychologist would have a more technical definition of these terms but please bear with me, for our purpose in relation to our subject matter these ones should do. Knowing these definitions, we can now substitute these terms into our equation above to get: **'a man is his mindset and mentality'** or more appropriately **'a man's mindset and mentality [will] determine who he is'**. It is not so simplified as there are other factors that come to play like his personality within him and external factors like his environment, circumstances at a point in time, access to information, resources etc but for as long as it rests on the individual himself then this equation holds true. You cannot know how many hours I have spent pondering questions like: can a human be controlled? And if so since a nation is a collection of humans then can a nation be controlled? And since the whole world is a collection of nations then can the world be controlled? And if so then how can a human be controlled?

Humans are complex beings created with free will, as far as bio-hacking into the brain and directly controlling a human with a remote controller as you would a robot I do not know how far the science of man has progressed with that and this is where I take a quick minute to address the overly religious ones who don't seem to understand. If man were created and emphatically he was as the proof is standing right before you, it means that there was a physical process of creation involved to get the physical product that you see today. In the right conditions this product can be studied, broken down and reverse engineered such that even if it never gets to 100% of the knowledge required to recreate the physical product which is a human in this case or replicate the total authenticity of the original product itself a great deal about the process of the product's creation can still be learned. The irony for me in all this though is the fact that the group of people who emphatically insist that the world had no creator are now growing meat in their laboratories recreating a creation process that they say has no original creator. Anyways, if a man's mindset and mentality determines who he is such that there can be a determined pattern of response from him to certain conditions, then certain conditions can be created artificially for him to respond in a certain way to get a desired outcome. Am I making sense to you? And since the mindset and mentality of an individual can be changed and influenced, then feeding that individual information to change their mindset and mentality that will in turn get them to act and respond differently to external conditions means that the individual can be controlled indirectly. In this case the information fed to change that individual's mindset and mentality becomes a command of sorts. This general process of indirect control of a human being is what I call psycho-hacking.

Now humans are diverse, granted 100% of the time with psycho-hacking you would not get everybody or get the desired outcome from everybody but when a fisherman casts his net he does not expect to catch every single fish in the river, he catches enough fish that he's able to happily return home with the harvest. Some will inevitably slip through the cracks or in this case the reach of his net but this is what guarantees that he gets a harvest the next time he comes anyways. Psycho-hacking does not need to work on every individual within the collective for it to be effective, all it takes is a good percentage of the individuals within the collective to steer the collective in a certain direction and keep it there. That said, let us get back on track, we have been demonizing the political ruling class as we should but we also have to look at the masses that allow themselves to be abused and exploited over and over again in an endless cycle. What has to be the state of an individual's mindset and mentality that they accept the treatment they are getting in Nigeria for so long? This question provides the basis for this theory as we try to uncover the factors that have shaped the mindset and mentality of the average Nigerian but before we do that I have to show you briefly my observations of the Nigerian psyche.

You don't need to still be told at this point that the mindset and mentality of the Nigerian masses is poor but these do not mean the same as intelligence with intelligence being the ability to acquire knowledge and skills and to apply them. To this extent I will tell you that the average Nigerian individual is very intelligent but intelligence alone does not automatically translate to a good mindset and mentality. You can have an un-intelligent person with a good mindset and mentality, likewise you can have an intelligent person with a poor mindset and mentality. Also I told you that the qualities of the Nigerian individual as a single never translates well into the collective as the masses. To illustrate this I'll take a scenario from combat sports which I enjoy watching. Let's say you have a trainee MMA fighter who is an impressive physical specimen like Yoel Romero with muscles in all the right places, intelligent enough to learn the science and skills required for combat sports in the gym with a good fight IQ too to boot. He is disciplined to a good degree, listens to his coach in the gym and seems to have all the tools to make it in the sport but with all that if he lacks the right mindset and mentality as a fighter he will never hit the pinnacle heights in that sport. Everybody wants to be a lion until it's time to do lion *shit*, if he does not have that shark mentality to go in the octagon and finish off his opponent then he'll never achieve true greatness despite his many good attributes. This is the importance of having a good mindset and mentality in the general scope of things.

I used to tell my friends that I would never become a freedom fighter for the Nigerian masses nor will I ever be stupid enough to give my life for them. But why? Do I not love them? In fact I do love them, very much so, but I also know them very well and it is for this reason that I could never give my life for them. What are the answers that Nigerians as a people give when questions are asked of them? How do they respond as a collective when life throws problems in front of them? They say when an animal is cornered it turns around to fight with everything it has and becomes very dangerous but when you push a Nigerian to the wall he turns to face the wall and tries to scratch his way through the wall; they will do any and everything else but confront the problem in front of them. Painful as it is it must be said, ours is a nation of cowards. One other thing that does my head in is the lack of gravitas from my people, when bad things happen within the society that requires collective attention and possible collective action there are always elements within the collective that fashion jokes out of the situation to make it a laughing matter distracting from the severity of what just happened in their midst. No matter how horrendous, people could have just died or be killed in an avoidable manner even children but you'll see young Nigerian men who should be sober and boiling within themselves to act to ensure that such a thing never occurs again making jokes about the situation. They are never serious about anything, so life too has decided to make their existence a joke right in front of their very own eyes. It is either that or they ignore the incident totally, I know that part of this reaction stems from helplessness but people have found out these flaws and are exploiting them. The wrong kind of people have unfortunately stumbled upon this innate flaw of the Nigerian masses and through the decades from the past to present they have daily tested the boundaries of it as if to say: how far can we push these people before they break? How long do we push them before they resist? And sensing no resistance they continue unopposed. The constrictor tightens its folds on its prey for it is no longer afraid of the sharp claws of its prey nor its sharp teeth, the venom of its prey presents no concern to the constrictor because all of those weapons are useless if they cannot be brought to bear in this battle so on and on it tightens its grip squeezing the life out of its prey, oblivious to its screams of agony. The prey on the other hand will become dinner in the stomach of the constrictor because it has failed to intelligently utilize the weapons nature gave to it. All that said, I want to look at some factors which I think have shaped the mindset and mentality of the Nigerian masses.

3a) POST-COLONIAL MENTALITY:

So, our ancestors were slaves; I know that people always like to say it was a long time ago but 1960 does not seem like a long time to me. I looked up and the sun hasn't missed a day since then, the clouds still sail lazily by and the birds did not stop singing because of this but these are the things that I think about every single day of my waking life and also something which I feel that most black people around the world today have somehow forgotten but to forget a thing does not magically erase that thing. When a broken bone heals it usually never goes back to how it was before. I would know because I have titanium in my leg and still have pains a few years after but surprisingly elite athletes break bones and are back running and competing at a high level in a year. This is due to the elite and expensive medical care and procedures that they can afford as elite athletes and multi-millionaires to help them recover that the average guy like me would not have access to which underpins the fact that great care, effort, intention and resources had to be applied to restore that broken bone. Even with all that the restored bone never gets to be the same as before, we have seen many promising careers sadly cut short after injuries. That said, why do you people think that this race can just get back to how it was considering all it has been consistently put through for hundreds of years? When you consider that the care, effort, intention and resources needed to build the broken down race was never invested in it in the first place the picture gets a little bit clearer.

Theologians and bible scholars have given us the breakdown and I would like to apply it here also. When God created Adam and put him in Eden, he gave him authority over the earth realm but you see Adam was a young being and he lost his authority. It is a spiritual law that you become a servant of anything you obey and yield yourself to so when Adam ate the forbidden fruit which he had been commanded not to eat by God his authority was transferred. When God enquired of Adam he said his wife Eve had given it to him and it switched to Eve, when Eve was questioned she dodged all accountability for the error and said the serpent had told her to eat the fruit passing it on to the serpent but if you understand spiritual things then you know that the serpent was actually just a medium in the physical realm so the authority passed on to the spiritual being that had taken control of the serpent which was Lucifer (**Gen 3**) and then God passed judgement on them. It would be thousands of years later in the new testament gospels before Jesus would undo that error by His death and resurrection so you can see the route of the transfer of Adam's authority. For the black peoples their rights had rested with their kings who were sovereign, so when the outsiders came and defeated those kings the rights of the black peoples were transferred to the outsiders who had it for hundreds of years, both for those in the continent and the others sold into the diaspora whose own were now in the hands of the outsiders controlling the territories they were sold into. When the rest of the world were signing public declarations of the rights of man for their peoples the rights of the black peoples was in the hands of the outsiders until it was transferred to the hands of the political ruling class where it resides till this day and who frankly based on my observations have only just held those rights in trust for the outsiders.

The implication of this is deep. You see man will only contend for what his under his charge, under his authority and his control. With the rights and authority of the peoples in the hands of the distinct political ruling class it creates a disconnect within the masses whereby you see the effects manifest in society where the every day black man does not feel the accountability and responsibility for his community so they are in a state of helplessness and powerlessness. This is why when anything bad happens in Nigeria the men do not even attempt to band together to take action, instead they look up to the government and blame the government because psychologically in their subconscious they feel that they are not in control of even their own lives and that the responsibility is not up to them. I continue to address the men on this topic because the man is supposed to be the head, the leader and the first line of defence for his family so if things have gone wrong like this he must be the first to take the blame for not securing his territory. What I am trying to do here is to rouse up the black man because the hundreds of years of tribulation have taken its toll. So while these rights and authorities rests in the hands of the political ruling class the masses are kept in survival mode such that they are never able to break out of the shackles of their day to day to stand up to the political ruling class and demand for their rights, this is what slavery in the 21st century looks like. Who has time for the dirty business of chains when you can use poverty instead from afar?

All those centuries of slavery, colonialism, lack of rights and authority has greatly affected, effected and shaped the mindset and mentality of the blacks through successive generations creating a dependency on groups and individuals outside of themselves, with different interests and different objectives separate from those of the Nigerian masses and by extension, the black race. What this has created is that these so-called African countries are more or less like imperial extensions of their colonial masters; they target the minds of the masses via a variety of tools like movies, documentaries and chief of all, social media. Do not forget, once you can psycho-hack the minds of a people you can influence them and control them. So like a horde of zombies they live from day to day, slaving through every means under the sun to buy foreign made products at exorbitant prices. These products are highly cherished by the blacks, there is no sense of shame or pain within them in their hearts for the lack of ownership of their own products. They do anything to get foreign made products which they covet and like their ancestors before them they lord these products over one another all the while ensuring commerce for their colonial masters. These people are Nigerians and other African nationalities, they swear they are patriots and love the country of their birth but unbeknownst to them they are looking out for the well-being and interests of other countries apart from their own; this is the magic, the beauty and the effectiveness of psycho-hacking on the mindset and mentality of a people via the post-colonial route.

3b) HYPER-RELIGIOUS MENTALITY:

> *'And without faith it is impossible to please God... in the same way, faith by itself, if it is not accompanied by action, is dead.'*
>
> *- Heb 11:6a/ James 2:17 (NIV)*

I will tell you like I was told, I encourage everyone to read the bible for themselves, cover to cover, at least once in their lifetime... it's a life changing experience. Ever since I stumbled on that watch making video which then led me to seek out plenty others just like it my conviction has not wavered, so I say that from where I stand every problem in Nigeria is solvable. If that were so then my approach to unravelling Nigeria's root problems is not just looking at the problems themselves but finding the reasons for non-engagement by the people because even if all the problems are solvable, nothing can be conquered until it is faced. The question I'm attempting to answer in this section of my theories is: why have this Nigerian masses, my people, not been able to seriously face their diverse problems to conquer them? One of the main answers to that question is because as a people they have a hyper-religious mentality that is running on steroids. What do I mean by this? It describes the mentality of a people who have firmly joined their hands in prayers putting them to no other good use and then putting their whole minds and thoughts and reasoning into their religions neglecting every other aspect of their society only for them to wake up and look around to find out that their society lay in ruins, and poverty has become their new name and their calling card and their new identity.

What do I mean by a hyper-religious mentality? It is the mentality of a people who major in false surface piety in a toxic, suffocating and all-encompassing manner that they leave room for nothing else to exist around them. The people that have this kind of mentality have succeeded in totally taking man out of the equation of existence on this planet and where they did not take him out completely they diminished his influence and his role in the physical realm that he is supposed to lord over to a level of unimportance and non-effect instead attributing all of his roles and duties to the supernatural beings of their religions in what I can only describe as a case of mass fatalism. The people in mass fatalism with a hyper-religious mentality believe that they have no significant role to play in the grand scheme of things, they believe that they cannot determine the outcome of things in their society around them or cause significant change but unknown to them they have simply committed the same error as the first Adam. Ignorant of their own power, they have simply relinquished their crown and their authority to subdue their environment creating a vacuum of authority and power that others have then stepped in to fill for them. The reality of the hyper-religious mentality is one of imbalance; it is that body builder that goes to the gym to work out vigorously training just one hand and one leg for all his sessions but still has the guts to be surprised when he does not get the form and the physique that he desired. It is that planet that has veered off its orbit maintaining the cyclical rotations and revolutions but headed to a fatal collision with another planet that will lead to its ultimate destruction. It is that chef that put lots of only one type of seasoning into the food and is surprised at the final taste of the meal... I could go on and on with this.

This hyper-religious mentality has made the people weak and reluctant to confront the problems staring them in the face instead waiting for miracles or otherworldly beings to do it for them. Let me give a brief example of what I'm talking about: 4 hyper-religious Nigerians are seated around a table to have a discussion, one of them places his mobile phone on the table but the table is imbalanced and the phone slides off the table and falls to the ground before he could stop it. Now the phone is on the floor but what do these hyper-religious people do? Do they bend to pick up the phone off the floor? No, do they examine the table to find the cause of the imbalance and try to rectify it to prevent more phones from falling off that table in the future? No, do they study the wood or material used to make that table and the conditions it has been subjected to, to find out the reason for its deterioration so as to apply this knowledge for future? No, instead they fall on their knees, close their eyes, start crying and praying to God to restore the phone back to the table for them but does the phone magically fly off the floor and back on the table for them? If I were God I'm sure that I would have grown weary of the excesses of Nigerian prayers by now, but He's a patient God and I'm a man. As a man their hyper-religious nature is nothing short of toxic and irritating to me at this point.

I am a spiritual Christian not just a religious one so I can tell you that this topic requires maturity and great care to handle. Like a brain surgeon at work we must carve this matter out delicately lest we do unintended harm instead of intended good. Religion is man's attempt to contact God while spirituality is God in man, God with man and God for man. There are many locations in the physical and in the spiritual realms, each operating under and regulated by their different laws but the superiority and the sovereignty of God over every law, every force and every authority in all the realms both the seen and the unseen is unquestionable. In fact, outside of Him there is nothing; no existence, no creation just... nothing. Man was put on the earth to rule it, the earth has its own laws and limitations set up and in force as part of its operations.

> **'The heavens are the heavens of the LORD, but the earth he has given to the sons of Adam.'**
>
> *- Psalm 115:16*

If in the process of man carrying out his ordained duties he runs into circumstances too difficult for him to handle then he can call for help and in response to his call God acts by suspending the laws and limitations of the physical realm causing strange things to happen. This is what is called a miracle, it is actually an intervention, an interference if you will, by the sovereign God in physical matters. This intervention can be as simple as an idea dropped in your soul to help you complete a task, overcome some difficulty or invent something in the earth, or it can be a set of directions to get you out of a particular situation. It can also be something complex as the rearrangement or the reorganisation of matter, the physical materials and the elements of the earth in a way naturally impossible and make no mistake, the human body is also one of those physical materials for man was formed out of the dust of the earth. All of these interventions can be done in certain scenarios to get an expected end and they show the sovereignty of God but when men want to sit back and cry for miracles on everything, even the things they should handle themselves then it brings the question: if God has to break the laws and regulations He put in place to govern the earth all the time for a bunch of hyper-religious cry baby-men and cry baby-women in a certain part of the earth alone then why did he create the physical laws and regulations of the earth in the first place? It is like parents who have birthed children, laboured hard to raise and train them to maturity only for the children to blatantly refuse to grow up or move out or fend for themselves, choosing instead to cry to their parents all the time for every little thing even the things they should be able to procure for themselves. Surely, this would be annoying, right? All of nature in the world of men and in the animal kingdom we see babies birthed and then go on to fend for themselves so over-dependence at the stage of maturity is unnatural and against the natural order of things as divinely programmed.

    Man is a spirit being that has a soul and lives in a body. For him to flourish in his time on the earth he must nourish these three components that he is made up of... if he focuses exclusively on one at the expense of the other two then he'll surely run into problems. Even if not all to the same degree or importance the fact remains that he must nourish them all to achieve balance in his life's journey. Because of the evolution of organised religion in the world today I cannot even ascribe it 100% nourishment of the spirit so I say 50%. When you consider this you'll see that hyper-religious societies that focus exclusively on their religion's service, 50% of the spirit neglecting the soul which is the centre for imagination and creativity, and the body which is the house; it is a spiritual law that a spirit cannot legally operate in this physical realm without a body so no matter how vibrant or how illuminated your intangible spirit is if your body is compromised you can no longer continue to legally exist here in the earth as a composite being. Instead your illuminated spirit will transcend to a higher spiritual plane of light while your physical body that is of the earth will return to the earth from whence it came (Gen 3:19b). The Word of God which cannot be broken states that we shall reap whatever we sow (Gal 6:7) so sowing into religion at the expense of everything else has created hyper-religious and superstitious societies where logic is scarce.

Now let me address the hyper-religious ones, you cannot be more Christian than Christ Himself for He knew that He had the power to walk on water and he showed it once yet He mostly used Simon Peter's boat to travel on water, a boat created by the science and technology of the time for his ministry just as pastors today are using technology to further the gospel to the ends of the earth and take it to never before seen heights. Why did he not keep walking over the sea on foot to preach to the cities He visited as He evangelized? Why did He not stand on water to preach the gospel to the people while they sat and watched on the banks? Yes He multiplied loaves of bread and fishes to feed multitudes in times of need for which He was almost seized by the hyper-religious multitude of the time who wanted to forcefully make Him their king so against the natural order set by God (Gen 8:22) they do no need to go to the farm again or go fishing or work for the rest of their lives but have a food multiplier they can always go to for food in the palace, why did He not succumb to that plan? (John 6:15) Yes He had the power to multiply bread and fishes but refused to turn stones to bread for His own consumption when He was tempted by the devil or do you think He could not? You have totally diminished the role of man on the earth but look at Judges 1:19 where prophecy had come that a certain people were to be eliminated from their lands but they could not be eliminated because they had iron chariots which were the equivalent of nuclear weapons, aircraft carriers and supersonic jets in those days, their technological advancement protected them from expulsion. These are the things I want you to meditate on. Thou overzealous and hyper-religious Nigerian Christian, you have to study the Word carefully so that you can learn properly, this blind religion you people practise is not the way forward.

If I may also address the African traditional hyper-religious practitioners; now if you were to combine the strongest *juju* from the Edo people and Yoruba land which you say have some of the strongest ones, to magically disappear from Nigeria and reappear in the factories and offices of say Apple without detection to steal the plans for the next generation of iPhones and tech and bring those plans back to Nigeria, undetected when you reappear, will those same powers magically materialize the modern factories required to produce the gadgets or will the new iPhones fall out already packaged and ready to sell from the mouth of a skull tied with red cloth in some blackened mud room somewhere in a forest? Will the *juju* also magically train the workers that will work in the factories and provide steady power for us to reproduce the gadgets? Will it create good channels to sell these products with airplanes and container ships to transport them to new markets and make Nigeria a tech giant of a country overnight? Will all these be done overnight by the beings you have worshipped, who have been drinking your gin and the blood of your sacrifices for a long time now? Or let's say you were to combine the *juju* from Kogi and Ibo peoples which you say is very strong and use it to supernaturally fly to the United States who maintain the largest nuclear arsenal in the world to steal nuclear plans right from under their noses and appear back in Nigeria that same night, will it somehow transform Nigeria into a country with nuclear capabilities overnight? I think you already know the answer to these questions before I finish asking.

To my Muslim brothers and sisters in the North and South-West, I will admonish you not to accept poverty and ignorance as your identity and your lifestyle because the elites among you that have imposed such conditions on you do not live under them. I do not claim to be an expert on your religion but I can tell you to open the history books and read, read about the brilliant Islamic scholars from North Africa and the Middle-East that spearheaded the golden age of Islam (9th to 13th century AD) who were credited with great inventions and advancements in the field of medicine, mathematics and many more. Time will not permit me to tell you about brilliant scholars like Ibn Al-Rassaz Al-Jazari of that time who is credited to be the father of robotics (*Awake!* November 2012 issue). You see, I told you I had always been a voracious reader from a young age and would read anything as long as there was knowledge to be gained from it. Around 2011/12 I had taken a liking to reading *Awake!* A Jehovah's Witness publication because of the science content they had which I found very informative and exciting but needless to say the Pentecostals around me which comprised of family members and friends did not like this new association of mine. I made sure that they stopped by the family compound every now and then and I would excitedly rummage through their stock to see if there was any new one I didn't yet have. They gave out the publication to me freely in exchange for anything I could give them which I must say was not much in those days but I always gave what I could, never taking it for free because even then at that age I could understand the pain and the resources required for evangelism so I could not take it for granted. Over the months I had built up quite a collection of *Awake!* as part of my personal library but the search for stability in life moving from place to place has seen me lose them. It was in that publication that I first read about the golden age of Islam which led me to do further study and educate myself on that fascinating topic.

    Yours is a religion with a rich history of research, riches and invention. If the history is too far back in time for you to relate to it then at least take a look at the Gulf states, look at Dubai and see what other Muslims like you have built up in the desert. I am not trying to say that all of life is materialism but I think as Nigerians regardless of ethnicity or religion we can all agree that we can and need to do better as a nation. The status quo is just certainly unacceptable! They created the Boko Haram and other terrorist groups in your lands and told you they were fighting against 'western' education but all these groups have brought to you people is more pain, more poverty, suffering and untold hardship. They steal your children from their schools, take your daughters in the hundreds into the forest, forcefully defile them en masse, rob them of their childhood by giving them bastard children to raise by themselves in an already harsh environment. What more can I say? Is it the bombings that have claimed the lives of more of your loved ones? Is it the insecurity and instability that they have brought to your region that the whole country is suffering from? Is it the fact that they forcefully make you pay levies in your own lands taking you back to the era of direct colonialism? All of this, and you refuse to condemn their acts because you all profess the same faith? I'm sorry, I consider myself an open-minded person but I simply cannot see the logic in this. As for despising 'western' education I have to tell all of us to learn how to separate ideology, religion and culture from knowledge. There are elements of Western ideology and culture that even I cannot stomach and will never ascribe to but we cannot all deny their dedication to research, development and their application.

This is the crucial part that hyper-religious societies always miss out on. My people are so hardwired and fixated on the supernatural and the extra-ordinary that they miss the simple ordinary things around them, they have the world right in front of them but they look up and keep their gaze up whilst they attempt to navigate this world. As gods on the earth have they given their time and attention to study the world they were put in to dominate and the laws it functions by to master and then manipulate these laws to their advantage? No, have they tried to discover the many elements put in the world and then use their relationship to ask help from the Maker of all things to find cunning ways to extract and utilize these many elements to better their time here? No, instead they are always asking and looking for these laws to be violated and broken all the time for their sake, there is an element of ignorance and selfishness to it all. They are exclusively fixated on the life after when their time here is done but I tell these hyper-religious people that a journey is way more than just its destination and that is what we are... man is actually a journeyman, we are just spirit beings on a physical journey but even at that we do have a physical journey to get through first.

Hyper-religious people ignore epistemology which is the creation of knowledge through study and the application of that knowledge in every day life, instead always praying for divine intervention in the affairs of men and are surprised when their societies lie deeply in poverty. I will state here emphatically that success in life for a man or a nation is not based on religion but applied principles, we can go deeper and I'll even tell you that beyond religion you can be spiritual and still be poor because sustained success is due to applied principles. There are principles like sowing and reaping. I use as an example the golden age of Islam. The people of that time were not successful because they were Muslims, in fact you could change the name historically to be the golden age of North Africans and the Middle-East and it would not change much. The people of that time gave themselves to study and research from which they gained much knowledge that they then applied to solve the problems they were facing in their society to better their lives and for that reason they will never be forgotten by history... It just so happened that they were devout Muslims. If it were just the religion then we would have had the golden age of the African traditional religion for the period of the African empires before they were destroyed, the time of Genghis Khan would have been the golden age of Buddhism, if so what would we call the modern times? The golden age of secularism and atheism? Anyways, my point here is on the role and the place of man in building successful societies and by extension a successful country, something that hyper-religious societies never seem to understand.

The society with a hyper-religious mentality is a docile society open to diverse manipulations. They have invested their all into their religions and have rightfully reaped super-mega religious organisations in return that build mega auditoriums while the whole land around them is suffocated by stark poverty, ignorance and suffering of the people. While you, hyper-religious people, under mass fatalism eagerly prepare for the life after your time here is done you must realise that you still have decades to spend here and you're bringing your children into this world that you've created for them. There abides the things of the spirit and the things of man, between them lies the soul realm like a bridge which houses man's god-like creative and transformative powers with which he can change his world around him... all of this power remains neglected and untapped still in Nigeria. As for me I'm always careful not to fall into the hyper-religious black hole despite the fact that it's all around me, my opening text for this topic which is made up of two verses of scripture joined together form the basis of my personal Christian walk, they keep separated in my consciousness the things that are spiritual and things that are of men, they also let me know the roles of the spiritual and my own role to play in my journey of life so I am not caught slacking. All that said, I maintain that the hyper-religious mentality of Nigerians has contributed to hold them back as a people and has restrained them from confronting the many problems they have so they will never make heaven with this mentality.

3c) POVERTY MENTALITY:

'And Satan answered the Lord, and said, Skin for skin, yea, all that a man hath will he give for his life".

- Job 2:4

The strongest instinct in a human being is survival. In fact, faced with extermination all living things will do their utmost best to cling to life. If a human who has been given the gift of free will chooses not to continue to play the game of life he or she can end it, but such an act would be frowned upon by those watching from the higher realms and will doubtless go without consequences.

When a man loses everything or when everything is taken from him he automatically goes into survival mode, and in that mode the remainder of his mental and physical resources are redirected towards surviving this gruelling period or phase and one of the things that keeps him going is hope. The hope that a tree cut down can still sprout again, and that a man cast to the ground can still rise again provided he's not killed because if he's killed then it's game over. This is true for men, women and nations, every human is a seed with the capacity to reproduce so men are representative of nations. You can see this from God's covenant with Abraham (Gen 17), and also even when David fought Goliath (1 Sam 17) that though it was two men that fought it was actually two nations at war.

Following all the natural laws like the law of averages, of times and seasons and of constant change this survival mode is supposed to be temporary; a transitory period and stage from which the man can then accumulate enough knowledge and resources to build himself back up to the next level and the next and so on but this process like all processes can be hacked and manipulated as we see in Africa to artificially create, sustain and maintain conditions like poverty, insecurity and instability necessary to keep the masses at the base level of survival mode in perpetuity. Notice that the goal is not to kill these people or to utterly destroy their nations, if that were to happen then the game would be up but they are kept just alive as a country in eternal survival mode. This is where the theory of the poverty mentality comes from because considering our subject matter you have successive generations born into this artificially enforced and prolonged poverty environment. They are born into survival mode, bred in it, they mature in it and are shaped by it to the extent where it becomes more than just a condition because that condition never changes so for them it becomes their identity. This identity shapes their mindset and mentality which in turn influences their behaviour and their reaction to the happenings around them in their societies, their way of living, culture and traditions including their religions and the way they practise it, all influenced by this new economy such that no area of their existence is spared, so thorough is this new identity that no aspect of their lives is left untouched by it. A negative reaction then goes into effect in the lives of these people where they begin to do the work of their oppressors for them, they birth the next generation and introduce them into their world and the conditions in it teaching them how to survive in this survival mode that they exist in ensuring its trans-generational continuity. In effect, it is a people specifically born and bred to be exploited, strategically handicapped, made perpetually vulnerable by their poverty identity and their circumstances and in that great battle between the political ruling class vs. them, they can never and will never win in this base state.

You have to look and see how this identity of poverty and survival mode does not change for these people, take a look at Nigeria, even when oil was discovered in the 70s and the billions of dollars that have supposedly come into the land since that time you would think that that was enough to eradicate poverty from these people and their lands but how wrong you are. You look at other places with this resource and the progress that they have made and you look at Nigeria, the powers that be have made the oil industry impossible for the masses to benefit from over the decades so her identity of poverty could not be changed by it. It is a scent that the average Nigerian is born with and will die with, and because man is man, some will fight with great struggle and through great pain to break out of this identity and wash off that scent but the far larger portion of the population remain stuck in it and in the general scheme of things those escapees account for nothing when you consider the general Nigerian equation so their effects on the whole are negligible and the status quo remains unaffected.

The unfortunate Nigerian masses who have had this foreign poverty identity forced on them with its attendant mindset and mentality are a small people, though not originally small they have been made small and kept small. You cannot stop birds from flying over your head but you can definitely stop them from building a nest on top of your head. Jesus Christ called Satan the father of lies (John 8:44) and he did not lie there but Satan spoke a psychological truth about man when he said man would give everything he had to survive (Job 2:4). Perhaps, faced with the Father of Truth he could not lie and when he said it God did not rebuke him. Lucifer, the being, was created long before man, I know that by his projection in the minds of many in the world today he makes himself look like he is equal to God or a direct rival who is just as powerful but in truth he is just another one of God's creation before He created man. Being that he was brought into existence before man he had had enough time to study the psychological make up and behaviours of generations of men from Adam up until the time of Job so he spoke from his experience of his dealings with sons of men when he said that even though Job turned out to be an exception to that, not the norm, all of humanity is not job even if the Father would wish it to be so. Funnily enough, even when he spoke that psychological truth Job disproved it for him but his assertion gives us a glimpse into the nature of man in survival mode. So when you consider the Nigerian masses that are perpetually in survival mode today they are a people who live day to day occupied with what they can get to eat for that day, securing shelter, how they can live and survive the day from the insecurity in the land then it's on to the next day to repeat the process . There is no sense of history for such a people, no long-term plans, no stability, no need for records for who can tell what will happen to their lives tomorrow? Whatever is left of their minds is occupied by many worries from the conditions and the manifold insufficiencies that have been imposed on them. They live and try to survive under a thick artificial cloud of lack created and regulated by the political ruling class and tailor made just for them, a thick black cloud that no wind of sophisticated problem-solving technology invented in the world can seem to blow away nor can the beam from the sun of oil boom or change in the price of crude oil and natural gas penetrate through to nourish the poor souls trapped beneath it. I must stress again that the poverty conditions of Nigeria and the other black lands scattered across the world are artificial, yes they are man-made created to keep these people trapped indefinitely and as for the case of our subject matter they can never fight or question the powers that be when they are trapped in survival mode which is why I called this artificial poverty a weapon of mass destruction earlier.

So this thick dark cloud that responds intelligently such that it cannot be displaced by anything not even by the many technological advancements around the world that could change the lives of the peoples under it serves a purpose for the political ruling class, it ensures that no man, woman, boy or girl in the land ever lift up their heads. If they look up they see the dark cloud and nothing else so they keep their heads low, backs bent in subservience, looking at the ground and scavenging the ruins of their lands for their daily bread. Can you imagine? A blessed nation that her seeds are supposed to live in the earth as kings, queens, princes and princesses have been turned into a horde of beggars and destitutes, this is destiny exchange and theirs is a sub-human existence. The peoples of these lands are conquered and broken peoples, the poverty as an identity was given to the generations that came before from which the moulding process started and took its roots so that by the time it has gotten to my generation it is so ingrained into the hearts and souls of these people shaping their mindset and mentality, it has become their norm because it is all they have ever known and this does not make them to ever question its continued presence in their lives. Sad as all this sounds it does not change the fact that the Nigerian masses have a poverty mentality and as long as they have it they can never aspire to be more than they are in the earth.

3d) CONCLUSION OF MINDSET AND MENTALITY: WEDDING DAY SYNDROME.

If the reaction of a people to external conditions around them based on their mindset and mentality can be studied and determined to a good level of accuracy then the external conditions that they are subject to coupled with their mindset and mentality can be modified and manipulated to get certain desired outcomes, this is what psycho-hacking is about. When you combine the effects of the post-colonial mentality, the hyper-religious mentality and the poverty mentality of the Nigerian masses then you can see why these people are able to keep on living in Nigeria without the country imploding all these years because if they had a collectivelly different mentality then they simply would not accept the conditions that have been created for them to live in. This is how they were made poor and this is how they are kept poor in this their broken and dehumanized state. Trapped in survival mode they exist in a different reality, a reality where they are pre-occupied with their survival and do not have the time for much else.

In this state, the people from the political ruling class that have accumulated the scarce resources of the land, resources which the masses cannot get their hands on become like gods to the masses and they are worshipped as gods by them. If they worship good enough sometimes a wad of cash is tossed into their midst by their gods who stand back and watch them scurry about and fight amongst themselves for the scraps like animals knowing fully well that the token and the experience will play into their minds the next time the elections come around. In such a society under this reality there is no regard for processes, only results. Now you know why they love and seek miracles so much. You are not asked how you became rich to know if the process can be replicated to benefit the society, no, as long as you mysteriously show up with money one morning by hook or by crook in Nigeria you are instantly celebrated. The bar is so low, it is a society ruled by superstition and wallowing in ignorance such that even though all the ingredients to make a successful nation exists in the midst of these people they just cannot make it happen for themselves.

In this their distracted state they fail to realise a lot of important things choosing instead to fix their minds on transient things of lesser importance. This is a coping mechanism of helplessness because they feel like they are powerless to effect change in the things that matter in their society. Don't forget, as I told you, under post-colonial mentality, that the authority of these peoples is fully vested in the political ruling class as handed to them by the colonisers. It is from this their obsession with social media and other irrelevant things that I coined the wedding day syndrome. Marriage is a big deal in Nigeria so when I grew to the stage where people my age and slightly older whom I had interactions with were beginning to get married and I was observing them it looked like they were so fixated on the few days of partying and ceremonies that signify their union than the decades they are meant to co-exist with each other after such that when real problems arise for them in the marriage long after the party has ended and the party goers have returned to their own homes these couples are ill-equipped and unprepared to deal with them leading to a hike in the statistics of failed marriages. This is not the only reason and my focus here is not on failed marriages because who am I to judge? But the wedding syndrome remains valid.

In their distracted state they are fixated on everything else but the small political ruling class who are then left to carry out their exploitation operations without obstruction, questions and the attention of the masses. But did the world stop for these people in their plight? They fail to realise and are ignorant of the fact that every nation on this planet is in open or secret competition with the other. Did the other nations halt their development in the race of life to allow these other impoverished nations to catch up? I ask you Nigerians, have your cries ever stopped you from being tormented, oppressed and exploited? Your answers to these questions will show you that your reaction of crying and pleading is not the solution to your problems. To solve these problems the general mindset and mentality will have to change, then the reaction and methods will change too to achieve a different outcome but until then you will remain where you are.

4. CORRUPTION:

> *'In a state of lawlessness, it is criminal to be law abiding.'*
>
> - *Gani Fawehinmi*

Ah! This one is the superstar among all the theories to explain what is happening in Nigeria so much that if you stop any Nigerian on the street and ask them why their country is the way it is, the chances are that this is one of the first answers you'll get from them. If you ask them what they mean by corruption they'll tell you it's the politicians embezzling public funds to buy houses and cars for themselves; this is generally known by everybody and while it is not a wrong answer it presents an incomplete picture which makes it just one of the blind men that went to observe the elephant if we use that analogy. If we took just his testimony alone without the benefit of the others unified you will see that though he's describing what he came in contact with and indeed he came in contact with an elephant, but his description does not match that of an elephant, only the part of the elephant he touched so in that sense he's wrong. It is until his testimony is combined with the others and properly constructed that one begins to get a picture of what the animal looks like. Similarly in this case I realised from my observations and study of the Nigerian situation that corruption itself does not exist in and cannot operate in isolation, it is not a root cause neither is it an end where the political ruling class wakes up in the morning and says that their goal is to be corrupt. When you look at it from this angle then you see that corruption is not a result but a tool and a means to achieve certain results.

I looked up the definition of corruption and it says that it's a 'process' by which a thing is changed from its original state to one regarded as erroneous or debased. Process is defined as a series of actions or steps taken in order to achieve a particular end. So corruption for me in the Nigerian sense is the series of actions and steps taken by the political ruling class of Nigeria and the Nigerian masses to further weaken the Nigerian masses in the country keeping her in a debased and erroneous state far from her ideal state. It is important to note that the Nigerian masses are not absolved from this but are also a part of the problem. If a debased and erroneous state of a thing exists then the ideal state of that thing exists too, we have never seen the ideal state of Nigeria in this present reality, some of us have only seen her in dreams and it is so different from what we see today that encourages us that she's still worth fighting for. She is weakened in this debased state and the political ruling class keeps her here because in this weakened state she can then be controlled and exploited without resistance. In this state she is thrown off her ideal course and everything is out of balance, so absolute is the control and power of this little group over the masses and so twisted is the artificial reality they have created now that in Nigeria up is down, down is up, black is white and white is black, blue, green or any colour the political ruling class with the money and power wants it to be. When a society has fallen to this point where the people cannot fight back for what they know in their hearts is not right then you know they are truly defeated.

> ***'Power don't come from a badge or a gun, power come from lying. Lying big [and] get the whole [**] world to play along with you. Once you got everybody agreeing with what they know in their hearts ain't true you got 'em by the balls'***
>
> *- Sen. Roark*
> *Sin City (2005)*

Gosh! I love cinema and the way stories are told on screen, so much that I intend to write and make movies someday in the not too distant future. I was young when I watched *Sin City* for the first time and it blew me away with its unorthodox style of film noir, its over the top dialogue coupled with the narration, the actors gave a good performance and the director deserves credit for his simplicity. It is one of my most watched movies till date and also one of my favourite movies of all time. Even at that young age when it got to the point where Senator Roark said those lines in the movie it always hit me in a certain kind of way, well they say nothing you learn is wasted so here it is. I repeat, when elected public officials who have been caught embezzling public funds stood before the Nigerian people and without shame or remorse said that the embezzled funds were swallowed in their offices by big monkeys and big snakes and the sky did not fall over our heads from the backlash I knew that the game was up. The Nigerian masses just made lots of jokes about the situation and went on with their lives like nothing happened, how much more can you kick a man when he's down before he loses all sense of feeling?

My opening text by the late great Chief Gani Fawehinmi gets a lot of criticism in online forums and when I checked to see that the criticisms come from 'western' people, you know, the first world gang who are just arguing about semantics I did not spend my time or my energy to engage. *'Oh, you can't be a criminal in a lawless society because there are no laws to break there in the first place, duh!'* *chuckles*. When you live in a society with a written constitution and set of laws but this society is controlled by a small group of people who totally ignore these laws and continually break them openly without repercussions or punishment imposing their will on that society through corruption then that society even with her myriad of written laws is in a state of lawlessness. When their power over that territory is so absolute that they can suspend the laws of the land at will and pull them out to punish their enemies and critics to teach the masses a lesson then it becomes very dangerous for you to follow the discarded laws of the land and go against the grain because that will essentially mean that you're going against the controlling powers of the land. In this peculiar scenario, this virtual reality created for these people, it can be criminal for you to be law abiding. I have nothing against online intellectuals, it's not like we're playing a game of 'who has the more corrupt country' or anything like that but your countries have mild corruption like your public officials embezzling money through some distant wars somewhere else so pardon you, you're not aware of what the man was talking about but in mine, in ours, the corruption we experience is pervasive and invasive affecting every facet of our lives. In such a society then that statement holds true and people that have been there know it to be so. The late Chief Gani Fawehinmi who spent his life fighting the system knew what he was talking about because he was from that type of place, I'm from that type of place too so I can relate, in fact I was born there.

The type of corruption here is general and it goes from the elected officials that abuse their office to embezzle funds to the common employee abusing his or her office for side gains which is hand in glove with Nigerian society. In society **corruption** is that guy urinating on the side of the street or the commercial driver that carries five passengers where he is supposed to carry four thereby inconveniencing the passengers, corruption is crossing the highway when a pedestrian bridge is just a few meters away, it is ignoring traffic lights, littering the street and drainage with pure water sachets, it is both the giver of bribe and the police officer that receives it, it is that driver driving without his/her seat belt on, it that child hawking tomatoes across town during school hours to support her family, that civil servant that goes to work very late because there is no accountability in the Civil service, that road safety official that collects money from a citizen and gives a fake drivers' license from the office of the commission in return, it is the election officials falsifying election records to manipulate election results, it is that man, woman boy or girl trying to use whatever means or connections he/she has beside true emergency to jump a queue for a public service and the list goes on. Following this train you will see that corruption is deviation, corruption is Nigeria and Nigeria is corrupt. All of these seemingly insignificant acts of corruption and more like them that go unchallenged in society set the tone and pave the way for the shocking big ones to happen because they have lessened the shock value and seared social conscience. It becomes a case of a place where little bad things have been happening consistently and concurrently so that by the time the big bad thing happens, the shock value and reaction of the people will not be much because they are already used to bad things happening day in and day out in their lives. This my people, is the true face of corruption.

> *'A great civilization is not conquered from without until it has destroyed itself from within.'*
>
> - Will Durant

Corruption is like a cancer in the body of the society slowly eating away at its vital organs on the inside and weakening that society from within, if 'a little leaven can leaven the whole lump' then when corruption is done on a mass scale as in Nigeria such that it becomes the norm then definitely you know that that society cannot flourish. I had a vision once, one of my pictures that come to me randomly but seem to carry great significance to my task and offer great help in terms of explanation to carry me through tough moments along the way when I'm stuck. This one was just a picture of absolute chaos that I thought had no meaning until I took the time to look at it properly and try to extract its message. It came to me one fine morning while I was lying in my bed contemplating life. I will try my best to explain here. Imagine one of those very bad Nigerian roads with pot holes, bumps, spoilt portions and damaged street lights lining. On the side of the road is a fenced field with harvests, the collective harvest of the people also representing the collective goal of the people in whatever form and this road just leads round a bend and ends at the proper gate to this field with people handing out rewards to those that eventually make it to the end gate. Along the fence a hidden portion has been cut open and is heavily guarded by uniformed men to allow a small portion of the rich and political elites to pass through the fields in a shortcut to the gate. Now, they stop on that short cut to fill their pockets, bags and booth with loot as do some of their guards and this very busy scene plays out in my creative region. I watch as most passers-by come down from their cars, negotiate with the guards and try to get some harvest for themselves, others try to get through the barb fence without being detected, and the bulk of the people have abandoned the race on the road to try to get their hands on the harvest through the fence or from those that have gotten theirs through the fence. Some head in the opposite direction for harvests in other settlements leaving their cars. As all this plays out the general harvest is just being depleted through different channels leaving nothing for the few that still try to go through the straight and narrow road to get to the destination.

As the general people that make up the society try different means to get their hands on the harvest, the bulk of the people who have come down from their cars turn to jeer and ridicule the few

who are still trying to go along the road dodging abandoned cars, negotiating with corrupt uniformed officials on illegal roadblocks that try to extort the motorists as they try to make it to the gate on this very frustrating road. This is as good a time as any to introduce to you the Nigerian 'wisdom' because Nigerians see themselves as very wise in their own eyes and I will give it to them that they are an intelligent people but intelligence does not make you immune to stupidity. The Nigerian 'wisdom' of the wise peoples of the territory sees every one trying to outsmart each other and beat the system in one way or the other for personal gain such that if you're not beating the system somehow and making some extra money for yourself at the expense of that system no matter the level you find yourself even if it's a crucial position in government or just some street side job, you're not wise or 'sharp' as Nigerians like to say which in effect plainly means that if you're not corrupt, in Nigerian society you are not considered wise; this should show you just how deep corruption has eaten into the individual and collective psyche of the people.

What this mass corruption does in the society is create chaos. Even though it looks wild and dispassionate I promise you that there is a method to the madness. If this chaos miraculously creates favourable conditions for the political ruling class but unfavourable ones for the masses then there is definitely a method and a pattern to it. The consequences of the corrupt practices of the masses can hurt an individual, a few people or maybe tens of people depending on the scale, and it happens daily. When all this is going on distracting the ordinary citizen and the real corruption takes place at the highest levels which affects the lives of millions of people they cannot even properly criticise because they are convicted in their hearts already as corrupt too so I guess you can say that a people truly get the leaders they deserve. In this chaos there are no working institutions to restore order in society and when you factor in the previous theories up till this point like the social fission, poverty, mentality and others you can see that the average Nigerian is powerless to change things in this set up. He is instead caught up in the motions of the chaos and standing on quicksand... in effect a prisoner to his circumstances. Everybody will have to start with themselves to change things and that will require unity but in a divided society like this one you can see that the divide and conquer strategy has been very effective So finally, when you take into account that great battle between the political ruling class vs. the Nigerian masses then you can see the vital role that corruption plays to further weaken the masses by creating instability for them and ensuring victory for the elites. This is why corruption is one of the vital reasons for the Nigerian mess.

5. ENVIRONMENTAL INFLUENCE: NIGERIAN FACTOR.

'When in Rome, do as the Romans do'

- *Old proverb.*

I remember watching a young Pastor Chris Oyakhilome with that ugly moustache on TV, doing the 'Atmosphere for Miracles' programmes in those days. I wasn't a Christian then but I knew what atmosphere meant and I knew a little bit about what miracles were all about but I didn't understand why miracles needed an atmosphere so I asked my mum the meaning of the name of the programme and she explained it to me. I would later carry that concept of atmosphere or environment into both my subconscious and my conscious interpretation and understanding of the world around me. The principle of the environment is simple enough, it looks at the relationship between an organism and the environment they are surrounded by, more specifically it looks at the influence the environment has on the organism within it. When we clean our house we're not just making it clean and beautiful to look at, we're also changing the environment of that house to make it difficult for disease carrying germs and other microbes to live and thrive there. Another example is a seed planted in the soil, before the seed is put in the soil it can spend weeks or months preserved in the silos with no changes to it but when its environment is changed and it's placed in the soil with adequate water and sunlight added then that seed begins to germinate. It doesn't stop there. If that growing plant is to grow and produce at its optimum level then the right conditions have to be maintained with its continuous access to sunlight and water, the weeds that would compete with it for limited nutrients in the soil need to be eradicated and in most cases manure or fertilizer has to be added to boost the nutrients in the soil that the plant can access and it still does not stop there. The plant has to be guarded against pests and diseases that would affect its growth and productivity if they attack the plant. I am no expert but from the little I know you can see how much the environment has to be regulated just for that plant to grow, thrive and produce optimally.

We hear all the time about some animals raised in captivity not being able to grow to the sizes they would have attained in the wild because of the small size of the confinement area like a small aquarium for a fish. I have a little experience about this as I raised catfish for some time using locally made wood and tarp ponds. All of these examples show the effect that the environment has on the organism. It was amazing to learn that even spiritual beings as powerful as they are needed the right environment for them to move and manifest both in the spiritual dimensions and in the physical realm so when Pastor Chris called his TV programme *Atmosphere for Miracles* he was creating the right atmosphere through praise, worship and ministering the Word of God to enable the power of God to move to his viewers and effect miracles in their lives through the person of the Holy Spirit. So if the spiritual beings needed the right environment to function how much more the physical beings which are a product of the spiritual?

For the average Nigerian, his environment is his house. As these people are a people targeted and marked for exploitation they cannot just be placed in any house but a house that's in line with the whole exploitation, subjugation and repression agenda of these peoples to ensure that the objectives are met. Man is a complex machine, man is an intelligent being, a formidable one but man can be beaten, so for man to be bested you need a higher intelligence than that man possesses for that time because he can grow and acquire more knowledge. What works for one will not necessarily work for another and when the one that is being bested starts to catch on to the methods by which he was beaten then you must move it higher or take it further to keep beating him. Now how do I view this theory of the Nigerian environment? I bring to your remembrance my experience with the watch making video and I draw my analysis out of it. When the complex mechanical engine of the watch has been built it needs a casing to hold it in place without obstructing the movements of its delicate parts as they move about to carry out their function. This special casing is designed to hold the watch engine in place, keeping it safe and assisting in its duties to tell time. There are different cases for different watch engines; some are small enough to be worn on the wrist, others are kept in the pocket, they get bigger to be hung on walls while the really, really big ones are in cathedrals but the principle and purpose of the casing remains the same which is, to house the engine.

You have followed me this far on this journey so allow me to point out the similarities between the analogies to you. The Nigerian masses are the different parts of the watch engine, the master watch maker shapes these different parts in a certain way and couples them together to interact with each other and function as designed. Likewise, the individuals that make up the Nigerian masses through psycho-hacking (religion, poverty, history, ethnicity, politics and propaganda) are designed to interact with each other and function in a certain way too. The watch maker then places his engine in a case to tell time but humans are far more complex than a watch, similarly the Nigerian peoples are domiciled in the Nigerian territory which serves as a casing for them but harsh poverty and mass corruption both of which combine to create a state of chaos for the people are added to the mix among other things. This makes them easy to be manipulated, intimidated, controlled, subjugated, dominated and then exploited by the political ruling class with little or no resistance from them. The intelligence, intention and design elements in all this makes it the right time for me to share my thoughts on social engineering with you.

5a) SOCIAL ENGINEERING.

When you look at society as an individual, it looks overwhelming, it feels like this big mass that has just come to be what it is by evolution where people just grow, change and try to live their best lives but when I look at society I see design, I see intention and I see control, all beneath the surface. The word 'social' relates to a grouping of people and their interactions while engineering is the action of working artfully to bring something about. The interesting combination of these two words will then mean the action of working artfully to bring something about in a group of people or in society. I like the use of the word 'artfully' in there because it connotes some guile and cunning in it all. Humans are smart beings but some of the questions I grappled with in my mind for a long time include questions like: can the human be bested? Can the human be controlled? And can the human be manipulated? The answer to them all is an emphatic yes! I come from Nigeria which is regarded as a third world country and I have seen barely literate people with an old laptop that has a low processing capacity and very poor inconsistent internet connections manipulate and scam highly educated, rational, logical and sophisticated thinking people from the first world of their entire life savings. I am not an advocate for fraud but just critically looking at this scenario you can see these scammers create a false atmosphere of trust, safety and security to manipulate, control and defraud their well-educated, logical thinking victims so I ask you my dear reader in this moment to think on this for a while and give me your answer to this question that will not leave me alone in peace: do you think that the human can be bested? I will request your answer to this question and your reasons for it when I see you.

Look around you at society, look at the roads and the way they are linked together, look at the roundabouts, look at the bridges and flyovers, look at the parks and the parking spaces, the pedestrian walkways and the bins for rubbish. Look at the different buildings and the way they are arranged - now tell me: do you think all of this just happened randomly or it was designed? Do you think that these things just fell into place on their own? Different materials chemically bonded together with different methods to put together stone, wood, glass and steel - do you think it was the winds that blew society into its current state? Your answers to these questions will give you some understanding as to why I'm always suspicious of the new age cult of the white lab coats with the fancy alphabets after their names. Those guys looked at the human being with his complex purposeful features and their conclusion was that the human was a product of random evolution. This is why I could never trust them when they started talking about booster shots but there are lots of people in society that would do anything just as long as it's one of the priests from this new age cult that says it's okay to do it. So pardon me for digressing but I was trying to present to you my argument that society, both, the built environment and lives of the people that occupy the space, are a product of intentional design which is where social engineering comes in and the act and art of drawing up the plan of this design for a society is called social architecture.

Different societies have different designs tailored to the characteristics of the people there, this is just like the watch maker designing different engines with different cases for different purposes. If all that were true then that means that the Nigerian society comprising of her built environment and the lives of her seeds within is also a product of intentional design. Dear Nigerian, I can hear your disbelief at this truth and to that I just want to say that I understand it. I also want to say that I can hear your many questions of this truth and about this truth and to those questions I say that there are answers. You see an answer to a question is a reply and a refusal to answer that question or a wrong answer given is also a reply. An action is an act and a refusal to act or a wrong action is also an act in itself. When we talk about design people think of the products running smoothly for some good purpose but that is not always the case, a design could also be something bad, I mean, people design weapons and bombs to kill other people and it sounds bad but the weapon could have been the only means they had to protect themselves. When I say Nigeria as a country is the product of design you might look at her and see nothing working and then take that to be the absence of purposeful design but that's where you're wrong because in her case she's designed to fail and what she is currently is exactly what her designers and planners planned for her to be. Sounds crazy right? The truth can be like that sometimes; what if I told you that we and by we, I meant your life, your properties, everyone you know and everything you own were all on a giant round rock suspended on nothing and endlessly spinning with other giant rocks like it around a… wait for it… around a bigger stationary giant ball of fire just burning away in the vast dark outside, what would you say? Would you call me a madman or would you think I was telling you the truth?

Take a long, slow look at Nigeria from top to bottom and I tell you that she is the product of carefully implemented design and who has the power, the authority and resources to shape whole societies and entire countries? That one would be a bit tricky to answer in its entirety here so for now I will just say it is the leadership of that society which in the case of Nigeria is the political ruling class from which the entire political leadership structure is derived. The environment speaks to people so when the average Nigerian says that they feel neglected, they feel no help from the leadership and they feel hopeless in their country and in the whole state of chaos it is in, the environment comprising the roads, houses and general infrastructures are in a dilapidated state constantly getting depreciated, worn out, sub-standard, constantly not fit for purpose but imposed on the poor citizens to cope with. These are the ingredients of the Nigerian environment that creates the Nigerian factor which is unique to the country as every other country has their own factor. These things are a yoke on the necks of the citizenry that they are so caught up in their day to day struggles that they have time or energy for nothing else, talk less of ever uniting and rising up as a people to fight their repressive and parasitic government. The overall run down state of the Nigerian environment is part of psychological warfare, it is a silent weapon but it speaks to the people every day and says things like this to them: *'this is it, this is your life and your reality', 'you're caught up in this life and you can do nothing about it', 'you have nothing and you are nothing and you are poor', 'you will die poor', 'you will live all the days of your miserable life here in pain and suffering and you can never be able to do anything about it'.* This is very depressing I know but these strings of messages are constantly transmitted by the Nigerian environment to the average Nigerian who is unaware of this from the time they are born until the day they die and it plays a vital role to psychologically set the tone for them on what kind of life to expect from their country, what is possible to do and what's impossible, and what the reality or the normalcy is in the country so that message tells them to get in line and you know as the saying goes: when in Rome do as the Romans do. All of this is psycho-hacking and social engineering taking place.

> **'But what do we have left once we abandon the lie? Chaos, a gaping pit waiting to swallow us all?**
>
> *- Lord Varys 'the Spider'.*
>
> **'Chaos isn't a pit, chaos is a ladder...'**
>
> *- Petyr 'Littlefinger' Baelish.*
> *Game of Thrones*
> *The Climb (S3 EP 6)*

Nigeria is unrelenting, she is in a constant state of crisis and chaos. One can only pity the poor souls trapped within her vicious vice-like grip, every single day of their lives they are taken through a roller-coaster with highs and swift dips, twists and turns of emotions and events that keep them distracted from the fact that the days of theirs lives and time on the earth are counting by, wasted, and that they are prisoners in their own country and can do nothing about it all the while getting exploited. This is their waking hour reality and it is one of silent, consistent and assured terror which sadly does not even hold any excitement close to riding in an actual roller-coaster. The days that do not come with drama and terror for them are deeply cherished by them but this sadly does not last because who knows what tomorrow will bring? This constant environment of instability greatly influences their lives and decisions and causes great mental stress but this is war, anything that will weaken your opponent and give you an advantage in the battle is a weapon and can be utilized. For the highlighted text above, I'll first say that I do not like watching series because I find them too time consuming and the waiting period for new episodes which is supposed to build excitement for the story does the opposite for me; it irritates me and because my mind wanders a lot the break in the story kills the momentum so my go to entertainment is a solid 130 minute movie with a good plot and exciting characters but both *Game of Thrones* and *Naruto* broke that mould and were able to slip through my defence; for *Naruto* I wasn't even an anime guy to start with.

In that famous scene, 2 of the more intelligent characters in the series were having a discussion and it was what they said about chaos that got me thinking hard. Lord Varys calls chaos 'a gaping pit' while Lord Baelish disagrees with him and calls it a 'ladder' instead, so which is it? You see, both men were right because chaos is both a pit and a ladder, it just depends on the perspective and who it's applicable to. In the Nigerian context chaos can be seen from 2 perspectives; the perspective of the political ruling class vs. the perspective of the masses. For the masses, the organised chaos in the society is the gaping pit they are trapped in and can't escape from, to them it is poverty, prolonged survival mode, insecurity and corruption which they struggle with every day and are occupied with, while for the political ruling class who have resources and means this situation is a ladder that presents many opportunities for them to climb and stay above the struggling masses in the pit while having the means to dominate and exploit them indefinitely. This is why I say that the Nigerian environment with the many hurdles it presents for the masses is another weapon in the hands of the political ruling class and could not simply be left to chance but was designed and enhanced. That environment in turn influences the growth and development of the average Nigerian trapped within it, so accurate is social engineering that within that environment the powers that be can estimate how high an individual can rise or how much he can make annually and like I always say, for humans, there will be exceptions who break that mould but exceptions are not the norm; matter of fact the exceptions justify the norm. Now let's briefly look at the elements of social engineering and their characteristics.

5a.i) SYSTEM:

I love football, and by football I mean real football, the one they play with the foot not that other one played with some funny looking ball that they pick up with their hands and then start running and bumping into each other like a bunch of drunk sailors at a bar fight. Football is war and my love for it stems from the tactical side of it. I love the fact that you can study the strengths and weaknesses of your team and then do the same for your opponent using that information to draw up a tactical plan tailored to that particular opponent that will give you the advantage to win the battle on match day. My main interest in football is in the tactical side of things which brings us to the manager and his coaching staff, they are the ones responsible for drawing up the tactical plans and setting up their team for success on a match by match basis throughout the whole season so naturally I love the great managers of our time. I love Carlo Ancelotti, the calm and gentlemanly Italian maestro, I love Jose Mourinho, the fiery Portuguese tactician, and even though Pep Guardiola is not my favourite character in the world you have to admit that as a manager that bald Spaniard is a genius. Honourable mentions include Sir Alex Ferguson who I could never get enamored to for some reason. Arsene Wenger was too docile a character to truly resonate with my soul but he's great too and we go down another tier to guys like Zinedine Zidane, who all due respect to his accomplishments always kept looking like Zidane the player to me even when he was a coach, Jurgen Klopp the big German. Thomas Tuchel is also great on his best day and Antonio Conte could have been higher on this list for me but he never won champions league and he tainted himself in my eyes by going on to coach Spurs. I pay my respects here and give my gratitude *slight bow* to the great managers that make football a worthwhile and engaging sport for me to enjoy despite the fact that football has become a money whore in recent times.

I am going to use what little I know about football as an observer and an enthusiast to explain social engineering because setting up your team as best as you can making in game tactical switches to get the advantage to try to win the match, then making shrewd and sensible use of the club's resources in the transfer windows to try to improve that team to go on and challenge for big things, is social engineering too. Now let's talk about the system, what do I mean when I say 'the system'? The system is intangible, it is the idea and the objective, the core and driving force that you want to implement on that social gathering. For a football manager it's his ideology i.e his own personal interpretation of how the game should be played and he can have influences and inspiration from outside but he has to discover himself as a manager and carve out his own unique system of how he thinks his team should play the game. So what is his system? Does he want to play offensive? defensive? Or a mixture of both? Does he want a possession-based team or he wants to play direct football? And if it is direct football he wants to play then does he want to go through the middle or have pacy wingers that will give his team width by hugging the touchline to stretch opposing teams' defences and come in from the side? He has to determine all these and many more within himself and even though in a match different scenarios occur that the players have to adapt to on the pitch the elite manager must have a clear-cut ideology and a clear style of play that he can implement on his team and that he can be associated with.

How does this relate to social engineering of a country? The ones who have the authority and the resources of that country which is the leadership of that territory have to come up with the idea of what they want to accomplish in that country with the human and material resources at their disposal. Many people confuse this with style of government so you hear many Nigerians say that we must stick to democracy at all costs and this is one of the reasons why they are so easy to manipulate as a people because they lack understanding of things, meaning that there is a high level of ignorance among the Nigerian people. The most effective style of leadership or government for any people is the one where the rights of the citizens are protected, there is justice in the society and there is an effective utilization of all resources of that people by the leadership to better the lives of ALL peoples within that territory and under that system. When you're a people that keep looking to indiscriminately copy ideas and systems from other people, just to live it up and drop it on yourselves then you open yourselves up to manipulation and other problems because a soulectomy can be carried out and you would not know it.

Soulectomy is the tactical removal of the soul i.e the vital working parts from any idea, system or thing that makes it function as desired leaving behind just the name and shell intact. So you can see that soulectomy causes deviation from the initial desired outcome to a debased and erroneous outcome so soulectomy is a corruption but within the confines of social engineering it is a tactical and surgical type of corruption that involves planning. How can I explain soulectomy to you? It is that family that have suffered much, trekking miles under the hot sun for the children to go to school, and the mother to go to the market and the father to go to and from work. They have been crying for a car and when the wicked car dealer who has long ignored their cries for a car finally has one delivered to them, he first takes out vital parts of the engine and the gear box then drops the beautiful metal shell with gleaming paint job on the doorstep of that family overnight knowing fully well in his heart that they are not driving anywhere with that car. What is soulectomy? It is that poor family shouting, singing, clapping and dancing around that car in the morning thinking that their prayers have been answered not knowing that their joy would be short-lived when the father finally gets in the car and tries to get it started.

Once again this is why I call political fraud because Nigeria is a crime scene in motion, unfolding day by day right before our eyes. Soulectomy is done every day in Nigeria that it has become normal now; for example the country is called a republic when it is not run like one, she claims to be a democracy when she does not operate like one, the electoral body in the country responsible for elections is called Independent National Electoral Commission and they went through the great trouble to add 'Independent' in the name there when everybody including themselves know that INEC is anything else but independent. This political ruling class have studied the Nigerian masses so much that they know putting such names there would pacify the people.

It is human will, not the style of leadership or government that makes a successful nation or society. If we look at history there were different successful leadership types that saw prosperity over the territories they were in control of before democracy. Kings ruled over kingdoms and just to mention it, one of the earliest forms of democracy in history was practised by the Igbos of South-East Nigeria. The problem of monarchies was that succession was hardly peaceful and brought about conflict and in-fighting that sometimes lasted for a long time and threatened to tear the kingdoms apart. Also because good dogs can birth bad puppies and succession in a monarchy is linear. One other major problem of that system was that some of the sons that succeeded their fathers were of a different disposition and temperament which plunged the kingdom into periods of chaos and hardship preventing a sustained growth and development in the kingdom. A new system was then designed where the powers of society are split up into independent institutions that balance each other out and the leaders have terms at the end of which their performance can be reviewed and it's decided by the people if they should be allowed to continue for another term. It's a brilliant system when it works but success of any system of government lies in the intangible will of the leadership in that government style which is their idea, motive or objectives. This is the system, the intangible part of social engineering which is the driving force that gives direction to everything else that follows.

5a.ii) STRUCTURE:

When the system which is the intangible idea or will has been designed and determined, a physical structure is needed to support that system and bring it to life in the physical realm. The structure is the physical representation of that intangible system that the people in the society can see and interact with. It is a well-designed set of interconnected and interdependent functioning parts or components all working together to bring that intangible system to pass in a tangible world. The system and the structure are one and the same thing, they are practically two sides of the same coin, just that while the system exists as an idea or will, in the soul realm, it becomes a structure in the physical. When that football manager has finished carving out his football ideology within himself, his ideology cannot run onto the pitch to play the game, he must then convert that ideology into a formation style using the correct number of players allowed on the pitch and having a defined primary and secondary role for each of the 11 players and their positions in that formation for the different phases of the game during gameplay be it the defensive phase in the defensive third or transition phase in the midfield and or during the attacking phase in the attacking third of the opponent his system must be expressed. Based on his system he must determine the shape and structure of the team when they are in possession or out of possession or if there are set pieces in different parts of the pitch for or against them and it's a lot that's why managers get paid the millions they get paid; all of this stems from his football ideology.

If he is a defensive manager he can structure his formation to be a 5-3-2 low block with 3 central defenders and 2 wing-backs, this can be changed to be a balanced 3-5-2 with the wing-backs shooting forward to support the attack by providing width, overloading the opponents' defence with extra men either to run defenders out of position or to provide the extra man for passing. He can also play attacking football which will see him draw up a 4-3-3 formation but there are variations to this too. It can be a defensive 4-1-3-2 with a lone defensive midfielder (6) shielding and providing extra cover for the back line or it could be an attacking 4-2-1-3 with 2 6s as a double pivot and an attacking midfielder (8) supporting the front line. He can decide to play 4-3-3 with a point man striker or he can play with a fluid false 9 who would get involved in the build-up of the game and interchange positions with other attackers. There are many permutations for the formations that the manager could play to bring his football ideology to life but note that all this would depend on the quality, the characteristics, intelligence, football IQ and ability of the players he has available to him in his team. I apologize to the non-football fans as I got carried away and it looked like I was rambling there. The thing is I love football and sometimes I wonder if I have what it takes to make it as a football manager. I wonder if maybe after this book I could try to study and sit for a UEFA manager's licence but I don't know, it might be too late for me to start afresh at this age to try to become a professional football manager.

The main point is that the manager sets up the team's formation according to his ideology but the important thing is that he sets them up to win. The most important thing in social engineering is the will behind the system, the will is the true driving force because you can set us a society to win and they win in which case your plan was a success, likewise you can set up that society to fail and they fail. Your plan was also successful here but because of the ill will behind it, it does not benefit the members of that society which makes it not a bad plan as far as plans go because it was successful but a bad unethical act. For example look at China with over a billion people which can be said to be the most successful country in the world for the past 2 decades now. They did not just go and borrow government styles to use throwing empty names around to fool their people but instead with the will to succeed and become prosperous already deeply entrenched in their leadership they designed a special system of government that better suits their values and their people which they practise. The fact that they were able to lift over 700 million of their people out of poverty becoming the largest economy in the world in the process is more a testament of their collective will to succeed than it is the style of government that they practise but the will alone cannot do that work so through their communist party structure they were able to translate that will into their society and the lives of their people and the results are clear for all to see.

When we talk about structure in social engineering I am not just blindly advocating for any particular style of government as the way out of poverty for Nigeria. You look at the surgical soulectomy carried out on democracy in the country leaving just the name intact and you can see that the system is very important in this set up. As far as structure goes the democracy practised in the United Kingdom is different from the one done in the United States. Both differ from how it is done in France which has differences with the way they do it in Italy and Spain but the underlying factor is the will which is to better the lives of their people. The structure becomes a guard dog to ensure that the system is not corrupted when it translates to implementation. The institutions in the structure provide stability and a strong foundation for prosperity. We are talking about the ideal scenario but if this knowledge will do anything for the average Nigerian it is to help you identify the components of social engineering in your country that have shaped your lives through the structures put in place. You can then reverse engineer these structures to get what the system and the will driving it is but that is an answer we already know at this stage because the results are evident for all of us to see. This is how the Nigerian factor plays into things, it would surprise you that ideas that worked excellently in other places to help them solve their problems over there, the moment they are brought to your own country they fail so miserably and you wonder why. Outside observers who don't know what is really happening under the surface will take one look and say it is because you are incapable of doing anything good for yourselves, they will say it is because you are unintelligent as a people or unwise or just a collection of damaged goods but that is why I have taken the pain to collate this in-depth explanation and I hope my attempt sheds a much-needed light to the whole world on the true happenings as it involves governance in Africa.

The structure is the case, when the watch maker said to himself *'I want to create a device that can tell time accurately'*, the structure is the engine of the watch with all the cogs and moving parts and the casing he put them all in to tell time. Dipping into my background, when the client took the approved plans from the architect and carried it to the building engineer and said, *'I want you to construct this building for me that would be 10 floors high and safely house people,'* the structure is the frame made up of connected beams and columns carrying all the live and dead load of the building including the lateral pressure and successfully transmitting it down to the foundation which in turn transmits it to the earth. Considering all these examples I insist that society is not a coincidence or a product of chance but of careful design, planning and implementation. There can be misdirection, certain aspects can be shrouded in mystery and secrecy but make no mistakes, no matter what country you find yourself in, that country is a product of design. The casing of the watch might hide the true designs and operations of the cogs and other moving parts that make up the engine of the watch but they are there and they are functioning properly. So is the case of the building standing tall and beautiful, the glass, plaster and paint might be covering the columns, beams and lintels but they are there doing their job, if they were not the whole structure would collapse. The soil has been back-filled to cover the foundations of that building so when you look all you see is the soil on the outside, tiles or whatever material was used for the ground floor finishing but even though they might be covered the foundations are there doing their job because if they were not then the whole structure comes tumbling down like a pack of cards. If the plan was faulty then you would have a faulty structure, likewise you have to look closely at the structures put in place in your country and how they are affecting your lives. Let's move onto the next one now shall we?

5a.iii) FUNCTIONALITY:

Hurray! our brilliant manager of Social Engineering Football Club (SEFC) is making progress; according to his understanding and preferences he has carved out his football ideology. He has also converted this ideology into a structure with brilliant formations in mind taking into consideration the different aspects and phases of the game, he has also studied and gotten all his licenses and necessary documentation not to mention the sweet 3 year contract he just signed with us at SEFC. It was beautiful, as the president of SEFC I made sure to be there as he signed the contract to communicate to him personally how important he is to our club, our ambitions and our project for the next few years as we hope to challenge for the title next season. We took a lot of pictures after he signed the contract with the logo of our club in the background along with the logos of our sponsors. All the sports news channels reported the good news even Fabrizio Romano and it gave our fans worldwide a lot of joy. As the president of the club I am happy with proceedings so far, the board is happy with the decision and my stewardship, shareholders are happy and shares are doing well in the market, all the staff and players in the club are excited for the new season starting next week and then in our last pre-season game to get the squad match ready, 2 of our star players go down with injury. Joshua 'JJ' Omuvwie our new striker and marquee signing for the season and hopeful longtime stalwart in our midfield Peter Jnr 'Engine' Omuvwie who is the engine in our engine room both go down and team doctor Zoe Omuvwie has just walked into the manager's office with a worried look on her face, bad news! Both players are going to be out for a long time perhaps missing as much as half of the season and the manager feels a cold sensation moving up his back towards his neck. As soon as the team doctor walks out of the office he looks at his notes containing his formation and game plan for the season and realises that he'll be without 2 key members of his squad for half of the season and that there is a huge drop off in quality with the backups they have in the team for those positions, what will he do? Because even if the transfer window still has 2 weeks before it closes, as the president I had already made it clear to him and the sporting director Mr. Atatre 'Money' Omuvwie that we have limited resources to budget for signings in this window but to make him happy the club had got him the striker he wanted after selling our striker for last season so now, what will he do? Sorry, what am I asking him that for? He's a fictional character so it's more like what will you, my dear reader, do in this scenario?

This is where functionality comes into play; the manager might have his ideology and drawn up his best formation but in terms of how it will all come together on the pitch he has to consider the quality and characteristics of the different players that he has at his disposal for the squad that he inherited. If he wants to play a system with wing-backs but inherited players more suited to fullbacks then you can see that he has a problem on his hands because it takes special qualities to operate as a wing-back. The player needs to have the stamina to run up and down his side of the pitch plus they must be good enough defensively to be able to provide support for the 3 centre-backs and he must be good enough as an attacker to beat his man, be able to deliver good crosses into the box for his attackers and be able to shoot to score if he finds himself in the position. This is a lot expected from a player in this role and a different profile from those of a traditional fullback so not a lot of players can play this role professionally at a high level in world football today. He'll have to adjust his system and his tactics taking into account the players that he has, how many of them are not just available but fit to play in the next match and he must do this consistently in order to succeed throughout the course of the season. On the part of SEFC we believe that we have provided him with everything he needs to succeed, if he still does not perform well he will mysteriously hear through the press towards the end of the season that club officials are already having meetings with possible candidates to replace him. He will be asked embarrassing questions about it by reporters and he will confront me about it. Of course I'm a professional, I'll deny it vehemently and we will even release an official statement from the club re-affirming our support for our manager and debunking the 'lies' and 'rumours' of his sack blaming them as the work of malicious reporters to destabilize the club and derail our season. It will all be a lie until it's not and he is finally sacked at the end of the season with the club putting out a short classy statement thanking the manager for his service and ending it with telling him our doors will always be open to him in the future. We will then announce his sneaky replacement less than a week later and of course as the president of the club I have to be there to take pictures with the new incoming manager after he signs his sweet contract, I am a professional after all and I have a club to run *lol* I'm sorry I couldn't help myself.

Now if we could just get back on track you'll see that the manager encountered a lot of problems when he tried to implement his ideas but he can always find creative solutions for them. He does not need to create the best club in the world, if he can do that it would be amazing but even if he were just able to stay in the game, get his team to play with pride and heart, finish the season in a good position on the log he tried, the consequences of him not doing so is getting sacked but in the case of a country the consequences of a combined systemic, structural and functional failure is what you see in Nigeria today. This is why I said earlier that her problem is a problem of organisation. The unfortunate Nigerian masses and the black peoples around the world have no country with a functioning system and structure all functioning for their interests and betterment in the world. In Nigeria their resources are extracted from them through diverse systems and structures leaving them without a voice and without covering in this harsh world so how can they perform? How can they compete with others as mere individuals when the others have collective covering? The manager lost some key players just before the start of the season what is the excuse for Nigeria? What is the excuse of the political ruling class as the reason why the country is in the state it is today? Can they say that they have truly tried their best but it did not work? These are questions for everyone to think on.

You can use the components of social engineering to fully analyse the government structure in Nigeria and you will arrive at the same conclusion that it is human will or in this case the political will of the ruling class that is the problem so it is one of those unethical situations where the plan is working successfully as planned and intended but it is a bad plan. What else will you tell me about my people? You want to tell me that they are not intelligent enough to build a successful country with them? The same people that were average students in schools here in Nigeria but have gone on to dominate in schools around the world including schools of the so called 1st nations? The same people that have emigrated to those countries as professionals in brain drain and are currently working in different companies and contributing to the growth of those economies, are those the ones you would say are not intelligent enough? You're going to stand in front of me and tell me they are lazy when not long ago as a people we were targeted for use as slaves for hundreds of years to work and start up some of the greatest economies we see in the world today? Are you really going to insult me and my intelligence to my face with that kind of talk? What is the reason for mother Nigeria chomping down on her seeds? It's because she was planned and designed to do so by her older kids so they can rob her while she's distracted with the task they have set for her.

5a.iv) CONTINGENCY APPROACH TO MANAGEMENT:

Contingency is a provision for a possible event or circumstance. The contingency approach to management is the continuous phase of social engineering that never stops because after the dominant will that is carrying out the engineering has been shrouded in a system and that system has been structured to function in the society it does not end there. There has to be constant monitoring and micromanaging done to the set up to keep it working smoothly and adapting to both internal and external conditions that will change. If this is not done then the entire set up will crash and fail. For the watch, the parts of the engine will be rubbing and moving against each other so there is bound to be wear and tear at some point. Periodic servicing and maintenance will preserve its working life span, also there could be damage due to use by the wearer which is unavoidable so proper professional repair and replacement of damaged parts will keep that watch working well. For the building there has to be periodic inspections, glass can break, wood can be compromised, metal can rust and cracks can also appear in concrete members due to loading or settlement of the new structure. Consistent checks, repairs and maintenance will prolong the life span of that building and preserve its value which is sure to rise with time. This is what a contingency approach to management in social engineering means.

In an alternate reality our SEFC manager did not lose hope just before the start of the season with 2 major injuries to the midfield maestro and his new signing striker who plays just the way he likes it and would have thrived in his system. He looks at what he still has left and takes stock. He still has 2 weeks before the transfer market closes, even though the club informed him that they have no budget for extravagant rascality in the transfer market, the situation is not hopeless. If he liaises with the scouting department he might get lucky and they find bargain replacements with old players whose contracts are ending and they are getting to the end of their careers. Those types of players might not be as physical as they used to be when they were younger but they make up for it with lots of experience. They can be snapped up as free agents on moderate wages that will not upset the wage structure of the club too much and he can convince the club president who will then convince the board to get behind the idea. Yes he can come and talk to me I'll listen, I consider myself to be a reasonable and supportive club president. Also he can promote young players from the academy in those lacking positions to train with the first team and the veterans, they will be inconsistent and will make a lot of mistakes due to their age but the experience will help them a lot in their development and, who knows? he can unearth some gems in the process. If he acts fast on this and he is able to keep the mood of the club and around the players upbeat then he just might get through the season in a good position on the log. He can also tweak his formation to play to the strengths of the players he has available, it's all about adaptability and balance. I just hope to God for his sake he's not one of those coconut head managers who refuse to change their formation for anything even if the sky is raining goals against their team. He can do this until his first choices return from injury but I do not expect players coming back from a long lay-off to just slot seamlessly back in but they can be eased in with their minutes managed in conjunction with the medical department, with a contingency approach to the situation he may yet get through the season with his job intact learning valuable lessons from these tests thrown at him; at the off season he can then regroup, reassess the situation and use the time off to plan together with the club for the next season.

All of those are for positive contingency approach to management in a positive social engineering process, unfortunately anything that has a positive also has a negative. In the case of Nigeria the political ruling class has feelers all over the nation, they know the conditions that have to exist to create the right environment and atmosphere that will allow what they are doing in Nigeria to continue so their job is to keep those conditions stable. It might surprise you but I can hear the doubts from some of you when you get to parts like this. These doubts especially come from non-Nigerians and people who have never been in this situation before. I hear your questions, questions like *'is this man telling the truth about his country?'* or *'is it possible for a government to do these things to their own people?'* And questions like *'if it is possible then how do they go about it?'* Well, we will answer your questions.

Nigeria the country like any other country is a closed system. The leadership which in her case is the political ruling class exerts their authority and rule over this territory, this is where their social engineering activities aimed at the Nigerian peoples trapped within start and stop. The dominant will within this territory is that of the ruling class, their system of choice is democracy that has gone through extensive soulectomy and they have the structure of the federal unitary system with a president at the federal level, state governors at the state levels and local government chairmen at the local level to bring their will to pass politically within the Nigerian closed system. I have gone through great pains to explain that the Nigerian masses within this system are put into and held inside a closely monitored and well-regulated artificial environment of poverty. Kept in this state within the closed system survival mode kicks in because survival is the strongest instinct in man and so the masses are so preoccupied with surviving the present day and entering into the next one that they have neither the time or energy to fight back or pay close attention to what the political ruling class are up to. This is the description of the closed system showing the first level of the domination of the Nigerian masses by the political ruling class. Left like this it's still a challenging system to beat that would prove daunting for the Nigerian masses but you know they are humans and will fight to find a way to beat it with time so the architects of destruction do not leave things like this. Like a cook adding ingredients and spices to a meal they are preparing to get the right taste they add more levels and layers of difficulty to the system with ethnic race, religion, political differences and any other thing that will cause unrest and distrust among the ranks of the masses isolating them within this closed system (individualism).

Isolated and having multiple levels of difficulties added to their woes within the closed system you can see that it has already become impossible for the individualistic masses to break from this multi-dimensional yoke placed on them but the architects of destruction are not done yet. Remember I told you that the different levels of difficulties all come with strings running deep into the masses and the strings are in the hands of the political ruling class. They tug and pull at these strings in different directions adding to the chaos within the closed system and further discomfiting the poor souls trapped within but that is not the end. Circumstances that I call 'instruments of control' because they have certain effects on the prisoners trapped within the closed system and elicit certain responses from them are then introduced intermittently according to the current status in the closed system. The average Nigerian would never think this in that they feel neglected by their government but the political ruling class have feelers deep within the veins that criss-cross the nation through which they monitor the chaos status which is like a meter that reads from low to high. The goal for them is to maintain a certain level of poverty and overall chaos so when the people start to beat the new level of hardship set for them in the country and demand better from their government or when they try to protest en masse, the chaos and poverty is like a tap in the hands of the political ruling class who have absolute control over the vital resources in the country. At this point, they can turn that tap high, low or off at will and they do this in response to their feelers and other signs they get from the masses.

    The instruments of control are then thrown into the closed system in response to signs that the masses are catching up. This plunges the masses into further hardship by increasing the chaos and poverty levels within the closed system dramatically and drastically within a very short period of time. They might turn the tap very high and the people will cry, complain, curse and beg and when they are beaten to the ground they turn it a bit low but never to the level it was before it was turned drastically up as if telling the masses that they should never ever have let the thought of freedom cross their minds in the first place. It is like that time in my vision I first saw them throw wads of cash into the struggling masses from their high building and I didn't know what it meant when I first saw it all those years ago, I had to dig deeper to find out. The instruments of control are but not limited to fuel scarcity and fuel price hike, increase in exchange rate to the dollar, ethnic strife, tokenism, religious propaganda, terrorism, insecurity, palliative and increase in the price of government services. I wish I could take each of these out as a sub-topic and do an in-depth analysis of them for you but we will get thrown far off our course and just pile up material and material. What I will do is talk about them briefly here and maybe intersperse explanations about them into other topics as we go along in the book. I'm guessing most of my readers are going to be Nigerians anyways so you're familiar with these things, as for the others you can always do a little research on the side, it would surprise you how much information is just flying about on the internet.

The Nigerian economy, day to day Nigerian life is dependent on oil. The Nigerian people for decades now think this is an act of stupidity, ineptitude, ignorance and failure on the part of the political ruling class but where they as a people see failure I see success, where they see chaos I see intention and design. The political ruling class do what they do and get away with it and if all they get in return from the Nigerian people is empty and harmless insults then it is a fair price to pay on their part. Every business and every aspect of Nigerian life is tied to fuel availability and fuel price making it the main artery in the country. They could have taken the money coming from oil to invest and develop other areas of the economy for Nigerians to thrive but in making oil the big dog of the economy they create a bottle neck and a funnel channelling the attention and livelihood of the large masses through this little point that they can then control. It is a wicked and brutal but effective strategy, so as a mechanism of control then they use their structure of the fuel supply already in place to manipulate its availability and price, then it affects the whole country throwing the masses into more chaos, the price of every other thing in the country goes up apart from the income and salary of the common man. In this way they have less money to spend and the value of their currency drops some more but when you're part of the political ruling class with a mountain load of money embezzled from the people these types of changes never affect you. So again, it's the case of the chaos being a pit for some and a ladder for others depending.

Nigeria is not a producing country so she imports the goods she consumes and most of the world trade is done in dollars adding to the power of the United States. In killing the Nigerian economy it leads to an increase in the price of goods. The people wake up one morning and the value of their currency in exchange to the dollar has gone down 300% and they are expected to deal with it and carry on with their lives. The ethnic strife and religious propaganda are thrown into the mix continuously and we saw its effects in the violence that erupted in the recent 2022/23 elections. Ethnoreligious strings are tugged and the people respond in what I can only call manipulation and psychological warfare. Create a fire, let it burn for a while and when the helpless people cry out for help in their pain you run in quickly with water to quench it and make sure everyone sees you while you quench it and you'll be a hero in their eyes, that is what happens in tokenism and palliatives. We have a parable in Delta state, we say *'you work like an elephant and eat like an ant'*. it is used to express the fact that you have done great work but got little reward or returns for the work you put in, in the same way the political leadership embezzles much from the people and gives them tokens to pacify them. For example they might build a road without drainage and get all the media to take pictures and report it celebrating it as a great achievement for humanity and a crucial step for Nigerians in the right direction only for the rains to come and wash the road away in a year's time after the cameramen, praise singers and politicians have long gone back to their houses. They are basically playing with the intelligence of the people, first they make them poor and then they come with palliatives, we know how much effect food has on a hungry man. Esau carelessly sold his birthright to his cunning younger brother for a bowl of pottage (Gen 25:29-34), and in John 6:15-25 we see a people almost seize Jesus to forcefully make him their king after he fed them so in effect create a desert for the people and when they're dying from their thirst you show up with drops of water for them in cups with your face branded on those cups and they'll worship you. This is too easy to see through and I wonder how the Nigerian people get fooled by all these childish tricks over and over again, decade in and decade out. Sometimes I wish the political ruling class had a more intelligent and vibrant people to contend against them, I would like to see how they'll respond when they are truly tested but alas they have these weak and docile people who are too tattered, battered, shattered and scattered to fight back to exploit, if you leave the Nigerian masses in this situation without help for another hundred years they'll still be there suffering and smiling.

5b) CONCLUSION TO NIGERIAN ENVIRONMENT:

This is war and sadly there is no middle ground for any of you to hide in so you must fight. You Nigerians need to wake up because you're sleeping on your bicycle, open your eyes wide and see what is happening all around you, this is social engineering at its finest; covert, silent, properly disguised and hidden in plain sight from its victims but very effective such that if you told them what's happening they would not even believe that it exists and it's happening right under their noses, it is brilliant.. I call it death by a thousand cuts. You insult these politicians every day and call them names from sun up to sun down but indeed you're all being played, even the most intelligent ethnic group among you, the Igbos, have been given the Biafra bone to endlessly chase all the days of their lives and you think these people are still just a bunch of stupid old men and women who don't know anything else but to service their greed? You have collectively made a big error and broken one of the cardinal rules of the art of war by grossly underestimating your enemy and you're rightly paying the price for it, your lives and the situation of your country is a testament of this fact.

Through effective social engineering the political ruling class have been able to create an enabling environment and atmosphere to give them a great advantage in their battle to subdue and subjugate the Nigerian masses for in which reasonable country can they do the things they do every day and get away with it? Can they stand in front of the Italians or the Spanish to say a monkey or a snake swallowed money in their office? Can they carry out the Lekki massacre without consequences in the United Kingdom? Can they try the rubbish we witnessed in the 2022/23 presidential elections in a place like France without the whole country burning to the ground in one night? Because you know the French people, I have serious problems with French involvement and conduct in post-colonial Africa and will be the first to tell them to their face if they asked me but you know that as a people liberty is their mantra and they would rather all die than stand for what was just dished out to you Nigerians without consequence or repercussions by your electoral body and your politicians not too long ago. When betrayal goes unpunished it gets reinforced, instead of acting young Nigerian men and women would rather congregate themselves on social media to make jokes and memes about their situation, a dearth of gravitas as I lamented earlier. What is it about the environment and atmosphere of those places that things like that cannot happen but it happens so effortlessly in your own country? When we say things like 'only in Nigeria' or 'only in Africa' we're right because of the unique atmosphere and environment created to allow such things to happen. I think I have said all I need to say and made my case about the environment as one of my theories, let's keep it moving.

6. THE CURSE OF BAD LEADERSHIP IN NIGERIA:

> *'I have never seen a business, a young entrepreneur [or] an experienced entrepreneur whose problem was solved by money, period! the thing that solves every problem is passion and I've seen people make huge successes without a dime in their pocket if they have the passion.'*
>
> *- Barbara Corcoran*
> *Shark Tank*
> *(S11 EP10)*

Many of what is generated in the world today as entertainment is garbage meant to fry your brain and make you dumber. To this end I gate keep my thoughts by being very selective about what I allow into my soul and being very transnational about what I consume even as entertainment. The simple questions I ask myself are: 'how does this benefit me in the long run?' or 'what do I learn or gain from this that would make me better or make my life better?' and only when I can conveniently answer these questions about an exercise or thing do I continue with it. This is why Shark Tank is one of my favorite programmes to watch, learning more about business in the process from people who have been there and done that. Barbara Corcoran is a very successful American business woman and investor, she's one of my favourite sharks on the show that I like personally and even though she was speaking on something entirely different from what I was working on when she spoke those words on my title text she captured my thoughts on political will so succinctly in words that I was taken aback, moments like this make me feel like the universe is speaking to me.

We Nigerians have a parable, in pidgin English it says: *'something wey elder see as he siddon for chair even if small pikin climb tall tree sef he no go fit see am'* which in English says: 'something an elder sees sitting on a chair even if a youth climbs a tall tree he or she cannot see it'. In his book *The trouble with Nigeria* the late great sage Chinua Achebe said the trouble with Nigeria is leadership. Well I have gone round on my journey and have come back to his point and I must say that I agree with him. We cannot downplay the importance of leadership in society, Confucius in his Analects said that *'to lead an uninstructed men into battle is to throw them away'*. To live is to do battle, to exist as a human is to overtly or covertly be in competition with other humans for scarce resources, all the way up to the family level and to the level of nations, so what is it about these peoples that they continue to be poor and disadvantaged in this battle of life? One of the main reasons is the pattern and the curse of bad leadership hanging over their heads like a cloud and refusing to go away. If it was outsiders that came for Joseph to capture him and to sell him into slavery then his brothers would have banded together to fight for him against the outsiders to protect their brother but in this case they were the ones selling him into slavery (Gen 37:18-36), the sign to the passersby says 'Beware of Dog' but the danger has been in the house with the occupants all the while.

I will cast blame on the masses for the mess that is Nigeria as they cannot be exempt and I have done so up to this point but the bulk of the blame must of necessity start from the head because the head is responsible, the head has authority, the head has taken the resources from the people, the head must find a way in times of troubles, the head must provide security, the head must at least create an enabling environment to give the body a fighting chance in the general battle of life but when the head cannot do all that it can be said to have failed but knowing what I know now about the human will and social engineering I cannot even say that the leadership of Nigeria has failed because in truth they did not fail, it is not a question of the head cannot do those things but more that the head will not do them. You cannot call the political ruling class failures as is the norm in Nigerian society when their plan is working smoothly so instead we say they took a different direction that is in contradiction with the direction that would have benefited the masses. Human will is great, in this case when it's concentrated and leveraging on political power of the land to become political will then it's powerful and power is the ability to do things.

Nigeria is not just a crime scene, she is also a graveyard; she is the place where great ideas and solutions from all over the world come to die and are buried. She is not meek in this act, she is a collector for she displays the bones and carcass of her many conquests proudly. How is it that ideas that have worked brilliantly in other places solving problems for others fail so miserably and become impotent when they cross into the Nigerian space? I would be a poor teacher if you could not answer this one by yourself at this stage. No matter how viable or genetically great a seed is it cannot thrive in a bad environment, how much more when that environment is intelligent and the elements are changed and tailor made to kill seeds? Who has the power to carry out social engineering in Nigeria? Nigerian politicians will give a million excuses as to why the country cannot work and in the same breath announce a raft of bonuses and benefits for them and their friends, why not? The environment is conducive for it and the people, utterly broken down as they are, are incapable of resisting so the shenanigans continue unopposed.

When I think about the predatory and parasitic relationship that exists between the Nigerian people and their leaders I liken it to a hunt and for me it's like a pride of lions ambushing a herd of buffaloes in the night under the cover of darkness. In the book *The Art of War* by Sun Tzu written hundreds of years ago to capture the essence of combat he talks about the importance of choosing the right time and place for a battle to give you the edge over your opponent, I only bought the modern version of it translated to English and I know a lot of the nuances he tried to convey were lost in translation but the core elements remain. I have seen footage of lions hunting at night in Africa and they start with psychological warfare, the lions approach the herd from different directions roaring and growling as they do so but note that the lions have the basics right in terms of choosing the right place and time to strike. For the time they do so in the night time when the prey have been running around all day grazing and are tired, wanting to get a nap and chew the cud, they are not the most alert in this state and as for the place they are attacked in the very spot the prey had chosen as a safe spot for the night to rest. This adds an element of unpredictability, panic and inevitability to the minds of the prey. In the thick darkness of the wild undisturbed by the bright city lights the sounds of the predators' war cry carries far and appears to be coming from everywhere enveloping the prey and sending fear down their spines. They hear the sounds, they know that the predators are out there but close by, they know what that means and what that means is that they know what's coming, that they are already under attack and that any of them could lose their lives and fall prey that night to satiate the appetite of the predators. The lions on their side have the advantage because reflective strips in their eyes which allows them to harness whatever low light is coming from the moon gives them better vision in the dark than most animals. They sustain this psychological assault roaring and growling continuously while circling the herd, heaping pressure on the prey in the process until they break under it. In their deep fear the prey do not hold their position as a group, they do not maintain their shape and in the panic some break rank and try to make a run for it. As they do so they are separated from the safety in numbers, they become isolated by the predators, making for an easy kill then they are eaten for that night. The escaping herd hears the screams and the cries of the poor victim for that night, its cries for help go unanswered, if it was during the day time some of the brave bulls sometimes band together to mount a rescue operation for a fallen comrade to rescue it from the jaws of death but not in this pitch blackness where they cannot see anything. The victim dies in great agony and is feasted upon by the predators but not before sending a chilling message to the rest of the herd through its cries and its death as if to say: *'any of you can be next'.*

    If we're to draw parallels to the Nigerian situation, you already know who the hunters are and who the hunted is so we'll skip the formalities there. The place of attack is in the very country of the hunted, a place where they should feel the most protected and safest but the time here is all the time, non-stop blitz chipping away bits and bobs until the prey are totally broken down. This is the boa constrictor analogy or the death by a thousand cuts scenario where they are attacked night and day until they fold giving in to the sustained external pressures; in this state they are easier to control and exploit. The psychological warfare of choice here is ethnic and religious differences, political differences, insecurity and the rumours of insecurity amplifying these conditions and creating an environment with an atmosphere that normalizes their direct attack of corruption to happen with as little resistance as possible. Am I satisfied with this? Do I feel like I've broken through to you? By your wavering attention I do not feel like I am getting my points across properly.

6a) THE ORDER OF THE DRAGON KEEPERS.

I know what you're thinking, *another analogy?* Well yes, some of these analogies are actually pictures or visions and I say to you that you have to thank my publishers who told me to tone it down else you would have been reading a book full of analogies mostly. The analogies show you just how much I've thought on these things and in how many different ways I've envisioned it, besides all that I'm African and we do love our parables. To what then do I liken the attacks of the Nigerian leadership on the Nigerian people? I see the Nigerian political class like a secret order of dragon keepers; they have the great dragon chained down deep in some dark dank dungeon, her mouth muzzled shut so she cannot breathe out fire, they keep her just alive in this weakened state, chained and imprisoned but they do not kill her. In this state the dragon cannot fly the skies and rule the earth, her environment and diet are regulated, her chains are checked periodically for any signs of weakness and this is the job of the secret order of the dragon keepers. This is a deviation from the intended existence of the dragon, destiny exchange and just the general slow sustained weakening of the people... the main job of the secret order of the dragon keepers is not to kill the dragon but to keep her weakened indefinitely so she can never be all she was intended to be in the first place.

The people of this world wonder and ask questions, they crane their necks and shade their eyes from the rays of the sun to see farther from their observation posts, and when they see nothing they look at each other with a bewildered look on their faces and ask their questions: *where is the great beast that is supposed to rise out of that place? For we saw her gathering herself and getting ready to take flight, where is she now? Where did she go? We were afraid in our hearts for we knew her coming was only a matter of time but now we look and can't see her, does anyone know what happened to her?* Well, the secret order of the dragon keepers happened to her and they have thrown new chains on her, kept her in a weakened state and maintained the conditions of her bondage so successfully that she cannot break the chains with which she is bound to take flight. They have dragged her into a dark dungeon away from the light and kept her there, in that dungeon there is no one to help her break the chains or supply the keys to open the locks attached to the chains, day by day she sits aching all over her body, her hands and feet hurt and she has become a shadow of herself, a corrupted version of herself.

There is no one to nurture her wounds from a thousand cuts inflicted by the priests of the secret order of dragon keepers from which her life-giving fluid is drained continuously day in and day out without stopping, there is no one to feed and nurture her the right diet for her to regain her strength so what can she really do in this state?

6b) CONCLUSION ON BAD LEADERSHIP:

You can look at the long history for yourself and you'll see that one of the greatest flaws of black people is that they have never learnt how to ruthlessly and decisively deal with betrayers and betrayals in their midst especially coming from their own. You can chalk it up to morals, forgiveness, empathy, compassion, naivety or whatever but this actually is a great weakness on our part because if as a people we were ruthlessly indifferent to betrayers then the message would have been sent out a long time ago and reinforced over time to the present. *The worm wey dey chop bitter kola, na inside the bitter kola e dey*, a little leaven leavens the whole lump, the dogs are in the house with the inhabitants making a mess of things, chewing furniture and pillaging the store room but no one has seen it fit to discipline them and to call them to order yet! Why are these people so comfortable in what they do for the entirety of their lifetime without fear of repercussions from the people? They live in the towns and the cities among the very masses that they persecute, they attend the same churches and mosques as their victims wherein they are celebrated as heroes, why do they not fear retribution? It may be because of what they know, they have come to know something that the outsiders who came to pillage before them already knew about these people, that sadly they let everybody in and they do not know how to decisively punish betrayers. If I killed a man or a woman that was exploiting me continuously I wonder what God would say to me after I was done with his or her execution.

The curse of black leadership is one of consistent betrayal and exploitation of their own people to serve and enrich others in the process and this runs deep. Look at the history, let's take for example Mansa Musa, one of the most prominent black leaders ever recorded in history. Mansa Musa of Mali is regarded as one of the richest kings ever, he has been quoted by many great black thinkers for many decades and every conscious rapper has name dropped him in their songs to promote black positivity but I never could get on that bandwagon. I have a very strict internal scale by which I weigh my life and the lives of other men so even if I acknowledge that no man is perfect my definition of greatness most likely differs from the generally accepted societal definition. What is king Mansa Musa's global claim to fame? He was said to have embarked on a pilgrimage to Mecca and on the way he had given away so much gold in Egypt and Europe that it had changed the economy of those places. Wow, what a rich man indeed! How typical of him, just another black leader that has taken the precious resources of his people in Africa to freely give to foreigners with no benefits whatsoever to his people in return, in fact leaving his people poorer in the process. While his loyal subjects were risking life and limbs in over a thousand mines located in Mali at that time as recorded in history to mine gold for their sovereign, he was busy giving it away freely to foreigners in foreign lands to show his generosity. I want to be respectful to authority and all that but tell me why such a man was not immediately taken into the village square and executed in front of all the people as soon as he got back from his missionary journey? Instead he made his way into the history books celebrated by the beneficiaries of his 'generosity'.

What was so bad and repulsive about his own lands that he could not gift his people the gold from their own lands? What is so repulsive about the land of Africa that even her own refuse to develop her? What chases goodwill away from these lands and the people within? I find it very disturbing indeed that as far back as hundreds of years ago the measurement of the greatness of a black leader was how much of his people's wealth and resources he could exploit and give away to foreigners and foreign lands. How does this differ today from the oil in Nigeria? Or the chrome in South Africa?

Or the uranium in Mali? Or the rare earth and other resources in Congo? This depressing list goes on and on and when you trace the movement of scarce and precious resources in any body of black people on the planet I bet you that you will find the consistent unmistakable pattern of outward flow. There just so happens to be conflicts and wars that are never ever resolved happening in these places causing great distraction for the peoples but the outward flow of resources from these places is never even hindered or disrupted in the process with all the conflict and loss of indigenous lives. You will just find religious groups, liberation groups or political groups at war with each other and even though weapons are not manufactured indigenously on the continent these groups always seem to be well armed and words like 'truce' or 'settlement' never ever seem to exist in their vocabulary. All of these yokes on the necks of my people and you mean to ask me why we are always poor and behind in the world? Do you really want to have that conversation with me?

While all this is happening you continue to get excuses, excuses and more excuses from the political leadership as to why nothing ever seems to work or will ever work in the land such that not even the most efficient factories in China can manufacture anything as fast as an African leader to manufacture a new excuse as to why things under his care, leadership and control cannot work. You name the condition and the African leader already has an excuse as to why it would not be possible to fix, and even when ideas that have worked well in other places are handed to him or her, he or she is sure with the cronies around them to first perform an effective soulectomy on that idea before giving it to their people such that when they eventually do the only thing that remains of that idea is the name and you wonder why nothing changes in the land. Truly, the elders did not lie with this one, *The worm wey dey chop bitter kola, na inside the bitter kola e dey* indeed!

What is their modus operandi to execute this will? All of the previous concepts come into play with social engineering where there's a dedicated system with a structure in place functioning to execute it. In this case it's a slow, crushing multi-dimensional move just like the boa constrictor analogy I used from earlier where the prey cannot fight back. I call it death by a thousand cuts where the political ruling class has applied so many little cuts to the masses that they are so discombobulated and bamboozled that they can never recover from the cuts to offer any type of meaningful resistance. These thousand cuts are made to vital societal arteries of the masses, disguised with distractions, masterfully done under an atmosphere of chaos and deep corruption that all serve to weaken the masses allowing the political ruling class to dominate, manipulate and exploit them… this is the curse of bad leadership in Nigeria and Africa in general.

7. UNDER THE VEIL OF SECRECY:

> *'O divine art of subtlety and secrecy! Through you we learn to be invisible, through you inaudible, and hence we can hold the enemy's fate in our hands'*
>
> - Sun Tzu
>
> The Art of War.

I continue to emphasize that what is going on between the political ruling class in Nigeria and the masses to create the reality of the country you see today is war and there is no middle ground to it for me. I view it as war, I approach it as war and I handle it as war, dear Nigerian you don't? Well maybe that's why you're all losing so woefully. In this war, as in all wars, secrecy plays a big part for success, one must be able to hide one's moves from the enemy so that the enemy cannot know it because if they do then they can develop effective countermeasures to nullify it. It happens across all dimensions of conflict: the spider's sticky webs are so thin that the prey does not see them until they are caught up in them, the crocodile stays submerged under water until its prey gets within its effective striking range, the lion creeps up on its preys in the day time even going against the wind to mask its scent, speed hunters like the cheetah on land and falcon in the air rely on their speed such that by the time the prey sees them coming it's usually too late for them to react appropriately to escape and we can keep it going. In boxing one of the most common things you'll hear about is 'telegraphing your punches' which is signs and tells a boxer makes before throwing his punches that his opponent can read to anticipate him throwing. A proper coach would coach out those traits from a boxer and even teach him to use them to confuse his opponent in a fight because you can't dodge or block a punch if you can't see it in the first place. In World War 2 most of you already know about the famous Enigma cipher machine used by the Nazis to mask their communication and the efforts of their opponents to crack that machine to have access to high level military and diplomatic communication, lots of movies have been created about that. Secrecy plays an important part in warfare, even in spiritual warfare we have praying in tongues to mask our communication to God such that the enemies like the monitoring spirits assigned to the saints only hear gibberish in such a high level communication but the Spirit facilitates a secure and closed circuit communication and connection ensuring that the message is delivered to the Source (1 Cor 14:2-15).

In the Nigerian situation, we see the effects of secrecy by the political ruling class in the way they conduct their affairs and the ignorance it causes on the masses so I've had to set time aside to look at it because it does have its own effect in the general Nigerian equation coupled with all the other effects acting simultaneously to create the effect we see today in the country. The political leadership operates in secrecy usually employing misinformation and misdirection which are all tactics in the art of war throwing the masses into further chaos and confusion and it's back to the hunt in the dark again. The herd are in the dark, they are the prey and they know they are being hunted but with the roaring and growling seemingly coming from different directions they are ignorant as to the exact location of the lions hunting them, they know what is happening but that extra element of ignorance heightens the dread for them further discomfiting them and giving more advantage to the hunters. Growing up in Sapele, Delta state we had an old dad in the home, coupled with the fact that people there spoke a lot in parables. We picked up on that growing up so I'll use one of them in this scenario to elaborate: *stone wey pesin see dey fly come no dey knack am for head o* which translates to 'the stone a person sees flying in his or her direction doesn't hit them in the head'.

The dark is the best place to keep a people if you want to manipulate them so to this end Nigerians don't even know what's going on in their country. The individuals that make up the political leadership know how to organize their personal lives and keep their records intact but when it comes to state business they become deliberately deaf, dumb, blind and stupid or not so much but you get the idea. In the special environment that has been created for them misinformation is also a weapon, the lack of records kept is a tool which means that there is also a lack of evidence to properly trace or track the wrong doings perpetrated daily and what's that famous expression again? Is it 'no body, no crime?' Or 'no body, no case?' Yes that one, and every now and again politicians gaslight the masses by repeatedly telling them that their country is broke and poor all the while misappropriating funds that should have gone to development and the people are not stupid, they can see the cars and the houses but without proper access to information they cannot really prove anything. When they cry out 'murder! murder!!' the politicians ask them: 'where is the body to prove it?' and they don't have a body to show in most cases and when they do have a body blood still dripping from it with all the evidence intact the justice system in the country Nigeria is waiting to make that body disappear or to cast so much aspersion with legal technicalities that the case is thrown out. So you see that the whole system is rigged against these people, the enforced ignorance on them has a direct tie to the wedding day syndrome because a lack of information about the ins and outs of their country creates a void which they have to then fill up with irrelevant things and all this compounds their sense of misdirection and helplessness in their own country.

Under the veil of secrecy is where the magic happens, the masses observe the veil and they are faced with a situation similar to that philosophical paradoxical question about the cat in the sealed box, is it alive or dead? The poor masses can only observe the veil from afar in their tattered clothes foraging for scraps in the dust, they do not look up because the skies above them are dark and their land looks barren, they have been plagued by many terrors for as long as they can remember and there is no champion to save or to protect them from it all. They are weak and are occupied with diverse worries about their existence but here is also this great veil in their lands that they are not allowed to get close enough to so that they can at least look underneath it to see what is really happening because it is heavily guarded. They can only stand and watch, there are noises coming from underneath the veil, rumblings and groaning which makes the veil to shake violently sending fear into the hearts of the masses. They are taken aback by it all and their curiosity is aroused so they still try to draw near, they ask questions among themselves, what happens underneath this great black veil? The magicians stand around the veil in their shiny beautiful uniforms bearing strange insignia of their sacred order. They address the people with calm smiles on their faces, they tell them they love them dearly and are doing everything to protect them from the terrors underneath the veil, and that they are working tirelessly to keep them safe. They tell them not to worry and that everything will get better for them and most of the masses are relieved indeed. They think in their hearts how lucky they must be to have these mysterious priests and priestesses from the order of the dragon keepers to keep them safe indeed!

8. RIPPLE EFFECTS THEORY:

> *'For want of a nail the horseshoe was lost, for want of a shoe the horse was lost, for want of a horse the rider was lost, for want of a rider the message was not delivered, for want of an undelivered message the battle was lost, for want of a battle the kingdom was lost, and all for the want of a horseshoe nail.'*
>
> — *Old Proverb.*

The ripple effect can be seen on a small scale as when a bored child sitting by the lake side playfully throws a stone into the lake which causes ripples moving out concentrically from the point the stone went into the water, when those ripples move to the edge of the lake causing the water to go over a line of ants searching for food whose path was normally out of the reach of the water and maybe drowning like four of them in the process before the ants re-adjust their path that was really unexpected. You might call it a reach but this situation is absolutely plausible, the child innocently playing at the shore of the lake has just killed four ants and didn't even know about it, the ripple effect is the domino effect. On a larger scale it could just be a tectonic plate settling down but causing a tsunami in the process that takes a few hundred human lives from the inhabitants of the coastal city destroying properties, livelihoods and businesses in the process but what can we say? That plate was just obeying gravity and settling down but look what has happened in the process; this is the ripple effect at work and this is where I coined this theory from.

In the Nigerian context the ripple effect theory refers to the continuous rippling effects and after effects of the actions and inaction of both the political ruling class and the masses on the general society since the society is the product of the people living within it. Such effects and after effects can be magnified or minimized to the point where they are difficult to trace as they ripple through the members and sectors in that society but the fact remains that a society is the sum total of the actions and inaction of those within it. External factors still play a role in the grand scheme of things depending on the vulnerability of the people in that society and the intensity of the external factors themselves but the response and reaction of the people within that society to these external factors go a long way to determine how their society turns out.

In previous iterations of this book the ripple effect theory had a more prominent role because we attributed a lot of the problems of the country to ineptitude, incompetence and ignorance but with the knowledge and understanding of social engineering I have had to strip it down just retaining the core elements of this theory. The general takeaway from this now is that in society as well as in life actions have consequences and the seemingly insignificant little actions could have the greatest implications positively or negatively, that is for good or for evil that come to affect us all. Money is budgeted for streetlights and traffic lights to control traffic in a particularly accident-prone street in a Nigerian city and as is usually the case with public funds in the country the budgeted money is embezzled through corruption and makes its way to private accounts. This means that the project is not done even after the government has made announcements through the media that it would be done. Two months later a woman and her 3 children were returning from a long hard day at her shop. Her mind is in a thousand places, she had made very little sales for the day to show for all her efforts because the customers complained that they didn't have any money, some of her long-time customers had come to beg her for credit and she had to refuse because she was still owing her supplier and needed to raise cash to pay back, her husband would be back from work now and home waiting for his dinner, besides she needs to quickly get through this dark part of the street as thieves usually operated in this area at night and she did not want her or her kids to come to any harm or even the little money that she had made from sale for the day to be taken from her.

    A man coming from work was driving through that dark spot, he had heard the stories in the news about the two cars that were hijacked in that very spot last month, he doesn't want to become car number three, there was an alternative route to take him home but it was a longer route and the cost of fuel had just gone up by 100% so he's just trying to manage. He has a strategy in mind on how to pass that suspicious spot, he'll speed past and not stop for anyone or anything until he was well past the area. So, the scene is set; the speeding man and the distracted woman with her children, he saw them too late and could not apply his brakes on time, when the car did stop and he saw the carnage in front of him all he could think about was the financial outlay and possible legal consequences which he was not capable of handling in his current state so he speeds off. Now if you were that husband and father waiting for your family to come to you how would you feel? If that man wakes up the next morning and decides to burn the whole country to the ground would he be in the wrong? Or if he decides to trace out the officials that diverted the funds for those projects and starts killing them and their family members would he have done wrong? He'll most likely be called a terrorist by the powers that be as they try to hunt him down. I'm a curious person and my mind wanders a lot so I would like to hear from you what you thought about all this and what you would do in this scenario if you were the husband and father.

9. BALLOON THEORY:

I am done presenting my main theories to you, this one and the one that is to come after it are just bonus theories to add colour to the picture. They played an important role for me helping me to understand what was going on in Nigeria because the Nigerian system is effective; despise it or say what you will about it but it does not change the fact that it's an effective system and the results speak for it. You cannot smoothly hold an estimated 200 million people spellbound in poverty and captivity for decades if you're not doing something right. All the 200 million people are not idiots, some must have sensed what's happening and those that were able to take themselves out of the game completely did so and moved to other countries where they felt they could get better opportunities to better their lives. The others' only crime in this is that they were either wilful tools in the system, couldn't escape it or simply did not present enough collective resistance to free themselves from it. I have never claimed to be an expert political scientist or analyst but all my life I have been an effective problem solver such that it was a pastime of mine to solve riddles and seek out little problems just to find solutions to them and I did all that in my own unique way which added to the thrill of the mental exercise for me... these are the same skill sets and enthusiasm that I bring to this Nigerian problem and my attempts to put all my findings in a book, this one you're reading right now.

To do this effectively I looked to the things around me for inspiration to help me explain what I was observing. The expert political analysts and scientists in Nigeria will always come up short because they are following the game, they are chasing it and they keep chasing it instead of getting ahead of it. I don't know if it makes sense to you but in always following the game they are caught in its wake and its mysteries which is what they analyse year in and year out then they dump all that on the Nigerian public, in this position of theirs they are never able to lay hold on the game itself. The game here that I see is something that is ever moving away and people are chasing after it, as it moves it releases things like steam and little objects which the people chasing after it catch and then try to analyse, you can see that in that way they'll never get proper knowledge about the main moving object itself and also they can be easily manipulated and misdirected by those controlling the game. It's like the missile that hit one of the many flares expelled by the jet fighter, yes it hit something but it was not the main target, its main target had bested it and gotten away giving it time to either escape or carry out its own counter-strike. These people probably have degrees where they sat in some university to learn the 'proper' way to analyse politics but the thing is you cannot analyse human will or political will as it has translated to this case using the methods they have been taught: **'The heart is deceitful above all things, and desperately wicked; who can know it?' Jer 17:9**. So they spend their entire lives and careers analyzing and chasing after this thing but never able to fully grasp it. Television appearance after television appearance but all the time the crux of the situation remains ever so elusive to them, so near but yet so far away. The real victims are the masses that get the wrong information and base their lives off of it. I am a cynical man and to me life is not so complex; it's either the experts and analysts are themselves innocently fooled by the game or they are placed in front of the TV to fool the masses that follow them by misinformation… the truth is in there somewhere.

    I'm a simple man and I'm no expert, I never said I was but when I look at the hands of the clock on the wall I can tell you the time of the day provided that the clock is accurate but I cannot tell you how the clock engine works. Now if the hands of the clock tell a wrong time and are always spiralling out of control and even going counter-clockwise then there is no amount of explanation or technical jargon the master watch-maker is going to throw my way that I would listen to him about that particular clock. The Nigerian system was not designed to work for the interests of the Nigerian people and it does not work for the best interests of the Nigerian masses but the designers of the system made it a chameleon where it acts like a real government system operating with the best interests of the masses at heart with a functioning structure that conducts elections every four years and puts out information that a real functioning government working for the best interests of the citizens of their country would put out, so when you look at it casually it looks like it's working. If you were to take a second look you'll see ministries and other government parastatal so you might walk away satisfied. It's when you take a closer look and look deeper that the whole game starts to unravel in front of you. In a society where everyone is occupied with surviving the day how many people can really look that deep? And even when they do look that deep what can they really do about it? It is to try to understand as I navigate the chaotic Nigerian political and societal landscape that I came up with the simple balloon theory earlier in my journey.

    The balloon theory comes from your normal birthday balloons and it states that when you pump air into a balloon it gets bigger and bigger and you can see it get bigger until it gets to a point where if you force more air in it will burst. Now even if you cannot see the individual air molecules in the balloon the swelling of the balloon tells you that air has been put into it, the technical guys can then come in to argue about the mode of inflation; was it hand pump, machine pump or was it pumped with the mouth? They can also go further and calculate the velocity with which the air was pumped into the balloon, they can argue about the type of gas pumped into the balloon; is it the type of gas that makes it keep going up and up and up until it disappears when it's released? Or is it laughing gas that teenagers inhale to get high at parties? Or it's the neon gas for party balloons that enhances their colour? You get my point, the experts will give you those details but everyone can see the turgid balloon in its inflated state and know that there's some type of gas inside it. This is the same way I look at Nigeria, I may not be an expert political analyst but we know that money comes in from crude sales daily and my argument using the balloon theory is that if that money is invested into Nigeria as a country and on the Nigerian people we would definitely see the signs in the society, it's as simple as that. While the politicians, their enablers and the political analysts in Nigeria argue all day and give excuses to confuse and entertain the Nigerian public I only look at the results and they tell me all I need to know about the situation.

    The reverse side of this theory says that when air is taken out of the balloon it gets deflated, becomes flaccid and eventually shrinks out. The trajectory of the balloon also follows the trajectory of man and nations, all of life looks connected to me and is open before me when I sit and observe from atop my 'simple' mountain. The balloon follows the survival mode, comfort stage, leisure and extravagance route of men and nations forwards and backwards depending on the motion, this is the path that civilizations before throughout the history of man has always taken; they start out, grow big, get to their peak and then they implode because when you climb to the top of the ladder where else can you really climb to? So when articles of the constitution are argued on TV or any of the other million excuses put forward by politicians and their highly educated hatchet men I think about the balloon and look at the state of the country to justify what has come in and of course there is a great discrepancy there. When a token project is being commissioned and is heavily publicised through the Nigerian media sometimes eliciting celebration from the beleaguered masses I think about the balloon theory and look at the state of the country and this simple yet effective theory has helped me stay grounded and kept me on track on this journey of discovery.

10. THE MOLECULAR THEORY OF WEALTH CREATION:

I still remember my chemistry teacher from my secondary school days, he was a short burly man that appeared to be quick on his feet, possibly he might have been an athlete in his younger days or he was just naturally light on his feet. We were young then, teenagers, but I remember he always seemed to wear the same clothes every day, to my young mind it didn't mean much to us as we students wore uniforms but now that I'm older and I think back I can surmise that Nigeria must not have been kind to him. I wonder where he is today because he was always nice to me and I pray that life had become kinder to him in his later years. I always think of all my teachers throughout my years, it honestly didn't use to be all of them because some were mean to me but as I grew older I realised that life was too short to keep carrying grudges from childhood. They were not bad and I reckon they were trying their best to mould us but we were young and stubborn and it might have been a bit difficult for them but I see videos of what students do to their teachers from supposedly 'more enlightened' parts of the world and I think we were angels as students in our time and our part of the world because we did not talk back or openly try to fight them. I appreciate all my teachers and I pray for God's blessings on them, I am a product of your efforts and someday I will seek you out and show my appreciation because I think in this world teachers are not appreciated enough.

I remember my chemistry teacher well but I sadly cannot recall his name for it was he who always talked about 'Van der Waal' forces between molecules in his classes over and over again until it stuck to my brain. Out of the three main science subjects I liked chemistry the least. Biology I could see and relate to, physics I could see and relate to but chemistry always talked about chemicals I couldn't see so naturally I struggled with it and my teacher was patient with me. You only felt the effects in the physical, the reactions took place on a level we can't see with the naked eyes but the effects were definitely there, if I put an acid on your skin even if you can't see the reactions taking place you'll definitely feel the burn. Well I did my best to try to understand it all but I think it was clear to me from the start that I would not have a great relationship with chemistry for the rest of my life but some things stuck from all those classes I attended and this is where the molecular theory of wealth creation came into being for me.

My molecular theory taps from the particulate theory of matter that states that matter is made up of little particles called molecules held together by forces, weak forces for liquids and gasses then strong forces for solids. The particulate theory of matter states that the molecules of the material are always moving and that the allowance of their movement depended on the strength of the forces holding them together hence the molecules that made up the solids could only vibrate while the ones in the liquids and gasses had more freedom to move all within the bounds of their container. When I started thinking about wealth creation at the early times of this work the pictures my chemistry teacher drew on the chalk board to explain the particulate nature of matter were activated in my mind and provided an explanation for wealth creation from the perspective of a country. The boundary that represented the container for the molecules became the territorial boundaries of the country as a closed system, the molecules became the people held together by strong or weak bonds also known as Van der Waal forces and I saw that life was nothing without interaction.

The molecules interact by vibrating, colliding against each other and against the inner walls of their container, and sometimes external pressure is exerted on the walls of the container leading to the molecules moving more and colliding more and sometimes there is a breach in the walls of the container leading to gains and loss of molecules. The introduction of external molecules caused more vibrations and collisions between the particles leading to the creation of energy in the form of heat, light or force and in all this I saw wealth creation in a country as a result of the coordinated interaction between individuals with ideas, raw materials, technologies comprising equipment for production and existing infrastructures in the society; it is the movement of people, goods and services within the country to create value... this became my molecular theory of wealth creation. This theory was very vital in helping me understand that wealth or poverty was not an accident because if you can influence the interaction between people and the other pieces I mentioned which are in effect the factors of production you can either create wealth or poverty within that closed system which is the country. I have touched on psycho-hacking and the different ways the Nigerian masses can be influenced so there is no need for all that, and with this I cap off my discourse on my theories.

RECESS:

Please remember that we're still in court and Nigeria is on trial here, me as the prosecuting lawyer has just presented my theories to explain what I think is happening to me as the judge and jury, and you as the audience and observers, and this short recess is to allow you collect your thoughts about the theories and run them over in your mind. I want you to turn them over in your mind and to acquaint yourself with them. I don't want you to just blindly accept them but I want you to be like me because I question everything so I want you to question the soundness and the integrity of these theories that I just presented to you, I want you to hold them up to your personal light of reasoning and logic and I'm curious to know how they hold up so I'll be expecting feedback from you.

We have been standing under the sun in this court on the streets so you can take advantage of this recess to stretch your limbs, relieve yourselves and have some light refreshment because when we reconvene I will be putting these theories to the test using the society or more specifically elements of Nigerian society as evidence to back or disprove these theories and we're going to do it together. My attempt to explain the Nigerian conundrum or the Nigerian situation does not end with these theories alone, these have laid the foundation and I will proffer more explanation based on my observation and analysis where needed but these ones already presented remain the main ones so at the end of it before I pronounce judgement I'll see if I have made a good case and was able to convince you of the strength of my case. Now gather around people let's get back to it then *hits the skull on the head* 'court in session!!!'

PART 1: THE NIGERIAN SOCIETY AS A HOUSE FOR THE MASSES.

'IF THE FOUNDATIONS BE DESTROYED, WHAT CAN THE RIGHTEOUS DO?'

- Psalms 11:3

INTRODUCTION:

There have always been successful and unsuccessful gatherings of humans in different forms throughout our history on this planet. Humans banded together to increase their chances of survival in a very harsh environment, kingdoms rose and fell, every human alive today has a long line of ancestors that somehow traces back to the beginning because that is the only legal way to exist here on this plane as people do not just fall from the sky. There has been so much trial and error through the ages that by these present times we have learnt from the mistakes of our predecessors by gathering information and utilising that information to swing the odds in our favour as it relates to building successful and prosperous societies. It is no secret in these times as to what makes a successful society, and where great challenges from the environment and other factors exist man has shown ingenuity through technology to provide solutions such that even if those challenges cannot be thoroughly vanquished we can at least have a fighting chance to survive, thrive or flourish in the midst of them. For those challenges that have not been thoroughly vanquished people have dedicated their lives and resources to study using existing information, technology and even inventing new ones along the way to find solutions to them but with everything available there still surprisingly exists for diverse reasons poor, failing and failed nations in the earth today.

This has been the motivation for my study; to find out why my country Nigeria and others like her are still poor and failing in a world full of possibilities like we have today where they could be so much more than they are right now. I approach the subject matter with a solution based mindset and mentality where everything negative witnessed in that country is just a challenge with different ready solutions that can be applied to combat them, and also with a concrete understanding of change that nothing is set in stone in life and that change is the only constant so the conditions that Nigerians have come to know and accept are not eternal, yes they are being currently upheld and maintained but they can be changed and as the late great African American thinker and writer James Baldwin succinctly puts it: *'not everything that is faced can be changed, but nothing can be changed until it's faced.'*

So we will look at a sample of elements of the Nigerian society that should be the foundation to build the nation, we will look at their current state giving you an idea of what it is to live like an average Nigerian in these present times and where applicable we will use the theories provided to explain the situation. I don't just want you to read blindly but I want you to read consciously asking questions as you go along and even comparing it to the same aspect of your own society because no society is perfect and you might learn a thing or two in the process and if we all learn a few things at the end of this journey then we're all the better for it. No need to linger anymore then, let's jump right into it.

INFRASTRUCTURE

'A rising tide doesn't raise people who don't have a boat. We have to build the boat for them. We have to give them the basic infrastructure to rise with the tide.'

- Rahul Gandhi.

    I think humans are amazing. I mean, if I created this planet myself with everything in it I could see just how I could be more than a little bit partial to humans. Not particularly strong when you compare them to the rest or fast or big but man reigns supreme; our true power is in our mind which gives us access and a connection to eternity. We are then able to draw from eternity and project it onto our physical plane to build the strongest, fastest and biggest structures effectively continuing the creation and dominion mandate. Left to our own individual strength we cannot accomplish much and that effect can be multiplied when you have a group of humans working together over a long period of time towards a common goal which places a premium on will, encompassing intention, focus and determination but it's the infrastructures which are a projection of our creativity to solve problems that takes our productivity to astronomical heights both figuratively and literally. Just like the different levels of existence it's all a building process requiring a strong foundation and then building layers atop existing layers on that foundation to construct the tower of Babel that we then climb on to touch the skies.

My opening text by Indian politician Rahul Gandhi builds on the saying **'A rising tide lifts all boats'** which was made popular by ex-United States president John Kennedy. *A rising tide lifts all boats* means that a growing economy will improve the lives of the masses in the country but Rahul Gandhi with his own saying has rightly pointed out that without the boats of proper infrastructures in place for the people the rising tide will not benefit them, in fact, those of us that grew up in places where boats are not built for the people have seen with our own eyes that the rising tide leads to the death by drowning of those of the masses stuck in the water who cannot swim or tread water anymore, nor are they fortunate like the few holding on to some piece of wood to stay afloat while the very few and the very privileged in whatever few boats there are, are raised higher by the rising tide. To drive home this very critical point I bring again to your remembrance the oil boom of the 1970s where almost every oil producing nation on the planet benefited heavily but with the influx of capital we have only seen the levels of poverty, desperation and suffering for the Nigerian masses rise and grow in leaps and bounds from that time.

I tell you this my friend, many a time have I sat and contemplated what kind of book I wanted this to be; do I just fill it up with complaints about the state of things in Nigeria? Now how would that differentiate me from every frustrated Nigerian out there? And they are right to vent their frustrations but what change has that brought so far? The answer is none and this is why we have to look behind the veil here to dissect the entire mechanism of oppression and give the people the ammunition of information about their situation but will it even this matter in the grand scheme of things? The answer is 'no' because I know my people all too well and the gravity of the predicament they are in but I've come this far and spent all this time on this work so I must see it to the end. The levels and the state of the infrastructures in Nigeria are definitely poor and we will talk about bad roads and the others in a bit but we have to dig deeper at the significance of why they are kept in that state. This is where we look at the double-edged sword called scarcity and its two-fold manifestation as both, instruments of control which on the one hand create panic which adds to desperation that is one of the ingredients of the chaos we talked about earlier, and scarcity as a bottle neck which is a means of control like in the movie '300' where the numerically disadvantaged Spartans funnel the larger Persian forces into a bottle-neck to strip off their numerical advantage in that bottle. In this case with scarcity the political ruling class are able to create panic for the masses and control (monitor and regulate) their economic activities at the same time reinforcing once again that the weaponized poverty in Nigeria is artificial.

The spices and the ingredients for wealth creation in a society are not a secret in these modern times, when you take a look at Nigeria you'll see that not a lot of infrastructural development has taken place after 1960 the year of 'independence'. What this means is that even the colonisers that put infrastructures in place to expedite their exploitation agenda and the extraction of the resources in our lands over to their lands have done more for Nigeria in terms of infrastructural development than the political ruling class in Nigeria which is made up of Nigerians themselves, shocking! Which is to say that if Nigeria was a human being she stopped growing after 1960 effectively trapping her in the body of a child which is an unnatural situation for all living things existing in this plane as we're all prisoners of time, we're trapped in it and are subject to its effects. Over the sixty plus years from that time the technology has advanced exponentially in other parts of the world but there exists a people still trapped in those times and of course I have my own questions for you about this: how can the people trapped in this situation not be poor? How can they favourably compete with other nations of the world who are working very hard at daily developing themselves? Have you considered the fact that prior to 1960 the country was under colonisation and the colonisers did not have her best interests at heart? Have you considered that whatever infrastructures they put in place was to make their work easy and they were here to exploit the lands and her peoples? Having considered all that can you also just consider the fact that not changing much and keeping things mostly as they found them the political ruling class in the country have only just continued on the exploitation mandate of the colonisers? Do you now see why societal observers in the past have called them neo-colonisers? Please, all I ask of you is that you spend a little time to meditate and think deeply on these questions that I've just asked you because when you do you'll see the patterns I highlighted at the beginning and you'll realise that these peoples and their lands have been on a deficit in terms of development for a long, long time.

Oh you poor people, you poor desolate souls, you have inherited old creaking pre-independence infrastructures which is inefficient and bad on its own but they are also insufficient because the estimated population of Nigeria as at 1960 is 44 million plus and now it is estimated to be 200 million people which is five times increase in people with little or no change to your lives, when the demand for infrastructures to create wealth outgrew their supply and availability in the country what was the solution? Was the deficit cancelled out? Was there ever a calculation or a visualization of this scenario where you perennially exploited Nigerian masses did not ever turn out poor and miserable? Who was there to hear your cries or offer you comfort thou unloved people? Was the world moved to stand still at your pain? Did they ever enquire the reasons for your cries? Your nonviolent nature as a people has cost you your humanity and they have taken advantage of your resilience as a people to push you through the gates into hell fire. Do not, I beseech you, rejoice amongst yourselves that the flames do not consume you, out of all the peoples of this world only you, black people, would accept this your existence for so long without change.

I must not give in to my anger but I still have to talk, there are those that will point out to the one or two bridges done here and there for the past three to four decades and my reply to you is that tokenism is one of the instruments of control in the system and also a dangerous tool for manipulation. It is so sublime that it's not quickly spotted and can be mistaken for kindness where people will say: 'at least, something was done'. We have a parable that says *'instead of the full nama-nama to run lost, make we still cut the tail take cook soup na'* which translates to 'instead of the full cow to run and get lost let's at least cut its tail to cook a soup with' which means that something is at least better than nothing and while this is true to an extent it does not account for widespread corruption costing an entire system its efficiency. Nigeria is a political fraud in progress and it sadly does not take much to pull the wool over the eyes of the Nigerian people; just a simple soulectomy here and there, a name change or a token dropped in front of them and thy are satisfied... Nigeria is truly the land of mediocrity. I'll give you an example, in the eighties the people cried that the cause of their poverty was due to improper representation and structuring of the country so the political elites created more states and local government areas by drawing more lines on the map and adding names and that was enough to satisfy the masses for that time but they have progressively gotten poorer as a people. Political fraud in progress, daylight robbery right under the noses of the victims.

There is a lack of realisation (ignorance) factor tied to all of this, Nigerians and by extension black people are not always able to discern the mechanisms of the systems and structures functioning all around them and how it affects them wherever they find themselves making them subjects, mere receptors and even victims to those mechanisms so they are not able to react appropriately. They just want to sing, dance and live the days of their lives in peace which is good but it sadly does not work like that, life is a battle and living is serious business. In my state I have seen scarcity used to great effect to cause further social fission and divide among communities. When they bring their tokens to present it to the people it is usually a Greek gift, for infrastructures like a road there is only one about to be constructed in a place with five communities who have existed as neighbours for a long time but there can only be one road. There is no manoeuvring to get more roads or a plan to satisfy the others but there is ONE road (scarcity) and it starts with the news filtering to the communities that a road is about to be constructed in the area. The poor villagers who are used to bush paths all their lives see that road as a great step up and avenue for development so they start to fight amongst themselves looking for their illustrious 'sons' and 'daughters' within the political government structure to influence the decision and have that one road built in their community and this fight causes further strife among them. When the road is finally constructed in the 'winner' community it does not end there as the seeds of discord have already been sown. It is like that father of triplets that comes back home in the evening with one toy, gives it to one child and then goes to sit down. Now when the whole family cannot sleep that night because of fighting and crying what exactly did that wicked and inconsiderate father think was going to happen? You can see that the theories and the instruments of control are all connected, here we just witnessed tokenism and scarcity used to cause social fission among those already poor communities (weaponised poverty), the people in the 'winning' community have the bragging rights as the first and only community with a tarred road in that locality but little do they all know that the road in question was poorly constructed and in a year's time when the rains come the road will be washed away. The bastards that gave them the Greek gift in the first place have come back for their property and all the people in that locality have just been played so you see? Political fraud in progress, smoothly and effectively executed.

    I have used roads as a prime example of infrastructures so much in this section that one would think it was only roads that makes up infrastructure in a country but that is not the case, using 'roads' all the time just shows you I'm Nigerian indeed because road construction has always been a Nigerian thing over the decades that's talked about all the time by Nigerians as an indication of development but every time they step out of their houses the reality of their situation hits them in the face and they are surrounded by bad roads. It is such a popular and effective trope that politicians still use it as a campaign promise to fool the people during election season. In these modern times the average Nigerian household still needs to dig boreholes and buy the pumping machine, storage tank with its supporting structure just to get water into the homes because there is no centralised infrastructure to provide water despite the whole southern coastline of the country bordered by the Atlantic ocean and the easy to access ground water reserves. Homes that are not able to afford this will have members of the family down to the young ones carrying buckets and other containers to fetch from their neighbours and carry back to their houses to satisfy their water needs. I saw this happening as a young boy playing in my father's compound in the nineties and I observed it still happening in twenty-twenties as a man. Same for sewage where each household has to construct their own septic tank because there is no centralised sewage treatment and disposal infrastructure in place anywhere in the country, and when the poverty in the land does not allow for proper servicing or maintenance and the septic tanks become full and overflowing I leave to your darkest imaginations the picture and the stench of the result to that household and the neighbours around them. If every household has to provide these basic amenities for themselves I cannot help but question the role, importance and usefulness of the Nigerian political leadership to the Nigerian people and their obligations in the social contract that exists in society between a people and their leadership.

In a sense all of these personalized infrastructural provisions by Nigerians for themselves is a metaphor of their isolation and individualism, the absence of these shared amenities shows a people without true cohesion which in effect is a people robbed of their people-power or simply their safety in numbers which we have talked about already. We also see death by a thousand cuts at play when a people have to provide these amenities for themselves because the extra money they have to dip into their pockets to satisfy these essential and fundamental needs is money lost. Well you can argue that it's not exactly money lost as they are providing these services for themselves to utilise but if they were part of a working society they could have channelled that money into their businesses which will in turn boost the economy of the country and their standard of living but here they are doing things for themselves that their government is supposed to provide for them so it's money lost to them because it could all have been avoidable in the first place. In this way you can see how weaponised poverty, corruption and general dysfunction can be used to keep a people poor and in lack. With these real-life scenarios I hope you can then begin to see how the theories play into the everyday life of the average Nigerian, it is one of constant loss in many little ways that may not seem obvious or bad in isolation but adds very big at the end of the day making it impossible for these poor, unserious and unfocused souls to escape the grips of survival mode.

INFRASTRUCTURE: TRANSPORTATION.

'Our transportation decisions determine much more than where roads and bridges or tunnels or rail lines will be built. They determine the connections and barriers that people will encounter in their daily lives, and thus how hard or easy it will be for people to get where they need and want to go.'

- Elijah Cummings.

The official line being given by the Nigerian government and repeated by the other governments of nations in the world is that Nigeria is a 'developing' nation but she has been called this for decades now and never ever fully developed to whatever they were alluding to; the imperfect caterpillar that never became a beautiful butterfly for whatever reason. The use of the term 'developing' there is just clever wording to deflect from the reality of the situation but even regarded as a developing nation what are the allowances that she's allowed in terms of the state of her transportation infrastructure? On the surface we all know that the transportation infrastructure is very poor, in fact I would say that Nigeria is about a hundred years behind in some aspects of transportation infrastructure and as much as two hundred years behind in other aspects but what good would it do us to go on just talking about bad roads and pot holes here? Your answer is as good as mine so the focus should be on the psychology behind having a terrible transportation infrastructure and also keeping it that way, the effects it has on the life of the average Nigerian and how it all fits into the functioning system of repression and exploitation of the Nigerian lands and masses by the political ruling class. The technology for development is not a secret in these modern times so how or why does a nation not apply it to their advantage? There is a lot to unpack here.

On paper and on the surface from casual observation the Nigerian government behaves like a working government and goes to great lengths to project itself as such, after all if they are going to keep successfully defrauding and fooling the Nigerian masses the way they have been doing without much opposition from them for all these decades then it is imperative to keep up appearances or as they say to fulfil all righteousness. To this end there are offices, ministries and different subdivisions of the government structure with people in them occupying different positions within the hierarchy, going to work every day and receiving salary. By all accounts this looks like a functioning entity but when I say it's not working I'm not talking about whether it's functioning or not, of course it functions, if not how else would it carry out its repression, dominion and exploitation agenda? So it functions but I'm talking more about the purpose of its functions, the ideology behind it, the objectives it is working towards and everything on ground despite what's on paper that's presented to the people and the world shows that the Nigerian government is definitely not working towards the good and the betterment of the Nigerian people, you can quote me anywhere on this. So when a question like: why is the Nigerian leadership not able to leverage modern technology to solve her infrastructural problems? If your answer is that it's because she's still a developing nation then I immediately know that you have been consuming too much mainstream media over the course of your life for you to have arrived at that conclusion so easily but in the true answer to that question lies the great predicament of the Nigerian people.

So we can talk about the bad roads with multiple deep potholes that fill up with water during the wet season and becomes impossible for cars to pass cutting off that area and this will do well to paint the dreary picture but it is important to note that the government in its functions must have awarded the contract for that road to be fixed years ago to a company and the funds released to that company to carry out the work. If it's not a private company then the government ministry in charge of that road on paper has been given the money to do it. The corruption in Nigeria is wonderful indeed, sometimes over the years that contract could have been awarded multiple times with the money paid out each time but the situation on ground does not reflect that because the work never gets done and this is one of the many ways Nigerians get exploited and shortchanged because where did the money go to? Those moneys have found their way into offshore accounts and fixed deposit accounts in other 'developed' countries of this world, the moneys have helped to boost real estate growth in these places putting food on the tables of many of their citizens and keeping their way of life alive. Isn't it paradoxical that the people that call themselves rich in this world cannot survive without the poor people and the poor places of this world that they despise? So in a classic case of destiny exchange the roads, rail lines, air ports, sea ports and other infrastructure that could have been leveraged by the Nigerian people are held securely in offshore accounts or used for housing developments in major cities around the world and also invested into some of the biggest and most successful companies in the world as shares bought all under the wonderful canopy of foreign investments and yet they do everything to keep us out when we try to emigrate to these countries not knowing that we're only looking for our stolen roads and bridges. *'My mother's children were angry with me, they made me the keeper of their flocks but mine own sheep have I not tended to'* indeed.

I will continue to stress that the origin and implementation of this infrastructural neglect in Nigeria is not by happenstance but by intention, this is strategy at play, clear cut cause and effect if I ever saw one. This is not just a bunch of greedy men and women trying to embezzle the money of a nation to buy the latest toys like bullet proof cars or high-end fashion and accessories churning out of the factories and displayed in the shops of the developed world, no, that is too simplistic an explanation for what is happening. They could have embezzled those moneys and provided the infrastructures then charged the whole country to use them and they still would have made money but they did not do that because the presence of those infrastructures in the country means that the masses can enrich themselves with it and get themselves out of poverty so that was not an option except in a few isolated cases that they could control. Surely you must begin to see the psychology behind all this by now? This is not just a bunch of ignorant and corrupt old men and women trying to embezzle money to wear the biggest jewellery at the next social event as the average Nigerian thinks. Where they see that I see an organised and focused group intent on keeping the wealth of the country strictly out of the hands of the ordinary citizens at ALL costs even if they have to lock it up far away or waste it, burn it up, anything at all but to let it fall into the hands of the average Nigerians. This is war and out of the chaos I see strategy, it is not just a war for resources but also a war for survival, the political ruling class are fighting for survival to preserve their way of life and maybe that's why they are so vicious about it but the languid masses are ignorant, like the careless frog in the slowly heating water they have been lulled into a sense of false security and calm but soon they will feel the intensity of the heat more.

They over price and over budget for the projects and while one would think that they would collect just the mark up funds as a regular thief would do and still carry out the projects. They don't, instead they steal both the mark up and the project funds littering up the land with incomplete projects... a graveyard of wonderful ideas indeed. You must look at the psychology behind all this, everybody knows the importance of good working infrastructures that the citizens can leverage on to boost their productivity and the economy of the country so if a person or a group of persons determine to sabotage the infrastructural development process of a country do you think they don't know the ripple effects that it will create in the society? Surely they mean to keep those people poor and in multi-faceted trans-generational poverty. The roads linking parts of the country are bad with potholes, without drainage or streetlights to discourage night travel or extending the productivity of the citizenry to night time hours. Whatever roads there are, are dangerous because of these factors mentioned and others making them accident prone and as if that were not enough they are unsafe with robberies taking place on them and kidnappings happening across them constantly and even if I laugh at this it is not out of pleasure but just because I see how much hard work is being put into chaos, insecurity and keeping the Nigerian masses in poverty. All of this is like an open book before me and I only marvel at how the rest of the country is not able to see through this thin veil of misdirection put in place just for them. It's like thee movie *Truman Show* (1998) played by comedy legend Jim Carrey when he starts to notice that there was something wrong with his community he was raised in. A country of diverse ethnic groups and regions does not have safe roads that can be travelled by the people of these different regions to know themselves more and further acquaint themselves. After sixty plus years together do you not see how poor infrastructural development ripples into isolation and further ethnic division? Am I reaching here or am I making sense to you?

With the lack of interaction seen in the lack of movement of people, goods and services within the country I bring to your remembrance the molecular theory of wealth creation, and in this state with the lack of movement the molecules are not able to collide to produce energy which in this case is wealth so it's like a stagnant water, harbouring disease carrying pathogens, squeezing every ounce of oxygen and life out of that body which means that the country is sick, dying... dead. The average Nigerian does not even know the levels of isolation they are subjected to in their own country of birth, they are so locked up in the yoke of their search for daily bread that has been imposed on them that they do not realise how very little they know about their environment and their very own country. They are born in the country, they live in it but the truth is that they are strangers in the country trapped in survival mode until they die making the country to look like an open prison to me, in fact the whole of Africa seems like a big open prison to me, Africa is the biggest prison in the world for the majority of the people within her.

They call them developing nations which is a cruel joke because the plan from the beginning was never to develop these countries. Nigeria which is the most populous black nation on earth with an estimated 200 million plus people has just over 4000km of rail lines and the state of the rail lines themselves with their insecurity truly must be seen to be believed. Most of those rail lines were pre-independence by the way but she's developing. Just imagine a country with the kind of resources Nigeria has but look at the state of land transportation, if there are no well- maintained transportation infrastructures for entrepreneurs to leverage on how will they improve their productivity and create wealth? You're expecting more than magic from these people because you know that Nigerians are overly religious and love the miraculous so much so Jesus turned water into wine but in this case you're expecting ordinary Nigerians to turn muddy water into vinegar, then vodka and then turn the vodka into wine which is impossible but surprisingly enough a very little amount still manage to accomplish that against all the odds thrown at them, the very supernatural ones among the bunch still find a way to break out and while this should be remarkable it underscores everything I'm saying because the general bulk are trapped in the net of the artificial poverty created for them and the few that break out from it are isolated and cannot really impact the situation much, in fact they become occupied with their own survival and growth after escaping the jaws of poverty in their country. We are carefully peeling away the layers of a very effective system at work affecting the lives of millions and millions of people and while we do this I want you to appreciate the design, intent and application of it all.

WATER TRANSPORT: This might feel like flogging a dead horse, transportation is transportation and we should be done with it but distasteful as this all is to me I must say that no single brush stroke of the painter on the canvas is wasted even if it turns out to be a mistake, at least the artist learns which strokes will not work in trying to create his masterpiece. I need to give you context and background for you to fully understand like I do what's happening here. The entire Southern part of Nigeria is bordered by the Atlantic ocean, from Lagos state in the South-west to Bayelsa in the South-south and then to Akwa Ibom and Cross River states in the South-east gives 850km of coast line so these people have lived beside water for thousands of years but are they masters of the ocean today? Expert boat builders? Leaders in all types of hydro-electricity? Master explorers and navigators that can circumnavigate the world? Masters in offshore drilling? Highest number of Olympic medals in swimming? Kings in commercial fishing? Looking at the strategic place Nigeria occupies in the African continent was she made a shipping hub for repairs and a place of rest for other ships to refuel while they travel the African coastline? No, if not all that then what are they? Let's assume that they did not have the resources to strive for all that but did they then do the next best thing by positioning themselves to benefit from their long coastline by making the country a tourist hub for foreigners to get money into the country? Well, you know the answer to that. If your aim is to keep a people poor and weak so that you can control them then preventing money from getting to them by whatever means is the way to go about it. The foreigner bit also works in line with the isolation strategy as these people are cut off from the rest of the world financially yet the average Nigerian on the street would tell you that these political elites are just foolish, ignorant and greedy old men and women, I am not disputing all that but we will soon know who have been the real fools in this relationship all this time.

What about commerce? The country has just one working commercial sea port which is the one in Lagos, it's pre-independence and the state it's in is another discussion, there's one or two other running skeletal operations for 'special people' with 'special' privileges but I want you to note the scarcity strategy at work here and how they create a bottleneck for resources and utilities to create lack and also as a means of easy control, monitoring and regulation. When they control and regulate the means of making money like this in the country then the masses cannot spring a surprise on them by taking advantage of them and casting aside the yoke of poverty imposed on them by becoming rich so they are able to effectively maintain the status quo in this way. Ships bring containers with all kinds of goods from foreign lands to the Lagos port, dump them and leave empty, I mean the ships and containers leave the Lagos sea port empty and why won't they? The Nigerians produce nothing so one could say that the containers leave empty because Nigerians have nothing to offer the world. Well that's not entirely true by the way because everything the world needs from them like their resources and culture is stolen from them so why bother? If I do not know these people as intimately as I do I would say they are useless too but I know them and the potentials that they possess and I insist that under the right conditions they can participate and contribute to the world but they do not have those conditions. Having great potentials does not change the fact that Nigeria produces nothing and relies exclusively on imports which is an ineffective way to live and run a country. This is one of the many cuts as it adds to the cost of these imported goods for an already poor people digging them further in the hole of trans-generational poverty.

AIR TRANSPORT: Nigerian aviation has suffered some of the worst aviation disasters in human air travel history. I just remembered something that brought a smile to my face right now as I write this. When I discuss and debate national issues with friends, they sometimes tell me that I use hyperbole and make extreme claims but I always remind them like I am telling you right now; what I state are the bare hard facts, facts that are so real that you could almost reach out and grab a hold of them as they come out from my mouth or in this case through these pages. I will tell you here like Peter Obi always says it, you can go check and verify them on your own if you so choose. For example the year 2012 was a really bad year for air travel in Nigeria, air planes and helicopters were falling off the sky and it was like a bunch of trigger happy giant-aliens in outer space were playing the classic 'Duck Hunt' with the planes. Those crashes took hundreds, if not thousands of Nigerian lives and destroyed many families but what I found most disturbing was that the crashes were for locally owned and managed companies that is Nigerian operated planes and helicopters. There was even conspiracy talks that some of the crashes were assassinations because of the high profile individuals involved in them but I cannot speak authoritatively on that. A house built on a faulty foundation just cannot stand and when you think of it this is the faulty Nigerian culture of mass corruption at all levels, negligence, mismanagement, politics, dinosaur status and ethnic race leading to nepotism where unqualified people are put in sensitive positions of power and influence due to their affiliations or ethnicity rather than their qualifications and capacity to function and deliver. The list goes on really and even though sometimes in life accidents can happen, when an avoidable accident happens then it is even more painful.

Another angle to look at is the expensive nature of aviation in Nigeria, this gives it exclusivity and is a status symbol rather than a service that could increase the productivity of a country. You look at Europe and some flight fares go as low as 20 Euros making them affordable but in Nigeria it is not the case, the ever-rising cost of goods and services in a very poor country makes it not readily accessible to the common man. The scarcity control mechanism can also be seen in the few airports that exist compared to the population of the country and the state they are in coupled with the quality and service they provide is a testament of the Nigerian factor. This means that it could be done well in other places but when it's done in the Nigerian environment, under the control of the Nigerian leadership for the Nigerian people it gets done in a different way, that is the Nigerian way because soulectomy gets done and all the consequences of the Nigerian environment and the Nigerian people play on that idea and concept that when it is delivered to the people and the world in general it has deviated from its original intended glorious purpose into something else regarded as ineffective and a failure. I could tell the poor souls that have perished in air crashes in Nigeria to rest in peace but when they look back from the afterlife and see the unprofessionalism and negligence that lead to their deaths I'm sure that they will not be able to rest in peace, what's worse? When they see that there were no proper actions taken by the bodies responsible for such things and those responsible for servicing and maintaining those air crafts that crashed in avoidable circumstances then for sure they cannot rest in peace. One other key loss due to the poor transportation infrastructure and service in the country is the absence of a postal industry, this shows the ripple effects on industries that are dependent on other industries to thrive and the jobs that would have been created and sustained in the process to work those services. This deficit sees international providers cover those areas but at a cost that is too expensive for the average Nigerian to afford and these are key services by the way. The lack of this postal service leads to a poorer economy and a harder life for the citizens. The lack of service leads to a lack of jobs and more poverty for the people leading to an almost non-existent middle class in the country and we could continue to draw these lines but not to drag matters too much, this ends my discourse on transportation in Nigeria but I hope I have painted a clear enough picture for you and that you can begin to use the theories I provided earlier to dissect the situation in the country through these examples and see the root causes along with the patterns they create that permeates every aspect of the lives of Nigerians leading to the catastrophic failure we see today in Nigeria as a country.

INFRASTRUCTURE: ELECTRICITY (POWER)

The generation, distribution and supply of electricity (power) to homes which Nigerians have come to popularly call *light* because that's how the bulbs light up has been a big problem in Nigeria since her inception. Your favourite 'developing' nation for more than sixty years of 'developing' has not been able to develop to the level where she can supply stable electricity to the homes of her citizens and it makes me wonder what else they are developing for their citizens all this while. I don't think the country has ever gone a full 24-hour day with uninterrupted electricity supply and there are parts of it that have gone months or even years without it and even remote parts that have never even seen it, if anything the state of the electricity supply is a metaphor for Nigeria itself. Please look carefully at the evidence I am presenting to you here, this is not the 1920s but the 2020s when technology is on a whole different level. Germany has announced that she is producing more electricity than her citizens need but Nigeria has not been able to provide a full day uninterrupted power for hers now for once in her existence, why is this? The places in this world that have this same problem are usually war ravaged places or places that have just been through a natural disaster like a volcanic eruption or a tornado that disrupts electricity supply and even then it is a temporary situation that is fixed quickly and electric power is restored for them but how does a country that has been in relative peace for decades with a leadership in place not be able to provide the infrastructures to bring drinking water into the homes of her citizens, effectively take away the sewage from their homes or give them stable electricity supply? Not from the first time of civilian rule to military rule and back to civilian rule over the course of her history has this changed now why is this? I mean the technology definitely exists and this is not some secondary school science book where I start listing off different ways electricity could be generated but even if the people in a country are so dumb that they cannot come up with things for themselves they can surely pay others to do it for them if those things are so important right?

War is violence, cold and unfeeling it does not care, hot and voracious it consumes. War is death, death to your enemies no matter the cost but how far are a people willing to go for victory? If the war is with outsiders then it is easier to identify your enemies but if the war is between members of the same body or the same household or country then it's more complicated because your enemies are harder to identify. They look like you, talk like you, dress like you, eat the same food as you, share deep ethnic and religious ties with you and live amongst you. They call you brother, sister and fellow Nigerian like they share a bond with you but all their tongues are full of lies and their actions jeopardize your very existence, so how can you identify them? And when you do how will you react? Whether they love the country or hate it is of no consequence to me at this point, what matters is what they are doing to this country and in a sane world it's high treason, plain and simple. I find it shocking that they are willing to even kill her if it means that they get to dominate, control and exploit her in the process, it's just the masses that are largely ignorant of this fact... it's war after all.

This is why I have chosen to make political will my primary focus in this work ignoring the many distractions that have been put in place to confound the masses and keep them in disarray while they are being exploited so that they can never know where their true problems are coming from. There is a big government body responsible for electricity generation and supply in the country called PHCN that is Power Holding Company of Nigeria which was formerly called NEPA that is Nigerian Electric Power Authority. They have played the whole name switch on it changing and rebranding the body but as always with these things it has not affected its agenda or its operations or its output. Creative Nigerians also gave their own names too, to them NEPA was Never Expect Power Always and when it was changed to PHCN it became Please Hold Candle Now. This body and others like it controlling other key areas of Nigerian society are very key vehicles used for the exploitation of the country's resources because huge amounts are allocated for them in the budget year in and year out that end up shared into private accounts of members of the political ruling class rather than being used for what they are intended and this is where I bring to your remembrance the saying that in a criminal state it is criminal to be law abiding. The intention of these bodies is actually to steal funds and on paper the money has been allocated, if you were working in one of these bodies and you decided to do the right thing and prevent those monies from going to those private accounts do you see how you'll be viewed and treated by the powers that be who are trying to embezzle those monies in the first place? So does it make sense to you yet or is it still vague? Now as for the common Nigerians they are not all stupid, they can see what is happening in the country just that they haven't taken the right steps to counteract it, they are trapped in a long dark tunnel where they are left to aimlessly and endlessly stumble and shuffle along. One of the main reasons that there is no light at the end of this dark tunnel for Nigerians is because PHCN does not supply enough or stable electricity to power that light. The consequences of the lack of stable power supply in Nigeria run very deep from running businesses to the economy to the daily lives of the people and I maintain that it is all part of the design to keep the Nigerian masses in survival mode.

DRUG ADDICTS AND THEIR INSATIABLE LITTLE BEASTS.

That the power supply in Nigeria is unstable is not news but that instability or the level of it is not uniform across the country. Some parts of the country might have relatively stable power supply and the people that live there might wonder what I am talking about criticizing the power corporation and the government not knowing that there are parts of the country where they go days, weeks, months without electricity and in the extreme cases even years. These places have all the wiring and sockets connected, and the inhabitants also have modern electrical home appliances that require electricity to function but see little or no action because the Nigerian government is not able to provide stable electricity supply for her citizens, not also able to have a national air carrier to subsidise flights for her citizens and I ask again; what is it the role of the Nigerian government in Nigeria? And the things they eventually do or make it seem like they are doing to help the citizens are done so badly that they are rendered ineffective.

You might be wondering what electricity supply in Nigeria has to do with drug addicts but this concept came to me when I went to spend some time with friends of mine that live in Lagos. The power supply in Sapele which is my hometown wasn't great and I complained about it a lot but when I got to my friend's place in Lagos I discovered that theirs was even worse. They sometimes went for days without *light* and when they supplied the *light* it was only for a few minutes. I remember countless nights over there and back home where as a light sleeper my night sleep was interrupted by mosquitoes singing high tunes in my ears, showing me the courtesy of first announcing their presence before they proceed to bite the living daylights out of me. They are usually kept at bay by the blast of air from the fans we have in our homes to cool the temperature as it's so hot in Nigeria. This blast of air disrupts their flying patterns, cooling the temperature in the room and giving us a good night's sleep in the process but without electricity to power the fans the mosquitoes are left free to roam at night and wreak havoc. This is the health angle to the power situation in the country that ripples into lack of proper sleep with its attendant consequences and malaria from mosquito bites for the inadequate health care system to take care of and it just goes on and on. The *light* situation was so bad at my friend's place in Lagos that sometimes we hadn't even finished shouting, dancing and celebrating the fact that they had given us *light* before they took it back cutting us off mid-celebration and we had to sit down again and wait, hoping. The combined effects of the hot afternoon weather in day time and the boredom could be tough on a bunch of young unemployed gentlemen who could definitely do with some fun in their lives.

We had to wait the whole day in the house on the days we were not booked in the studio to record with practically nothing to do and in the evenings we had to dip into our pockets for hard earned cash (earned from where you might ask) to buy fuel for the generator to have some relief at night before we dozed off. It was on these constant trips to the fuel station with the empty gallon that I began to notice the excitement and anticipation building up in me because I knew there would be *light* from the generator for a few hours that night. At least we could charge our phones, laptops, get some much-needed excitement from the Play station 3 and also get to watch a little TV. This feeling was akin to the feeling of drug addicts when they are going to buy the drugs because they know what the outcome of the trip would be, a fix, joy, excitement and in the end relief. The feeling was magnified when I saw different people from different walks of life with their small gallons coming to buy their own fuel, some in cars, others just getting back from work and the fuel station was like an unofficial meeting place for Nigerians from different neighborhoods who have gone out for the whole of that day to look for their daily bread in the harsh, poverty ridden country and now have to dip into whatever they got from that day's earnings to buy petrol to put in generators they bought themselves to power their homes because their government could not adequately provide that service and that infrastructure for them. This is another one of the cuts again as to how the people are kept poor because the political ruling class by defaulting on these services and infrastructures forces the people to provide it for themselves as they are essential services and in doing so repeatedly they dip into whatever little they have. It is a perpetual process and a perpetual system that is effective when your goal is to keep a people in poverty.

So as I began to observe these meetings of different Nigerians at the fuel stations in our constant evening trips and to meditate on my observation that was when the image formed in my mind of the Nigerian people as a bunch of fiendish drug addicts crowding to the fuel stations to get petrol while their generators which they relied on to give them power became insatiable little beasts that always hungry and never got satisfied no matter how much you fed them. These little beasts always seemed to have their mouths wide open because we just kept pouring the petrol in and they rumbled away and a few hours later were empty, asking to be fed again which means to be refilled with petrol from the petrol station which when you looked at it was really just money from our pockets just being thrown into the mouth of a necessary evil in those little beasts. This is the level of the average Nigerian's reliance on petrol, it is so integral to our daily lives so imagine doubling and tripling the price of this vital substance without a moment's notice or artificially making it scarce. When you have the power to do this then you can control the lives of the people that are so dependent on it and that's why I listed both fuel scarcity and fuel price increase as control mechanisms by the elites over the masses in the ongoing war.

CONSEQUENCES:

The personal discomfort experienced by Nigerians in their day to day lives living in the country is not the only consequence of an irregular power supply, sure disrupted sleep cycles and mosquito bites are bad but they are nothing compared to the real consequences and loss suffered as a result of this condition.

A) SOCIAL ENGINEERING: if Nigeria were a house made up of 1 million sandcrete blocks cemented together with doors, windows, ten thousand pieces of wood and twenty thousand pieces of roofing sheets cut to different sizes and nailed together all designed to be supported by seven key concrete pillars as the foundation what would be the most effective way to tear this house down if that were your intention? Would it be to come with a sledge- hammer and try to tear it down block by block? Well if you tried that you would be seen by the owners of the house and the inhabitants as the enemy and they will band together to fight you off, besides that method would take a lot of time and they would start rebuilding and repairing as you're destroying the house so that might not be totally effective but if you were able to attack the foundation of that house through the seven pillars supporting it then you could bring it down in an instant but wait, I have told you before that the destruction of Nigeria as a country is not the goal here. That would be foolish, why would these people ever try to completely destroy such a sweet and docile money maker for them? That would be the most stupid thing to do in the world but if you were a part of the design and build team for that house then you can deliberately mess up the foundations in secrecy so that when the house is completed and they are loaded, they will start to fail. When this happens and the house is shaking with cracks appearing everywhere throwing the inhabitants into disarray, deep fear and chaos. You can then magically appear with a head pan of mortar with a trowel and try to fill in the cracks in the foundation and the walls so it looks to the ignorant inhabitants of that house that you're trying to repair and fix things but deep down you know that the house will never stand strong because you and your pals never designed or constructed it to do so.

When I dissect the Nigerian situation in my mind I do so from a social architecture and social engineering point of view. First of all power is the ability to do work and there are thousands of ways to loot and exploit the country while giving her stable power supply in the process so the question becomes 'why'? Why was it so necessary to take that too from her and her citizens so religiously and consistently all these decades? Is it the famous ineptitude and greed of the political ruling class that the average Nigerian thinks is the cause of everything wrong with the country? These people know how to build lavish mansions for themselves but when the time comes for them to build infrastructure for the country that would benefit the citizens they suddenly become inept? How's that logic working for you by the way? Countries in the dry desert have stable power supply, places in mountainous regions with snow, high winds and all other extreme environmental conditions have stable power but when it comes to tropical Nigeria it becomes an impossible feat to achieve? Please make it make sense when some of the neighbouring countries have stable power supply, or when parts of Nigeria are generating and transmitting power to these countries and they have stable power supply while the generating country does not. Please make it make sense when the country only generates between four to six thousand megawatts in total and when these infrastructures are mostly pre-independence ones set up by the colonisers. This could go on and on but I hope I was able to show intention, foreknowledge and even design in the lethargic power supply in Nigeria and its part in the artificial poverty of her people.

B) MANUFACTURING - THE ABILITY TO CREATE: The hyper-materialism among Nigerians and blacks in general is a by-product of lack and scarcity because they simply lack the familiarity of a creator's abundance. When I talk about creator's abundance I am just trying to say that people who grew up in and around a car manufacturing factory and saw a new car roll out the assembly line every hour or so and then moved into storage with hundreds or even thousands of other new cars from that assembly line all their lives will have a different outlook and mentality towards cars compared to a person far away that only got to see the finished product as put together by the designers, manufacturers and marketers. This is also another angle to the poverty mentality and survival mode, when the electrical and industrial revolutions happened in other parts of the world the Nigerian peoples were still living under colonialism and whatever technological advancements that came in those times were used to further exploit them as a people so in essence we missed that train and were stranded at the train station. When the colonisers from outside left another new wave of colonisers from within seized control of the country and they have been running things ever since till the present day so their interests are similar to the interests of their predecessors leaving the peoples and their lands neglected.

If the interests and objective of the Nigerian people as a collective was to develop industrially using the abundant resources in their lands as a catalyst then Nigeria should have caught up to the rest of the world by now, I'm not saying she would be ahead or dominating the whole world but she would have at least made some strides but instead she has sadly regressed. A person can say sweet words to you from sun up till sundown but their actions will tell you more about their intentions than those many words. If the intention of the political ruling class in Nigeria was to develop the country and her peoples then stable electricity supply would have been a key part of whatever plan they would have come up with but the current situation is plain for all to see. The simple tools that man invented to make his works easier have evolved over time from mechanical to electrical and then the automated machines in factories around the world all using electricity as their source of power to function, heralding again the importance of electricity but a country in 2024 cannot guarantee uninterrupted power supply for 24 hours hence they are left 100 years behind their competitors and this is one of the major reasons Nigeria does not have an indigenous manufacturing industry.

The being that man was crafted after is a creator which makes man a creator also, it is one of the prides of man to be able to create so if you take out that ability one can say it's a form of dehumanisation in its own way. I could probably write a whole book on the ripple effects of the lack of infrastructure to supply stable electricity to Nigerians and the absence of an indigenous manufacturing industry but let's stick to topic because we still have much to talk about. The absence of an indigenous manufacturing industry means that these people do not make or produce anything, which means that they have not been able to benefit from the immense advancements made in manufacturing and production in the world and this absence leads to a decreased productivity for the Nigerian people which in turn leads to poverty and continues to fuel the importation culture that currently has the country and her peoples in a chokehold. What this also means is that with the great insecurity plaguing Nigeria the people cannot even invent, make or produce things to defend themselves leaving them weak and vulnerable as a people to the elements of their environment. A country of about 200 million people that produces nothing looks like a ripe harvesting ground for countries that actually manufacture and produce goods, a massive market country which is the stuff that the wet dreams of the manufacturing nations are made up of. The picture of the lions and the buffaloes flashes in my mind as I write this, an already poor people are made to buy finished products with the mark up of shipping and transportation to get to their shores in the first place and these many cuts add to the slow demise of these people. So when I say that the shipping containers return empty it is because the country has produced nothing internally to export, if there are exports it's usually raw materials and resources shipped out at peanut prices to foreign lands to be used to manufacture goods that are brought back to be sold to the people at higher prices; the woes of these people are only multiplied.

C) IMPORTATION OF GENERATORS: You cannot live in these modern times without electricity so when you live in a place without electricity or with really poor electricity supply of just a couple of hours a day or even minutes then you have to supplement it with something else and that's where the insatiable little beasts come in. The Nigerian environment and the Nigerian system as designed for the average Nigerian is one with many deliberate faults and each fault is a cut that takes a little bit more money out of the pockets of the already poor people ensuring that they stay poor and in survival mode indefinitely. In trying to provide electricity for themselves they start to buy generators and I'll tell you from the start that these little beasts do not come cheap. This cuts across the board whether for domestic purposes or for business and industrial purposes so if you were to add the cost of the industrial generators to your overall business cost along with the daily cost of running it by fuelling it, maintenance costs and parts then you can see how unsustainable it becomes to start and run a business in the country. The lack of a manufacturing industry means that these little beasts are imported parts and all, they were ranked among the top six things imported into the country which tells you that it's big business indeed and which of the two warring classes has the capital to engage in this type of business? The political government structure ensures that electricity supply is not stable while their friends in the political ruling class provide the generators for profit, isn't it all a nice big scam of a country?

The political ruling class on their own have access to the resources in the country and can afford the big generators with the fuel to run them or in the most cases they are connected to special electric lines running through the country that have some level of stability in terms of electricity supply but this is only reserved for the elites as the poor Nigerian masses are excluded from it. The political ruling class runs like a parallel state in Nigeria, it is a small country within the larger one with its own system, laws and rules separate from those of the larger, the price of admission to this exclusive mini-country is money and they are able to effectively exclude the general masses from the lifestyle they have created for themselves with money and it works. That is why I said at the beginning that the most important thing in all these topics and discussions is resources; where they are taken from, where they end up, who they are taken from, who takes it, how it's taken and how it's used, those are the most important things, everything else is just a distraction. If the importation of generators into Nigeria is such a big business with big players and big investments made into it then common sense and logic tells you that there is a conflict of interest here because it is in the interest of the powerful people involved in this business to NEVER see constant electricity supply in the country, for the day it happens is the day their lucrative business ends.

On a personal level the absence of stable electricity supply makes it difficult to live in the country. I love Nigeria but I hated that aspect of living in Nigeria with a strong passion. The noise from the generator sets of the different households in the quiet night time which should be for rest and relaxation was a nuisance that constituted noise pollution especially for a light sleeper like me. They say Nigerian men are not romantic during night work in the inner room but I don't see how a man living in an apartment complex with up to ten generators performing a symphony of disconcerting noisiness at 11pm can whisper sweet nothings into his wife's ears while he is performing with her that night, he'd have to shout it at best to get over the noise of the generators (*OH BABY YOU'RE SOOO SWEET!!*) while she has a bewildered look on her face *lol*. On a serious note the generators are expensive and with the high level of theft in Nigerian society this made people to keep them in the house while they ran all through the course of the night and in this way unlucky individuals and sometimes entire families have been killed by the buildup of carbon monoxide in their homes from the exhaust of the generators they kept in the home to prevent thieves from getting access to steal it at night while they slept. In this way among others like electrocution and immolation from petrol explosions generators have added to the needless loss of Nigerian lives because if the electricity was stable they would not be needed in the first place.

D) COLLATERAL DAMAGE: Yes, yes, collateral damage you might ask, is the PHCN fighting a war with the Nigerian people? In a manner of speaking but leaving the battlefield for a minute here, I noticed that over the decades there have been other huge ripple effects from the actions or inaction of the PHCN and the national grid they administer which is always collapsing. This has transformed into domestic collateral damage when you consider the countless domestic appliances that have been damaged by abrupt power supply and failure, low voltage supply, higher than normal voltage supply and that peculiar strobe lights style flashing voltage supply they do sometimes that mimics lightning or Christmas lights and is somewhat beautiful to observe when it happens at night with the lights on but is very destructive to electrical home appliances and light bulbs. You name it we have seen it all growing up in Nigeria; we have seen sudden surge in voltage from normal or nothing that instantly heated up the filaments in the light bulbs that they started exploding one by one like we see in the hollywood horror movies before we could get to the switches on the walls to turn them off. We have seen voltage supplies so low that it was better to just turn all the light off and light a candle or lantern for that night if you don't have petrol in the generator, that is even if that home owns a generator in the first place but most homes do, they have to as it's a necessity in Nigeria. Nigerians are always paying for the inadequacies of their government, their resilience is used as a weapon against them further tightening the noose and pushing them deeper into the hole of poverty and suffering because the assumption is that they can take it. No matter how hard the conditions are the average Nigerian will take it without complaint, protest or revolt.

    To combat this type of power supply Nigerians have taken to buy all kinds of devices like stabilizers, surge protectors and all kinds of solar devices just to have some degree of stable power supply in their homes... something that should have just been as simple as plugging into the wall outlet. These devices do not always come cheap as they are not produced in the country but imported which is more money out of the pockets of the average Nigerians. I cannot in anyway cover all the collateral damages of irregular power supply to the Nigerian people else this book will not end so the best I can do is to paint you a picture. There is just not enough space or time here to go into the level of corruption in the PHCN and their dealings with the average Nigerian people, from high estimations of electricity bills (estimation, gerrit?) to loss of equipment like replacement of damaged transformers which they pass the cost onto the poor people and it goes on. Cases like the transformers when the people cannot come up with the money because they just don't have it, they are left in darkness for months and in some cases years as I told you earlier. When you check on paper those transformers have been allocated from the office and reported as provided to the people. For damaged appliances we had damaged flat screen TVs at my parent's house that I will one day take to the PHCN office to request compensation or reparation in this case because they were damaged by unusual power supply by them but who am I kidding? I'm pretty sure that if

I got a naira for every appliance that the PHCN has damaged in the country over the past decades I would be contesting with the richest man in the world right now. Housewives and mothers also know that they have lost perishable food stuff in the refrigerator because there was no power for that appliance for days. All this waste is money going down the drain which is a loss to the average Nigerian and God hates waste, I do too. The appliances are expensive to buy because of the mark-up of the importers and the weak naira purchasing foreign finished products, the perishable food stuff are also expensive for the common Nigerian on the street because nothing is cheap and the society is in deep poverty so how will the Nigerian masses survive Nigeria? If I ask you the reasons why power supply is the way it is in Nigeria at this point will you be able to tell me without looking?

INFRASTRUCTURE: COMMUNICATION.

The consequences of the slave trade and colonization periods still echo through time to the present day and the after effects are still playing out and being felt both by the victims and those that profited heavily from their pain in different ways. I know, I used to be a strong critic of those that call to those times as the cause of the problems of the black race today until I took a closer look at the facts to understand what really happened and now I can say that the past cannot simply be wiped away like writings on a chalkboard, those things happened and the problems today are from back then and today into tomorrow because it's a continuous thing. What the past did is to create a destructive pattern in the trajectory of black lives, it is the pattern of exploitation that has stagnated to people caught in it such that while the rest of the world carried on and developed black people were kept in limbo, their upward and forward trajectory was violently stopped in its tracks and they were thrown into suspended animation and left in a vulnerable state. This is the negative aspect of the balloon theory at work where the air is continuously sucked out of the balloon. We do not want to just lay all the blame on the outsiders and their deeds because black people are just as responsible for their predicaments as they have not been able to band together to mount a serious resistance to the forces acting against them in the world even in these present days, they have not even been able to identify the systems and the forces controlling their very existence in the first place and this might seem like victim blaming but they are human after all, humans with the capacity for deep critical reasoning not just things or animals.

In this world there are two groups of people, they are the actors and reactors; the actors make things happen while things happen to the reactors that they can only react to hence the name and black people have been reactors now for hundreds of years. The black problem is not genetic but sociological and for those that are versed in these types of things they know that we can always trace it to the spiritual too but we live in a physical world so we focus on the sociological aspects. No one, no doctor, scholar or scientist, can honestly look at the black man or black woman as a specimen in comparison to any other race in the planet and try to suggest with a straight face that we are somehow genetically inferior or deficient to the others so no, the problem is sociological and it's on a global scale. I would have just said that the problem of the blacks in Africa is sociological but when you look at it there seems to be a subtle global push to keep wealth out of the hands of our people. There I go again with hyperbole, right? Well I say look at the United States, they had a portion of black population that were willing to work their factories but they decided to take all their operations to Asia rather than keep it in their home soils for the descendants of the slaves they brought in earlier to work on their plantation to benefit from saying that they could produce cheaper in Asia but the Asians were smart though, they were patient and quietly learnt the technology from the Americans. Whatever they could not learn they outright stole and today they are a direct competitor to the Americans even surpassing them in certain aspects as is the way of life because the student must surpass his teacher. This is still a developing situation and I am excited to see how it all plays out but the Asians have been a great people with a rich history for thousands of years but they definitely had been in a slump for an extended period of time so I would not be out of place if I said that racism against the blacks in America contributed to this shift.

Anyways kudos to the Asians because it's one thing for an opportunity to present itself and another thing for the person to recognize that opportunity and to take advantage of it. Even if they have diversity they do not have the magnitude and intensity of the diversity that the Africans have and the challenges that can come with it when it's not properly handled. Also they do not have the setback of a thousand years of slavery, exploitation with the century of colonization, the attendant problems and after effects working against them but obstacles must be faced not turned into excuses. Also they had the one key thing the Africans today do not have and it cannot be underestimated, it is a country that is a legal entity where the leadership and the people are working together as one with a common interest to better that country and the lives of the people in it, for them and their generations to come. This bit here is very important and cannot be overlooked, this is one of the key boats among others that's supposed to offer protection, give opportunities to and lift the people up at the high tide but the Africans do not have that at this moment so they are exposed and vulnerable. What does all this have to do with communication? When I talk about communication in Nigeria I am talking about telephone, internet, mobile phones, their infrastructure and their development in Nigeria as influenced by the Nigerian factor. For a people trapped in suspended animation while the rest of the world evolved and advanced the trajectory of the development of things in Nigeria is always different. When the telephone landlines and accompanying infrastructures which were developed by the actors finally made its way to Nigeria it did not proliferate nor was there any technology transfer to the people to learn how to make it for themselves gaining the ability to modify it, further develop and evolve with it.

What we have seen with technology in Nigeria is that no matter how vital to development, business and lifestyle that technology is it is imported into the country in its finished form which is usually substandard to the rest of the developed world, is scarce to come by in the land (remember scarcity!), is highly priced (cuts and losses that combine to create poverty for the people) and most likely becomes a status symbol that only the elites can afford. This whole process that I've just described to you is a pattern of operations and I'd like you to take note of it because it plays into different sectors of Nigerian life and I'll develop it further or give it a heading at some point and expand it to be an additional theory to explain the situation of Nigeria as it's that important to our subject matter. First of all this pattern shows you one of the modes of exploitation I have been talking about as you see that resources are being extracted from the masses when these technologies are brought into the country. Now how do these technologies come into the country? The elites bring in foreign companies and go into back door agreements with them that the Nigerian masses are not privy to (secrecy!) as regards their operations, pricing and employment of staff and that becomes a money maker for the group within the political elites responsible for that particular racket. Of course they remit a percentage back to the hierarchy of their organisation but you see the picture. There is so much to unpack here it's tiring for me, mentally draining even but surely you must see the picture for yourself at this stage. Foreign company with Nigerians employed as cleaners and drivers while the sensitive operations of the company are handled by expatriates, basically the profits go back to the home country of that company and its staff so all of that is more extraction and what do the Nigerians get in exchange for all this? You can see how far removed the average Nigerian is from the matters that control their very lives.

So the fact that only a few can afford the technology in the first palace shows you the importance of poverty for this system to work. Money becomes a barricade and a shackle, it is used as a limiter and a control mechanism carefully crafting and shaping the lives of the masses. Never forget that to import such new technologies and infrastructures into the country would cost a lot of money and who has the capital and the resources to undertake such a venture in the country in the first place? You guessed it right, it's the members of the political ruling class and in that way using capital and weaponised poverty they are able to maintain a choke hold control over the country, her operations and the vital pillars that hold her up. Now if there are no foundations in the first place what is there for the people to build upon? These political elites through the government which is a microcosm of it are able to set up a ministry or a board or an authority backed by government power to oversee that sector seemingly on 'behalf' of the Nigerian people so in this way political fraud is smoothly carried out without resistance because if anyone in the masses would dare revolt and challenge what is happening it would seem like they are trying to fight the government of the country itself. For electricity you saw the PHCN, for communications it's NITEL (Nigerian Telecommunications Limited) and you have others like them for different key sectors of the country. Seems they were all changed to private companies or so but it's the old name change trick. When you see the Nigerian government change the names of any of such bodies it's the old magician's trick of deflection so you have to pay close attention so you don't fall for the trick. The top hierarchy of these bodies that can influence key decision making or operations of these bodies in any way possible are flooded with members of the political ruling class and with this done their control over the country Nigeria is absolute! The African rock python has its helpless prey firmly wrapped in its coils and it will not let go, there is greed in its eyes, raw greed and glee, its forked tongue continuously stabs the air around it trying to taste it and look for more prey, more opportunities and more ways it can exploit this country, and it is secure in its position, it knows it's secure because its prey is too weak and drained to fight back at this point.

    The current situation in Nigeria is carefully crafted, it is made to look chaotic but that chaos is a lie. If you know how to look and see then you will see the dots all in the chaos, if you start to connect the dots then patterns will emerge and if you read the patterns you will be able to travel through time and see how we got here. If you are able to see how it all got to the present then you can travel ahead in time to see the future and you don't need to wait for the end of this book for me to tell you what I see. If nothing changes in Nigeria with the way she is set up and being run then for the next 100 years and beyond she will continue on this trajectory and only get worse as time goes on, her people and their descendants after them in a perpetual bondage for eternity. Anyways as for the quality of the communication services provided in Nigeria I would just say that a NASA probe is able to take pictures in Mars and send back to earth with little to no problems at all, there are scientists in Antarctica which is barely inhabitable and they are able to communicate reasonably well but sometimes if you put two phones side by side in Nigeria that's on the equator and try to use one to call the other most times it might not connect and the internet services are no better too. Other countries have made these services available and even mandatory in some cases but the poor Nigerian masses are still struggling to afford the services and when they do the services are substandard. Nigerians know this and that's why the average Nigerian has more than one mobile phone with different providers just in case you are trying to reach them if one doesn't work then the other might work. Many a business deal has been lost because of this, now how are they supposed to compete favourably with the rest of the world like this? Well what about the service providers you might ask? These are international companies that provide great services in their home countries but their allegiance and obligations are to the political ruling class not the masses so why should they be bothered to do anything about the poor service they offer in the country? In this way you can see the Nigerian factor at work whereby an idea or in this case a company that has worked well and is still operating well in some other place fails and does not do the same in Nigeria because it's Nigeria so how does the average Nigerian compete with the rest of the world?

You cannot really write Nigerians off, even pinned to the ground in the fight of their lives they have still managed to free a hand and throw punches back. With the odds stacked against them they have still managed to scam millions of dollars from foreigners using the slow internet services and limited resources available to them but why does it seem that these people are driven to crime? It was Tupac Shakur that said *'they wonder why the rose that grew from the concrete had damaged petals'* so in the fight for survival crime has become an outlet and a way of life. What will you say to the drowning man that grabbed a hold of his rescuer and would not let go? Now if him and his rescuer who can swim end up drowning together would you call him a murderer? Would you call him wicked or will you consider his situation that led to the unfortunate tragedy in the first place? This is the Nigerian factor, the environment that has been created for these people to survive in and we have Nigerians that have done great things in the fintech industry and I think my people still have a lot to offer in IT but poor, substandard and terrible telecommunication infrastructures available to them, politica government induced limitations and bottlenecks amongst other things has been a hindrance and a limiter to the ascension unto their higher selves as a people.

AGRICULTURE

I must keep on writing, oh yes I cannot but continue to search out and write, I must feel out and fish out the subtle vibrations of this reality with my spirit so I can know them and understand them fully as best as I can and also share as much of it as I can with you. How is it that a people living in over 923,000 square kilometres of green fertile lands cannot feed themselves? It's even worse when you have desert dwelling nations producing in abundance for their people on one hand and even exporting food while you see a nation with green fertile lands having two great rivers running through the heart of her lands providing natural irrigation having her people starving and still having to import food, what comes to your mind? If anything this mysterious situation describes Nigeria perfectly; it's the continuous contradicting pattern of stark lack in the midst of great abundance that continues to pop up in every area of Nigerian society and just will not go away that's why I insist that the poverty, lack and scarcity in these lands are all artificially manufactured and sustained for her many peoples. It is the false identity given to these people, a clear case of destiny exchange where they have had their clean clothes taken off them and a filthy garment made of rags forcefully donned on them to wear and parade around in condemned to be the scum of the earth for all the days of their existence. Social engineering is the process of creating specific conditions in a society to trigger certain responses from the people in that society to shape it in a certain way or take it in a certain direction and to do this you need power, authority and resources to make the changes and to sustain them.

Sustenance is very important when you want lasting effect because left to their own devices all living things will take a different direction; for example if you have been cutting the grass in your yard in a certain shape to make a walk way for 10 years and you stop doing it the grass would grow out of that shape and cover the walkway. If you want to maintain the shape you might cast a concrete slab as a more permanent walkway to keep the grass from growing in that area and this is what sustaining the walkway is about but the day the slab is broken and removed the grass will start growing again over time. The scenarios differ, for the grass the slab has done the job and for a tree a weight might be used to bend it in a certain direction and the tree keeps on growing such that when they weight is finally removed later on the tree keeps growing in that way on its own because it's stem is bent already, it is the application of these diverse tailor made strategies to different aspects of Nigerian society impacting Nigerian lives to create the current conditions we see today that points to intelligence and intention behind the problems. These might not be the greatest examples but I do hope they create some form of context in your mind as to the idea I am trying to communicate.

I will forgive you as a foreigner or even a Nigerian born and bred in Nigeria for that matter if your remedy to the low agricultural production output in Nigeria is to list out new farming methods or cheap and affordable fertilizer brands to purchase to help the local farmers but if that's your answer then you haven't really been paying proper attention to what I've been saying about this country the whole time. I do not doubt that these technologies and methodologies exist in the first place but as I explained earlier with the theory of the Nigerian factor, those technologies and methodologies that have worked magnificently in other lands will fail magnificently when you bring them to Nigeria because of aggregated human will that has become controlling political will in the country. One of the greatest problems of black people is that they are reactors and the authority to decide their own fate and destiny in this word does not yet rest with them as a people which in effect is a lack of people power, and even if a chunk of that authority rests in the hands of people with black skin that look like them the interests of these people sadly do not align with the interest of the larger body hence the war of the political ruling class vs the masses that I've highlighted to you earlier in this book.

To show you the game and political fraud that was played on these smart people in the area of agricultural production I would ask that you kindly take a short walk with me through history back to colonial times when the prime need was for agricultural products. The main aim of the colonisers who had the authority over the territories and her peoples in those time was for her agricultural produces and mineral resources so they directed their efforts into agriculture and Nigeria was a leading producer of cocoa, rubber, oil palm kernel, groundnut among many other cash crops with economic values which were exported to the home lands of the colonisers to benefit them and theirs. So bountiful was the harvest of this land that the infamous groundnut pyramids made up of sacks of groundnuts stacked up in big pyramid shapes are a testament to this but what changed over the years? The pyramids of Giza stand till this day but the groundnut pyramids in Nigeria have all disappeared so what happened? I know you'll argue that the Giza pyramids are made of stone while the Nigerian ones were made of perishable agricultural produces and you'll be right in that but it still doesn't change the fact that there was a great decline in the country's agricultural production output from those times till these present ones and we have to look at some of the mysterious causes and effects of this decline to fully understand.

Nigeria's high agricultural produces were the main cash cow for the colonisers and this continued into independence era with the new black colonisers continuing the exploitation mandate, however this changed drastically when a new cash cow was unearthed in 1970s with the discovery of oil in Nigeria. Now the Nigerians from that era and others who have studied these things will tell you that the rush for and focus on oil which was definitely more lucrative led to the decline and death of agriculture in the country and there is a lot of truth in that but when you look at it strictly from a resource and exploitative point of view then you see how the focus was shifted to exploit the more lucrative crude oil and agriculture had to die. Not to say that because crude oil was more lucrative then agriculture became useless overnight because you will soon find that people cannot eat and live on crude oil, the death of agriculture was a slow and painful one. If you try to think of this logically you will miss it and you'll not be the first person to fail in this, what you need to know is that in the control agenda over Nigeria it is paramount to the controlling party to have the resources and wealth of the country to go anywhere else and into any other thing than into the hands of the masses and the people of the country even if these resources have to be wasted or burned. Even if they go into the hands of foreigners it's fine, just as long as it does not find its way into the hands of the ordinary Nigerians because for this current system of domination and exploitation in the country to work poverty and scarcity are key ingredients to weaken these people, without these ingredients you cannot easily control them.

As to the methods they employed to kill agricultural production in the country the older Nigerians who lived and operated in those days know what happened, my father was a major trader in oil palm kernels in those days and I still vividly remember what he told me as a young boy about the destructive Nigerian marketing boards created by the government to control different aspects of Nigerian agricultural production. I spent a lot of time with him and asked him lots of questions and every question I asked he always tried to answer as best as he could. You'll have to do some digging on your own if you want detailed information especially for the young Nigerians who are ignorant about these things. For our generation they tell us that it's the terrorist attacks on farmers that killed agricultural production in the country but that's just another bold-faced lie from the mothers and fathers of lies in this world, terrorist attacks while a great example of how insecurity works in the grand plan and general Nigerian equation to create poverty and chaos is not the main reason for the decline of agricultural production in the country as it's more of a recent development. The Boko Haram insurgency in Nigeria was first recorded in 2009 and by that time agricultural production was already well and truly dead in the country, terrorism and insurgency like vultures were only new layers and dimensions added to pick at and scavenge on its carcass to ensure that it stayed dead (sustainability).

I sadly cannot go into full details here about the operations of the marketing boards as that would be a full book on its own but thank God for the internet, there are writings from different sources to balance the information you get and some from even British observers who although their country benefitted immensely from the activities of such boards and their exploitative activities in Africa were able to honestly record the activities of such boards and document them for future generations and the verdict is unanimous. They were used to create monopolies on cash crops, tax the farmers thereby discouraging production of select crops, abused by the politicians to enrich themselves, fund their lifestyles and political activities and they destroyed the livelihood of ordinary Nigerian farmers and businessmen from those days. There was widespread abuse and corruption with those boards and bodies like them are the precursors to the ministries and boards like the water board you have today. You can see that such methods have already been used in the past to great effect and by now the political ruling class knows what works and what will not work in the country. This is clearly social engineering at work creating policies that systematically destroy economic activities thereby creating poverty for the people in the process. You young Nigerians that think that your battle started in 1960 are in for a rude shock, you need to put the social media aside sometimes and read, those of you that have 'founding fathers' that you idolize might not like what you find when you open the history books. The marketing boards have been in operation from the 2nd world war period which is a good 2 decades before 1960 so you can see that this group have been in operation well before 1960 as I told you earlier in this book so there is a lot to unpack and understand from the past to fully understand the present Nigeria as you see it today.

These boards and ministries are created then select individuals are put in the controlling hierarchy to oversee their operations and the agenda of their creation which never seem to bode well for ordinary Nigerians. The story has been the same from the beginning; in the case of agricultural production while the marketing boards carried out their destructive operations, stagnation, retardation and neglect saw to it that the indigenous manufacturing and technology in the country did not advance to follow global trends of mechanisation and research in agriculture to improve agricultural practices world wide. If the aim of the country was to improve agricultural production within her lands then the discovery of crude oil would have been a big boost to that because the funds that came in from oil would have been used to finance agricultural operations but it was instead killed off as soon as another cash cow was found and the scarcity principle could not have too many of these cash cows lying about to create a bottle neck for control purposes. The Asian countries that came to Nigeria in the 70s, 80s and 90s to learn oil palm planting and production left with seeds and seedlings in the bags and pockets of their emissaries but today are global leaders in the production of palm plantation and palm oil production while the lands they collected the seeds from are languishing in trans-dimensional and trans-generational poverty, and all I can say is, what is life? Life will puzzle and humble you when you look at it. If you couple all this with government neglect in not supporting farmers with fertilizers, subsidies and other programmes to help their very important work in society then you can see how we got here, terrorism and insecurity were just merely added later as sureties. Please pardon me if you're tired of hearing or seeing this at this point but I must add it again in case some have missed it the last times I said it; the poverty in Nigeria and many of these African countries is artificial and man-made, thank you.

I am trying to get into your mind to see what other possibilities you might conjure so I play devil's advocate and on your behalf: are the people lazy to work on farms? I try my best to have my emotions in check when I respond to you that for a people that were hunted and enslaved for their ability to work for hundreds of years that argument will not stand. Then why don't the individual people farm to boost agricultural production? Well society has become more differentiated and with the survival mode heavily in force due to poverty the people are locked in finding their daily bread so the farming is mostly left to the farmers as it is done even in the developed societies as they are called but some people still engage in different forms which sadly is not enough to cover the demand. To wrap things up here I'll just say that it would be impossible for me to cover every area of Nigerian life in this book so my hope is that in the areas that I do cover you are able to see the patterns and have enough understanding to answer your questions about the areas that I eventually do not cover. That said, let's move on to the next one then, shall we?

EDUCATION

"My people are destroyed for lack of knowledge: because thou hast rejected knowledge, I will also reject thee"

Hosea 4:6 (KJV)

There is a popular saying that goes like this 'knowledge is power' and there is no reason to disturb or distort it in its original form but the severity of our subject matter requires that we go deeper into all things so now I say that, 'not all knowledge is power, rather it is applied and utilized knowledge that is power.' Looking at that modification you can see that there is latent knowledge and manifested knowledge, look at the man that somehow gets the knowledge that his building will soon collapse but does nothing about it either through procrastination or impediments by his immediate circumstances, if that building eventually collapses and he perishes in it then that knowledge he had about the impending doom did not serve him in any way and was useless but if he was able to get pillars put in place to save the building and repair the cracks or just evacuate the building altogether when it becomes obvious that the structure cannot be salvaged then that manifested knowledge served him in some way by saving his life. If the statement that as a man thinks in his heart so is he is true pointing out that the convictions and dispositions of an individual as expressed by their mentality and mindset will determine their decisions and behaviours then it is important to study the information that are fed to that individual to craft his or her mindset and mentality which in turn shapes how they interact and respond with the circumstances of their environment and the people around them. There are several layers to this that might seem confusing but there is a direct pathway linking it all because Nigeria as a country, dysfunctional as she is, is still a closed system but she does not exist in isolation so what kind of information is the Nigerian fed from birth that eventually normalises the dysfunctionality to them as they grow up until they eventually accept it as normal?

That question and others like it are some of the things I've pondered for some time because I subscribe to the school of thought that says that the human mind is like a clean slate when they are born as a baby, *tabula rasa* it's been called, which is like a lump of clay to be masterfully shaped into whatever form by education fed to it and it's that form the individual will maintain mostly as they grow up. I know people can change but they rarely do, the bible says '***train up a child in the way he should go and when he is old he will not depart from it***' (Prov 22:6) and I quickly connect that to a Nigerian proverb that says '***na when fish still soft naim them dey bend am o, because when e done dry if you try to bend am e go break***' which in English translates to 'it is when the fish is still soft that you bend it, if you try to bend it when its hard already you'll break it'. I'll have to provide context if this parable is to make sense to some of you; now I know that all the doctors and the big psychologists in the 'developed' nations all advocate for letting children just grow up as they like and do what they want but we were raised in an African setting that's big on discipline and this parable like the other one I mentioned from the book of Proverbs states that parents must start to discipline children from a young age and set them on the right path because it will become harder to do as they grow older. The Nigerian proverb is culled from the old African method of preserving fresh fish whereby they were bent into circles with the tails going into the mouths most times, salted and bamboo strips with sharpened tips are pierced through them to make rows out of them before they are slowly smoked over an open fire with a mesh to remove moisture making them hard in the process. They can stay for longer periods in this state and are sold like that. I can remember as a child my mother buying lots of fish preserved this way and even though I was a good and obedient child, my siblings and I couldn't resist pinching off bits of the fish to snack on sometimes because they were just so delicious in that brown, round, salted and hardened form. So this parable is saying that it's when the fish is still fresh that you bend it into any shape you want because in that hard and dried form if you try to bend it, it'll break meaning it won't work. These examples for me point to the fact that you have to mould the minds of children so they can grow up to become productive members of society and this is where the importance of education can be seen.

Education though, is not just for children and as a student of life I believe that we never stop learning until we die so my focus is on the information that the Nigerian gleans from environment/society throughout their lifetime, how it shapes them and by extension has contributed to the Nigerian situation today. It was Mark Twain who said **'I have never let my schooling interfere with my education'** effectively separating formal education in institutions with fixed term duration where certificates may be issued to informal education that takes place outside of such institutions. Both forms of education are important to the development of individuals in a society and since a major cause of the problems of black people today is sociological, talking about the development, structure and functioning of their societies it becomes imperative to look at the education that the Nigerian receives because society is a reflection of the mindset of the people within it. How is it that these so called 3rd world countries in Africa can remain 3rd world countries for so long even when their designation was changed to 'developing' nations? Why don't they ever advance and become better? Do the brains of the people in those countries develop like the brains of the people in the 1st world countries? Do they have the capacity to be taught? Do they have good schools? Do they have enough teachers in whatever schools they have to teach the children in those schools or do we need to send teachers from the 1st world to the 3rd world to help them out? These are some of the questions driving this section that I hope we'll have answers for at the end of it but to properly look at education within the Nigerian context we have to separate it into formal and informal education.

FORMAL EDUCATION:

The pattern of the story continues. When we talk about formal education in Nigeria, the public school system is a mess and the vultures of Nigerian society have found their way there too to wreak their havoc of corruption and degradation in an area that should have been left out of the Nigerian shenanigans but alas, here we are. I must admit that I had a much, much lower valuation of schooling in Nigeria when I started this project but time and first hand experience have changed that into what you'll read in this finished version. I have had to re-evaluate the correlation between the schooling system, the state of the schools and the overall situation in Nigeria as we see it today. In the decades after independence Nigerians have proven to be consummate scholars, my father belonged to that old world and they believed strongly that formal education was the key to greatness for the blacks especially as we were playing catch up as a race. As a product of the private school system in Nigeria my siblings and I were fortunate enough to be carried by our parent's personal sacrifices for our education but I guess the people of that generation were blindsided by the political ruling class of the country that hijacked her destiny and some of them were fortunate to die early because they did not live long to witness the latter stages of her evolution and see with their own eyes the accomplishment of this destructive and parasitic group.

Formal education is very important but I have to ask the question: to what extent does schooling affect the outcome of a country? There is a ministry created to oversee public education in Nigeria, like all the other ministries they have a presence in all levels of government in the country, an organisational hierarchy, big buildings with offices and staff employed who report to work daily and a robust budget allocated and reported on paper but the state of the public schools at all levels from the primary to the secondary and then to the colleges, polytechnics and universities all tell the true story if you care to take a look. There are government schools where the classrooms have no roof and the children are exposed to the elements, there are no tables and chairs in some of these classrooms and the children are forced to sit on the bare floor or on mats spread on the floor to be taught, there are even some of these schools that the buildings are so dilapidated that the teachers and students are forced to carry out their schooling activities under trees because the thirst for knowledge is so strong in these people and I can testify to that. There are instances where the buildings are constructed without fences and gates or adequate security which leaves them exposed to vandals and looters that will progressively cause the deterioration of the facilities until they become run down but it's not all bad because this presents another opportunity and business is business for the businessmen and businesswomen in Nigeria so these projects can be re-awarded down the line by the the political ruling class to themselves and the cycle continues unbothered. With all these negative interference from the top on their lives it has not killed the Nigerian spirit. Nigerians still have a strong desire for formal education as a means to better themselves, a fish can never outgrow the tank it's kept in so surely the environment plays a huge part and the decay coupled with the rot in Nigerian society has spread far even into the educational sector but there is still a high level of schooling going on in the country. This sadly as with other things in the country for the everyday people is the rose that grew out of the concrete with damaged petals scenario not the one placed in fertile soil with all the nutrients and sunlight it might properly need plus the pruning required for it to blossom unhindered so the Nigerian factor has an effect on the students and the educational sector but my question comes up again: how has all this gone on to affect the outcome of Nigeria as the country we see today?

The first seeds of doubt were sown in my heart when a dear friend of ours who we went to school with was fortunate enough to be sent to Canada by his family to further his studies. We did not hear from him for a little over a year but when we did we were excited and chatted happily amongst ourselves but it was something he said during our conversation that stayed with me till this day. He told us that he was currently dominating his class academically in school over there in Canada, how easy it all was and that he wondered how it would be if I came over there. Now he said this because we attended the same secondary school and while he was an average student back then I was an A student so he said this innocently in passing and while I was still in Nigeria at the time I was in 'observer' mode so naturally I took that, internalised it and quizzed him a bit more on how the experience was for him over there as a student in a school in a 1st world country. You see, we were always made to feel like we were nothing both by Nigeria and the rest of the world so we had inferiority complex, we felt like it was because we were failures that's why our country is such a failure, we felt like we were doing things wrongly that's why our country was the way it is but something died in me that day. It was like a veil was pulled down in front of my face, some respect died that has not been resurrected till this day. When the reports started to pour in from others in places like the UK, other countries in Europe and the United States of how students from Nigerian schools have gone to schools in these '1st world' countries to dominate there shattering decades and sometimes even century-old academic records in the process the glass container was totally shattered for me.

    My brain was in overdrive; here were children who sat under trees, some sat on the floor because they had no desk and chairs, some had to cross rivers on their way to and from school every day, some had to walk kilometres on their way to and from school sometimes on unmotorable roads which were flooded, some had to pass through dangerous bush paths to get to school, some were flogged and sent back home on occasions because their parents could not pay school fees, some were flogged and sent out of the class because they could not afford textbooks in a society ridden with poverty and I could go on, our sisters and daughters sexually abused by lecturers in our higher institutions for marks because they are covered by a corrupt educational system in a corrupt and morally bankrupt country but you did not break the Nigerian spirit. Behold mother Nigeria, look on the many scars you have inflicted on your own children but you could not kill us all, here we stand before you and before the whole world. These people have survived all these and many more not listed here with the opportunity to go to these developed countries through scholarships or other means and they gave a good account of themselves. They did not receive a brain transplant as they landed in those countries, they did not get mind augmentation drugs, it was the same people but the only thing different for them now is that they are operating in a completely different system which even though it can present its own form of limitation for them over time has allowed them to showcase their abilities so I ask my question again: how has the state of the educational system in Nigeria contributed to the deplorable state of the country today?

The results and reports from our students in the diaspora if anything shows that we have the potentials for greatness if properly harnessed. The state of the schools and the schooling system while bad cannot be shouldered as the cause of the decay in the country because they are victims or more appropriately collateral damage of the war between the political ruling class vs. the masses whereby keeping the masses uneducated or poorly educated gives an advantage to the people that seek to dominate them. In the 'developed' world the children there do not attend schools as they did in the past because of debts from fees among other reasons, they go for training in specific roles with certifications and add that to experience which is enough for them. The students in the diaspora report that they have more of their African brothers and sisters along with Asians in their lecture halls than the local students so what does that say about formal education? The formal education is not perfect in Nigeria, it is heavily theory based as they have killed any form of practicality from the schools giving the students knowledge but giving them no way for them to utilise the knowledge also within their immediate society so that knowledge remains generally in latent form. In this case knowledge cannot be converted to power, it is taught and in the minds of those it has been taught to it stays there with the potential to create power but without the means to express the knowledge in society they have effectively and intelligently short-circuited the educational system in the country. Do you still think that the things in Nigeria are just happening randomly? The mechanical engineer graduates with the degree and finds a job in a bank as a cashier, the electrical engineer finishes from school and opens a boutique to sell clothes that were imported into the country, the chemical engineer graduates with her degree and becomes a social media influencer or worse still a lifestyle blogger doing stupid things on camera because that's how they get their coins so the effect of all that desire for knowledge is effectively neutralized because people have to eat and survive somehow.

If they get lucky they are able to travel out of the country to a better place with a better system where they are able to utilise the knowledge they gained from school and this has led to the brain drain where the top talents from home and on the continent all have to move to foreign countries outside of the motherland to actualise their dreams. It is an aberration and an anomaly and I will speak more on it later but first let me wrap up on formal education. Schooling in Nigeria was a false bottom for me, the state of it is another entry in the growing list of metaphors to describe the state of Nigeria as a country and how things are being done here. With the way I have described it to you, you can see how the simple idea and process of formal education has been rendered ineffective in the country due to the Nigerian factor and this also applies to other sectors of the society too.

INFORMAL EDUCATION:

I consider the informal educational sector to be an even bigger loss to the Nigerian people than the formal educational sector. This is because although the government schools are in shambles you still have the private schools that operate at a high level but sadly these schools are not within the reach of the average citizens as they cost a lot but the fact remains that they are there and they exist. For informal education I have taken a broad and loose approach to encompass all knowledge imparted outside a normal school environment in the country. They are vocational skills passed on by an experienced practitioner to apprentices by instruction and practice in private workshops for business and government established skill acquisition centres for a period of time until the apprentice is deemed as fit to strike out on his/her own to carry on the practice or trade having gained enough knowledge and experience in that particular field or skill. These include auto mechanics, tailoring, hair dressing, make-up, baking, welding, masonry, carpentry and a whole lot of others. The Nigerian society is a pit and 'limitation' is her middle name. In a modern world where development is driven by electricity, information technology, concrete, steel, iron and glass how does a country that does not have stable electricity or a proper indigenous IT industry, has a monopolized cement industry and one that does not manufacture her own steel, glass and other materials favourably compete? Look it's bad enough if a country does not have the natural resources and capabilities to manufacture these materials needed for development, many countries do not and cannot, but they still find creative solutions to these challenges but it's the worst when a country has the natural resources and the capabilities to manufacture these materials but does not because of politics, the politics of repression and the manufacture of poverty.

The sad story of Nigeria continues to be written in ink and in blood, the very blood of the forsaken because every Nigerian that has died an avoidable death due to the inadequacies of Nigeria as a country is a murder committed by the political ruling class. Children have been kidnapped in the hundreds at a time from right inside their school premises, some have been struck down by reckless drivers on their way to or from school because they had to walk long distances and the list goes on. All they ever wanted was to get an education to become better versions of themselves. People continue to ask me: why are there no jobs in Nigeria? And my answer is always the same, simple as ever: the country is not working because if it were working it would require people to work it so there goes that. The informal educational sector is trapped in survival mode with the rest of the country. Nigeria has no indigenous manufacturing industry and sadly the knowledge of manufacturing is not widely spread in the country for the people, they have no production culture so in essence have no real knowledge to pass on down to the coming generation. It's a country that relies heavily on importing finished goods from other countries for her survival through a single shipping port in Lagos for 200 million people, do you get the pathetic picture already or do I need to keep painting? The one steel factory in the country was allowed to die, same as other factories that were built around the 80s, whatever little manufacturing is done is not widely done and is done by a few people mostly with ties and links to the political ruling class because when you so effectively create poverty for a people with you controlling the resources who else would have the capital and resources to start anything of that magnitude in the country without your involvement in it? Another way they carry out this control is by licensing. The Nigerian government is a subset of the political ruling class so through the government they are able to control who gets the licence to do what so their control is absolute in the territory because they have the backing of political power behind them.

So in the informal educational sector Nigeria has no indigenous steel and iron industry, no indigenous glass making factory amongst others, the people are restricted to baking, hair making, rapping, clothes selling, internet influencer roles and other opportunities like them that while good or okay to survive on they cannot really drive the economic growth in the country. So and so wants a table or a bed made, Mrs B wants her hair done, mister A wants his house painted and such, the productivity of the people have been greatly limited and truncated by this, this is just as disastrous as the absence of stable electricity supply in the country and they work hand in hand to ensure that these people never escape the survival mode that they have been so conveniently placed in. Your car broke down? Oh poor you, the level or tradesmanship in the country is so poor and backward because of the Nigerian factor. This is due to the fact that the tradesmen have to practise in Nigeria with the knowledge, skills and materials available to them, sometimes I just have no words to describe the hatred I have for Nigeria. If you look at it from a spiritual background these are the destinies of people cut short, does it make sense to you yet? I don't know why I feel like I'm not exactly getting my points across to you properly. Look, if anyone of these people have the skills and the destiny to be a great welder for example who would have advanced the field of welding through mastery and innovations they could never attain their best version of themselves in their own country because of the many limitations she offers so despite the designation of that individual's destiny from the spirit realm it has been truncated by the environment they are born into, get it? Now multiply that effect for tens of millions in other fields and see what a catastrophic human resource waste is being politically engineered within that country and others like her. This is why you have the massive brain drain that has been happening in different forms for centuries now and these people are a loss because where they would have elevated their places of birth with their gifts they are pushed to contribute to the other lands and countries they emigrate to and those ones take the credit, all because they know they have no conducive environment in their home countries to be all they were destined to be initially. It is a sad thing for a society, a community or a country to always have to look outside of themselves for fulfillment, to have your young with the energy and strength in their bodies losing absolute hope and faith in your society knowing that leaving it is the only way they could ever become anything worthwhile in this world. It's never easy to be black because wherever it is they are escaping to racism and xenophobia is waiting for them with open arms but what would you have them do? The choices are simple: it's to sit back and have mother Nigeria swallow you up and spit out your bones or run away and take your chances in faraway lands... choose your destiny wisely and carefully.

So to wrap things up here, the limitations of the informal educational sector should be pretty much clear to you by now. You can get a Nigerian carpenter to make you a nice table or chair, you can get a Nigerian painter to paint your house for you and depending on his or her skill levels they'll do a great job for you, you can get a tailor or fashion designer to make a pretty native dress for your wife and she'll deliver but if you need to service a refinery for crude oil or produce steel and iron needed to create the parts of a factory that would use any of the many raw materials and natural resources found in the country to create finished goods to a high quality for exportation then you'll draw blank stares, where is the stable electricity supply to power that factory in the first place? You'll need to have a generator imported at a ridiculous price plus shipping, transportation and installation costs then there's the little matter about the daily costs of buying fuel for that generator and we haven't even looked at the cost of setting up the factory or paying the staff yet. In this way the political ruling class is effectively in control, they do not need to move house to house to know what the citizens are up to because they know and they know because they have painstakingly ensured the extent and the limitations of their capabilities perfectly.

FINAL THOUGHTS ON EDUCATION IN NIGERIA:

Most Nigerians view formal and informal education as different things but that's a misconception, I see them as the inseparable different faces of the same coin as they are meant to complement each other. There is a stigma on the informal sector but I think both need to come together to elevate Nigerian society. Culture is the way of life of a people, it encompasses the customs and traditions of their different ethnic groups but that's not all, it's the sum total of their lives, what they do and what they are capable of doing with the things available to them. The Nigerian culture as it currently stands is one of no production, dependency, breeding a victim mentality, it's a culture of dehumanisation, one that primes her people for exploitation, domination and repression. What's more? These people don't even know it and it's passed down from generation to generation. You might not agree with me now but think about it, if it were not so then the people would resist what's happening in their country right now but they seem to have accepted it and live side by side with it as the norm. How did I get to this conclusion? I asked myself that if a child is born into Nigerian society and spends a considerable time in the society going through the school system how's that child guaranteed to turn out in terms of their mentality and mindset due to the education they get from the Nigerian society? And the answer was simple, they'd turn out like the Nigerians we see in Nigeria today which is a people just one level above zombies. It's harsh and painful I know, it's not entirely their fault or making I know but it is what it is if a people are entirely locked indefinitely on survival mode then they are not exactly living are they? They are just surviving and existing and that's not what humanity is all about.

The extremely theoretical nature of the formal educational system in Nigeria is limiting in that it does not produce original thinkers and problem solvers, rather it produces literate people who are able to regurgitate what you fed to them. All of that is good but the country is in need of people who can think outside the box to tackle her many problems. The lack of research and development means that these people are at the mercy of whatever is handed to them by the 1st world countries which is not the position you want to be in when you're supposed to be competing against these people in the first place. There are no facilities for research neither is there a budget because even though the budget shows on paper that it's been set aside by the government, it has actually been embezzled and used to purchase luxury properties in New York or London with no one living constantly in them so there go the destinies of the Nigerians who should have been researchers and innovators.

> **'It is the glory of God to conceal a thing: but the honour of kings is to search out a matter'**
>
> Proverbs 25:2

The state of the public schools in the country is terrible but it's not the worst thing that could have happened. Don't forget they got Ivy league graduates and put them as technocrats in Nigeria and they all failed to perform because the way a country is set up to operate is more important than the beauty of the schools her children attend. Some of them succumbed to corruption and I ask you ever so humbly: what good is an Ivy league certificate in the face of the rapacious, ravenous and voracious Nigerian political corruption? Oh thou proud Ivy leaguer, what will your pretty certificate on the wall do for you in that office when you're finally faced with that roaring ferocious beast called Nigerian corruption? Many like you have come before and were marketed as saviours to the masses, they came in their pretty suits, spoke English in their fancy foreign accents, but

when they were weighed on the scales they were found wanting, so passion trumps certificates in this case. The Nigerian system in its design and operation is one of aggregated human wills to form political will, the country is a business deal and the interests of the business men and women come first. Sadly there have not been enough books written about this system of prebendalism yet to be taught in school. In conclusion, the public schools in Nigeria are in a deplorable state which is a shame because they could have been used to educate the young minds about the challenges and problems they'd face in their society as they grew older. The Nigerian masses have given up hope on their situation and just folded in submission so there is no push back.

HEALTHCARE

'Is there no balm in Gilead; is there no physician there? Why then is not the health of the daughter of my people recovered?

- Jeremiah 8:22

I bear them witness here that Nigerians are a religious people and some of them are truly spiritual in their religion but the main danger of an overly-religious mindset, an hyper-religious one for a people is that they tend to disregard the physical entirely for the religious to their own disadvantage I might add. Galatians 6:7b says that: **'A man reaps what he sows'**, so you place 2 things in front of a man and tell him that the one on the left is very good while the one on the right is good also; if he chooses to place his focus entirely on the very good and ignore the good then that man will not have balance in his life because he will reap the benefits of the very good thing and will be found lacking in the area of the good thing. So what is the implication of this? You will end up with a society of people who are hyper-religious but that society lies in a mess, now is this exclusively the fault of the people? Surely not, but as with all things they also had their part in it. One of my favorite stories in the bible is that of King Hezekiah as told in the book of Isaiah 38:1-5, it is a testament that a man in the earth can affect spiritual proceedings and in this case it was through prayers and supplications. I have heard this story preached many times by pastors and apostles both great and small about the importance and power of prayers and supplications because the man Hezekiah was sick and word came from God to him through prophet Isaiah that he was going to die but instantly he prayed to God and God spared his life adding 15 more years to his life. It's a beautiful story and you should read it for yourself, now you might already be wondering at this point where I'm going with my sermon when I'm supposed to be talking about healthcare in Nigeria but please, let me finish first. So, it was not until I read the bible for myself that I discovered that way down in verse 21 of that same chapter after the prophet had come back to deliver a new word of life from God to the king that he asked for medical treatment for him so he can recover. We humans, though spiritual beings have to exist in this plane as mortals for a time and a season; so if we disregard our time here what was the essence of being here in the first place? What will become of us during our time here?

    My spiritual walk though is one of balance, so even if I am quick to show you that king Hezekiah still needed medical attention after prophecy was given to him I must also point you to the woman with the issue of blood who had gone to many doctors and physicians spending all her money in the process but they could not cure her until she touched the hem of Jesus' garment and got her healing by faith (Luke 8:40 - 45). Would you then argue that the physicians she had been to were not good enough? Anyways, healthcare in Nigeria is readily available but not necessarily of a good standard, quality is too expensive for the masses and only reserved for the rich. Money is important everywhere in the world but it's the way it's used in Nigeria that deserves mention here. In Nigeria money is used as a barricade to keep certain people in and others outside, it's a gate that lets some in and keeps others out, it or the lack of it can either be the chain that keeps people in bondage or the bolt cutter that cuts it to set them free, it could be the blindfold that keeps men from the truth or the eye opener that reveals it to them... in this way the political ruling class operates almost as a separate entity within Nigeria, it's a state within a state, a little country within a country, an authority unto itself as the smaller country and externally unto the larger country. There is no in-between, you're either on or off, there is no middle class in Nigeria and if there were whatever is left of it is dying anyway so there's only the political ruling class and the masses, and as a citizen of that accursed place you either belong to one side or the other.

Services like healthcare, education and others are just the ripple effects, they are collateral damage of the battle to show you what Nigerian society has been degraded to and the nightmare that the average Nigerian has been made to live in. The average Nigerian has many cuts on their body, they are constantly leaking blood which is their life's force and their normal level is a weakened version of themselves, they are operating on a low level not because they are low but because they have been pulled down to that low level and kept there by forces greater than them that they've not even been able to properly identify yet or come up with strategies to combat. They are just poor reactors to the forces that shapes their lives, survivors and not in a good way, a people who have been stretched to their limits and beyond but are still being stretched as their natural resilience which should be a positive for them has been made a negative unto them, they are thrown into the dungeon and expected to adjust, to acclimatise themselves all the time to whatever gruesome conditions are laid out for them without complaint or resistance and in this weakened state they are somehow expected to still compete with the rest of the world who are doing their utmost best to win and to stay ahead, how can they compete? How can they manage it?

The Nigerian healthcare services for the masses is generally very poor. Just like the private schools there are private hospitals who provide a high quality service that comes at a high price that most Nigerians just cannot afford. As the Nigerian saying goes **'soup wey sweet, na better money kill am'** which in English means that 'the soup that turns out sweet requires the money to buy the spices and ingredients that make it sweet in the first place'. There is a consistent theme running here which I expect that you would have caught up on by now, everything the Nigerian government touches dies. They have many ministries, authorities, boards and the likes which act as capillaries and appendages touching every meaningful area of Nigerian existence by which they effectively, consistently and systematically choke out the life like a boa constrictor on its prey from every area of Nigerian society and existence such that their reach is absolute! There is hardly any escape except you leave their sphere of influence which is the Nigerian territorial space then you might have a chance to thrive but if you stay back mostly you'll be choked out by the poisonous cloud that they cast over the people in the space. You have a long coastline so why do you have only one sea port working? Why is the technology from that one working port from pre-independence times? Why are all your schools in such a deplorable state? Why do they keep regressing? Don't you want our children to be properly educated? Why are all your infrastructures in such a deplorable state? Why do you keep allocating budgets to fix these things yet they never get fixed for the people? Where is all the huge sums of moneys announced in the budget for these things and others going to? Why do my people have to suffer and be made to experience great pain just for you to enjoy? Why do the cost of government provided services keep rising when you know these people are poor? They have given everything even their human dignity, is that not enough for you? Are you not yet satisfied or do you still want more? You have taken everything from them and even when they have no more to give and they cry out for mercy you totally ignore them and squeeze them to get some more out of them, why?

When the high ranking members of the political ruling class in Nigeria fall sick and are in need of healthcare the former colonial masters like England and France are always waiting on the sidelines, eager to provide help and fulfil the Hippocratic oath of providing quality healthcare for all regardless of skin colour or dick size but even in the UK healthcare is not readily available to most UK citizens as they have to wait months but there's always room and bed space available for your favourite African politician that has a headache, do you doubt me? I've lived there for years so I know what I'm telling you. These African politicians are traitors to their own people but will always find love and care with the colonials because they have to keep them healthy and strong for the mandate and the agenda that has been going on for hundreds of years. When they exploit the black race and African peoples where do you think the resources are going to? Well I'll give you a hint; it's the same place the resources of the African continent have been going to for the past 500 years so try to figure that out. I fear no man or woman under the sun and I'll continue to speak my truth until the day I die, what's the worst that can happen to me seeing as they can only hurt my mortal body? There's an uncanny romance between African dictators and traitors of the African people with the Colonisers but we'll have more to say about that in a bit because we still have to look at the nature of healthcare provided in the country. When the children of the political ruling class want to go to school they send them to the Colonisers and other 'developed' nations where they pay exorbitant fees to those institutions while the schools at home which are rotting away are reserved for the children of the masses, who's fooling who here? And when the elites or their children need healthcare or some other services they are taken to the same people; the Colonisers and their capitalistic friends across the oceans but the masses are confined to the death traps called government hospitals and whether they live or die is entirely up to chance and the God they serve then you wonder why these people are overly religious? It's because somehow they know that they have no one else to depend or rely on except God.

    I'm staring at the blank canvas in front of me and you have a total view because you're staring at me from behind staring at the blank canvas. I have a wet paintbrush in my left hand that I've just dipped it into paint... you're a patient in a Nigerian government hospital laying on an old, rusty hospital bed space that your family had to pay extra for in bribes denying another patient and their family in the process who would require that bed space but they unfortunately could not come up with the extra bribe money that the doctors and nurses were asking for off the record so poor them, right? You're on the bed and while you're hooked to probably the only oxygen can in the hospital to pump life giving oxygen into your lungs to keep you alive the lights go out! The PHCN had just cut off power to the area that the hospital you're in is located at that moment, all is not yet lost right? There is a chance that maybe this might be one of the government hospitals that have a working generator on standby but sadly this is in the middle of fuel scarcity and the hospital staff were not able to procure gasoline or diesel required to run the generator to provide power for the hospital that night so one moment you have the members of your family around your bedside with anxious and worried looks on their faces and the next you've crossed over to the other side and your ancestors are welcoming you prematurely, is this a reach? Your children who could have had extra advantage with an extra parent around to shield them from such a harsh society just had that taken from them altering the course of their lives in the process, do you think I'm too dramatic about this? First of all let's take a moment of silence for the thousands if not millions of Nigerians lives that have been lost in this way and others like this due to the inadequacies of the Nigerian society. What makes this even more painful is that a lot of them were avoidable deaths, do you think I'm reaching here?

I cannot even begin to go into details the horrors I've personally experienced in Nigerian government hospitals or even the stories we heard with some even making the news and popular blogs. I've had to quickly drive home with a friend whose wife was in the process of delivering their baby, to pick up their personal generator set to power up the hospital so that the doctor and the mid-wives in the delivery room can have light to see as they are delivering their baby. There have been times when the flash light from mobile phones have been used to complete operations in theatres because the electrical power supply suddenly went off, the list goes on really. The pharmacies for drugs which Nigerians call 'Chemists' have sold fake, sub-standard imported drugs which have been sold to unsuspecting people with symptoms in the past that they have taken and still died. For the sake of balance some of the chemists did not know that the drugs were fake as they were supplied these drugs by people they have done business with for a long time. The truth is there have been crackdowns that have seen a reduction in such practices over the years but the story goes on and I hope I have painted an accurate enough picture to communicate to you about the state of healthcare in the country. The blacks are blessed with good genetics so you're better off not falling sick at all in the first place than falling sick and having to rely on the health care services available to the common folk in the country, that's when you know how faint and easily erasable the line between life and death really is. You are put face to face with death and you get to see how cheap a black life really is even in these so-called modern times and you get to see how easily your dreams, your aspirations, your pain, your hopes, your sorrows and your light can all be put out.

As for the training of the doctors and nurses it's like I highlighted when I talked about education in the country and told you that it's done at a good level or even at a high level theoretically but when we move over to the practical side of things that's when they see that things are done differently. This is why a lot of them try to branch out to start their own private practice but when they do they find out that it would cost a lot to do things the proper way due to a lack of the basics, a deficit in infrastructures in their immediate society, a lack of indigenous manufacturing which leads to importation of equipment if they can even scrape together the capital for them in the first place to start with and all those costs are sadly pushed unto the consumers, the clients, the patients and their families hence the high cost of private healthcare in the country. The medical professionals still in employment are always going on strike because of the treacherous conditions they are made to work in or the peanuts they are paid to do so. In the midst of the drama the ones that are able to do so find a way to emigrate taking their knowledge and skills with them into the waiting arms of the developed countries which is a loss for the 3rd world countries but do the leaders care? Why should they? If they ever fall sick all they need to do is travel out of Nigeria and they'll have the same people attending to them under a different employer so it balances out for them, it's the masses who have nowhere to go that suffer the loss.

Oh where have they put all your hospitals? Where are the modern medical equipment that should keep you poor, unloved and despised people healthy? Nigeria, where are your ambulances and your doctors? They have been put in fixed deposit accounts in Switzerland or some off shore island without taxes, they are tied down in properties in North America, why? Because you have to keep suffering and be poor in this world, why? You poor black Africans just have to be for this world to work. The money and resources from Africa have to go anywhere than to be re-invested back on African soil. Mother Africa knows, put your ears to the ground and you'll hear her heaving and quaking from deep in her bosom, she knows she's being ignored and neglected by her own children, she wonders to herself and has her own questions: is she not pretty enough? Not caring enough? Has she not tried her best to be a good mother? Then why do her own children continue to betray her and treat her so? The wealth and resources of the African continent will be dumped into the Atlantic ocean, shot into a black hole in space or set ablaze to be burned completely into ash if that's what it'll take to keep it out of the hands of the Africans themselves and this has been on for more than half a century counting to present times.

The warriors of the Nigerian healthcare sector still appear every now and then to remind us of what we can be. None other represents this more than the immortal Dr. Stella Ameyo Adedevboh (1956 – 2014), a truly great Nigerian, a physician who gave her life to prevent the spread of Ebola in Nigeria in 2014 by detaining patient zero of the virus in Nigeria, businessman Patrick Sawyer, a Liberian citizen who flew into the country with the virus from Liberia. The brave Dr. Stella held him under quarantine despite pressures from the Liberian government to release him to walk freely in the Nigerian public which would no doubt have spread the virus and led to unpredictable but grave number of deaths in Nigeria starting with the overcrowded Lagos and then spread to other parts of the country. I shudder when I think about what could have been had this woman not made that brave and crucial nation-saving decision and stuck to it because we all remember how devastating the virus was in Liberia. I have a very curious and peculiar mind so I would also one day like to personally ask the Liberian authorities the reasons for their continued pressures for his release into the Nigerian public when Mr. Sawyer was quarantined knowing he already had the virus. Sadly, this brave woman contacted the virus from patient zero in the process and died days later paying the ultimate price for her loved ones and her country. The healthcare system was and is nowhere near ready to deal with that kind of threat so that tells you the significance of what she did for all of us. There was no proper equipment to test and check for the virus but against all that she stuck to her gut feeling to quarantine him which by Nigerian standards meant keeping him in the hospital she operated from without proper equipment to handle the threat and protect herself at the same time *sigh* what a country! She must have known the dangers involved but persisted and had she been a coward she could have abandoned the situation to save herself and let the nation always sitting on the very edge to plunge into total chaos and catastrophe but that was not to be the case with brave Dr. Stella. It is for this reason that I honour her and hope that future generations get to know of her sacrifice for her country, she was a true Nigerian hero indeed in a nation without true patriotic heroes. She left behind her husband and son; respect ma, sincere thanks and may your soul continue to rest in peace, you will not be forgotten, amen.

*Dr Stella Ameyo Adedevboh, (1956 - 2014),
A true Nigerian hero and Patriot.*

THE CURE:

It's been a while since I used an analogy, I did so many of them at the start that I had to hold back but I think it's okay if I drop this one here. Just imagine for a moment that humans all over the world had a sprain problem and sprain being a physical problem impairs the use of the affected limb or joint causing great discomfort and pain. The blacks in their usual manner would explain the sprain away to their kids in one of their numerous folklores as one of those things in life that the gods gave to us that we must live with and in true resilient manner they will then try to adjust their lives to the sprain. The whites in their inquisitive way would study the sprain, fiddle with it, carry out research and tests on it until they eventually come up with a cure for the sprain. The cure would then be applied with great results in the land of the white men freeing a lot of their people from the sprain problem which means that they are already ahead in this problem, then they would eventually decide to pass the cure to the black man in their lands who has sprain too. The 'passing' down of the cure could be in the form of sales which is commerce that would further enrich the white man or some selfless and philanthropic white men might just decide to cover the cost and it gets passed on for free. So anyways, they pass the cure along to the black man but there is a problem... the cure is not working or even if it is, it is not working effectively. What could be the reason for this?

That cure could have landed at the Lagos port for free and some high- ranking individuals in the political ruling class through the puppets and sleeper agents they had previously installed in the organisational leadership hierarchy of the government agencies responsible for things like the cure could have them hoarded in warehouses secretly getting the first doses to their family members and friends, the supply and availability has to be controlled to create scarcity don't forget that. Then they can put a price on it to make money off the already poor Nigerian masses, if the cure came at a price then they can add their mark up to it keeping it further out of the reach of the Nigerian people and you can see that money has been effectively used as a barricade to keep the masses from the cure. 'Oh but, what would be their motivation to do that?' Well don't forget that these 2 groups are in a war with the political elites dominating and exploiting the masses for control so it would not be in their interest to see the masses cured of their sprain and running around freely because then they could run their way to freedom effectively ending the way of life of the political elites. These are not the only tricks they have in their bag though, they could just perform soulectomy on the cure to make it ineffective now how would they accomplish that?

The thing is that while everybody had the 'sprain' problem, the white man had his on his left hand while the black man had his on his right leg. You have to take into account the Nigerian factor i.e the unique characteristics of each society so the cure appears already made as a finished product on the Nigerian ports which means they have no idea of how it was made or the steps it took to create it and they do not have the knowledge or the capabilities to create this cure for themselves or even make modifications to it which puts on them the disadvantage of ignorance and dependence because whatever is it in that cure? Something could have been slipped in there on the shipments meant for the black lands and no one would be the wiser and we have to keep going. Never mind the hoarding, price barricade and the other shenanigans that would have affected its availability and proliferation to the average Nigerian but the blacks take this cure and start to apply it to their left hand following the instructions given with the product and are surprised to find out that they are still limping. So you see a product or an idea that has had great success in other lands reduced to rubbish in the black lands, the international media would not cover it properly and the message that gets put out into the universe would be how these people are useless and nothing good could ever come out of them and that would be that. While all this drama is playing out the Japanese collect the cure, study it, break it down and try to recreate or re-engineer it from scratch.

Well they are one of the remoras attached to the big fish so they could even have the formula of the cure passed along to them to recreate for themselves and their people, the Chinese will try to copy the cure and make a cheaper version of it to satisfy their multitude population. They will test and apply it to their own people with great success even going ahead to make some changes to it and combining it with their native acupuncture that they have done traditionally for thousands of years to try to get better results. In this way they have been able to combine a new technology or methods to their existing ones to combat a new threat ensuring that they do not lose their identity or traditions in the process and this is how the world works. It's something that black people have not been able to have for themselves and it shows around the world. People take care of their own but the average black man or woman or child is a vagabond in the earth and they as a people have just not taken enough time to look at this very crucial flaw of theirs but the effects are witnessed all around us every day. When the Chinese finally succeed in making a cheaper version of the cure the Igbos would go over there to import it back to Nigeria to sell it, they would be hailed as business geniuses by the people because they would have helped cover to an extent the deficit of the availability of the cure to the Nigerian masses that their leadership would not do for them. This would further enrich them as a people but would add no significant benefits to the Nigerian people as a collective in the long term in helping them get better at preparing, tackling and solving further sprain problems and others like it and this is no fault of the Igbos, it's just business for them. They are not the political leadership of the country so the expectation or responsibility to solve such problems and develop the country in that manner rests with the government but this is just the way things are.

SPORTS

'It is only the offspring of slaves that allow America to be competitive athletically. American Olympic gold can be measured in negro sweat.'

Dr. Joseph Goebbels

Inglourious Basterds (2009)

The whole world and the nations within it are in open or secret competition with themselves so who do losers who came into the competition unprepared have to blame for their continuous loss? Now, is it not even the more painful when the losers had obvious advantages over the competition that they failed to capitalize on in the first place to give themselves an edge? In terms of preparedness as an advantage in competition this reminds me of the parable of the ten virgins told by Jesus Christ in Matthew 23:1-13 and how 5 of the virgins came prepared to wait on and meet the groom while the other 5 missed out because they came unprepared and did not carry extra oil for their lamps. The consistent contradictory patterns that we have seen in every aspect of Nigerian society are also glaring in sports when a country of 200 million physical and genetic specimens just cannot seem to produce athletes and teams that go into world competitions with other nations to dominate and win medals or even to compete favourably for national pride, dignity and bragging rights.

I know that for some people it's just 'sports' when the athletes of the nations of the world compete in the Olympics and other global, continental or regional sporting events but the performance in these competitions can also be an indicator into the health and status of the countries. A bad performance could be the case of a nation with a little population and not enough sample size to select athletes to create a team for that competition or it could be just a bad year for that nation sports wise, it could also just be some countries having the advantage in certain competitions like height in basketball or a disadvantage like traditionally hot countries participating in winter sporting events but even with technology artificial equipment can be used to mimic the competition's conditions in the hot countries for the athletes to train, practise with and to develop their skills to still compete favourably with the winter countries while for other countries bad performances in sporting events could point to other more sinister and deep lying problems; whatever the case is nobody likes to lose at the end of the day.

    My interests in sports is not just on the medals and the glory of winning competitions over rivals, all that is good and makes for good banter but my interest is in the fact that sports is a big global business involving the movements of large sums of money as salary, winner's prize, participation fees, bonuses, revenues from sponsors and many more so I try to see how much of those are flowing into Nigerian hands and if they aren't we have to look at the reasons why. As often with sports the viewers get lost in the excitement of the sporting event, patriotism or love for team that they do not care to look at the movement of moneys involved in those competitions. By following the money it's important to see who gets what in these events and why they get it so the question remains on why a good chunk of that global sporting money is not flowing into Nigerian hands. If Nigeria is said to be a country in poverty, and she is, you would wonder why she is not doing more to position herself to get a larger market share of the global sports money but then with everything we have discussed thus far it is easy for you to picture the state of sports in the country as influenced by the theories I presented to see the reason why. Like in the case of education you could have argued that the people from the country are just dull, dumb and intellectually incapable of being educated but these children have gone on to other schools around the world and dominated, giving a good account of themselves in the process so that argument cannot stand. For sports you could also have argued that maybe the people are not athletic enough despite the way they look physically but the athletes have gone on to compete in different sporting events under different nations representing different flags, jerseys and badges and they have won important things in the process so what's the problem? The common denominator in all this is their home countries. It is a terrible thing I repeat, when the young and vibrant people of a country cannot look within themselves but have to constantly keep looking outside of that nation for fulfilment, completion and for them to ever become anything in this world that we live in. What is it that's peculiar about the country that differentiates it to the others these young people are running to? Deep in their hearts they know it, and it is general knowledge that their chances of greatness would be truncated if they were to stay back in their own countries, this is the brain drain we have been talking so passionately about because for each one these talents that leaves for greener pastures it's a loss to the home country; dear mother Nigeria, why dost thou keep eating thine seeds?

My opening text is fictitiously attributed to the Minister of Propaganda, Dr. Goebbels during the Nazi regime in Germany. As a black person, you might become quickly offended by the strong racial undertones in that quote but I say do not let your emotions distract you from the message the quote carries. I feel like I have to present to you some history and background so you can understand the significance of that quote. The line was used in the movie *Inglourious Basterds* by writer and director Quentin Tarantino who always uses racial tensions for effect in his movies. This particular movie of his featured a fictional take and outcome of the 2nd World War but it retains some real life characters that existed during the time and the person that inspired this quote was a real life person, an African American athlete called Jesse Owens who won 4 gold medals during the 1936 Olympic games setting a new world record for the 100m sprint in the process at the time. This black man's contributions and achievements will forever be under that flag but It's astounding the amount of racism and abuse we've allowed ourselves as a people and as a race to endure in this world at the hands of the other races. The Americans would claim that Hitler had snubbed Mr Owens and refused to congratulate him like other athletes of different colours after his wins but by his own account Mr. Owens said that Hitler stood up and gave him a friendly Nazi salute when he walked past his booth on the last day when the athletes paraded around the stadium to greet the crowds who had come to watch the games. Guess who did not even provide him with proper running shoes as one of their athletes to begin with? He had to run his races in German made Adidas shoes and when he got back 'home' to America he was not even invited to the white house by then US President Frank Roosevelt to be congratulated like the other white athletes nor was he even sent a telegram. As if that was not enough he had to use a side entrance to access the building where a banquet was organised in his honour because of racism in the very country he just represented and won all those medals in their name. A movie was made to tell this great black man's story called *Race (2016)* but you know that as is their manner real events had been 'dramatised' to present a more positive outlook. This is not even my focus but I feel like we have to preserve certain truths for ourselves and the generations to come after us so that we can stay reminded; the falling of the brown dry leaves whereafter they are gathered to be burned is a warning to the green leaves.

    I'm trying my best not to get sucked in to do a full blown piece on Mr. Owens so I'll just provide some more little details about his life and move on. After the publicity surrounding his record breaking performances at the '36 Olympics Mr. Owens could not compete any more as poverty made him drop out of school so he could support his family. Not even the hard work he had put into his performances or the 4 gold medals he won could protect him and the point I just want to make is that from a black perspective both Nazi Germany and the United States were discriminatory towards him and this is why I have never been able to buy into the 'Nazi Germany was bad while the allies were good' narrative till this day as a black man, but guess which of the countries black people are still being gunned down in broad daylight in till this very day? I'll give you a hint; they like to open their mouths wide and scream empty words like 'freedom' and 'democracy' all the time. Anyways, my main focus in that opening text is the part that says: **'American Olympic gold can be measured in negro sweat'**, I know it's derogatory and offensive to black people but it acknowledges the fact for me that under the right conditions black people can compete, win and get paid in sports so if American Olympic gold is measured in Negro sweat what is the Nigerian Olympic gold measured in? Have they any gold to be weighed in the first place? What's the situation like in Nigeria today?

The story is the same and there will unfortunately be no exception for sports. In fact, I could have copied and pasted one of the earlier chapters just switching the name to match the current header and you'll have your story but that would be too repetitive so I had to switch up the formula; even the side piece on Mr. Owens was one of that so as not to bore the reader. Where people see just plain chaos in Nigeria I see a machine, a living breathing dynamic machine designed to fulfil the purpose it was created for. If it is certain that things will not work here until you move to some other country then it means that something is wrong here to begin with. People ask me why there is so much unemployment and poverty in Nigeria and I tell them the same thing every time that it's because the country is not working because if it were then she would most definitely need her citizens to work her and they would get paid in the process; this is the molecular theory of wealth creation. How was this situation achieved? They continuously took all the money out of her from all the sectors and like a boar constrictor choking out its prey they let her die a slow and drawn out death only that the purpose is not really to kill her in this case but she is dead already, Nigeria is a dead country because certain types of existence are just as good as or even worse than death. I heard a saying once and I don't know who said it but it says that some people died in their twenties but got buried in their seventies, this properly explains what I mean when I say that Nigeria is a dead country already.

When the political elites take out all the money and the resources from the different sectors of society they are essentially killing that sector. The people who are supposed to be motivated to work and earn in that sector will no longer be able to do that because of the poverty and the fact that they have to make a living somehow which means that whoever is embezzling money out of the different sectors of Nigerian society know exactly what they are doing and what will happen to those sectors and the people in the country after they take the money out. People of the masses who should have been athletes, coaches, trainers, nutritionists, physiotherapists, team doctors, chefs, grounds men and women, those in charge of kits, referees and officials, ushers, security, mascots and many more working directly with the athletes cannot exist, when you think of other associated professionals like those that grow the special foods the athletes would require, truckers that supply the foods and other equipment around the country, then those that make the sporting equipment like balls, nets, bats, shoes, jerseys, whistles, flags, red card, yellow card, watch, chairs in the stadium and this list goes on and on and on, you begin to get the picture. This is destiny exchange where an entire economy and productivity of a people is being sabotaged in real time with incalculable loss to the Nigerian people who without the funds cannot give their all in that particular field. If they somehow exist despite all these challenges then their numbers are greatly reduced and it becomes a case of the rose from the concrete with the damaged petals where they might never be able to showcase their very best. This is due to time lost just trying to survive the harsh conditions they were born into that greatly hampers their development and hinders their performance. In such a case where they do come up against athletes from other countries that do not have to worry about these same things but to train and practise to get better you can see that it would take extraordinary talent and grit to level the playing field if ever.

In this way you can see that the continuous embezzlement of the Nigerian resources by the political ruling class is a strategic social engineering move designed to create a specific type of environment of poverty and lack that will have waves of ripple effects spreading out to cover the entire nation like a net or a blanket. In that way if you were an aspiring footballer, the members of the Nigerian elites do not need to come to your house to break your legs in person to kill your dreams. Just by the environment that they have created and continue to maintain and sustain it will ensure that despite your skills and your desires there will be a lack of opportunities and proper modern equipment for you to attain the heights of your dreams, am I making any sense to you? As for the hunt you can see the elements of isolation whereby Nigeria is not part of any sporting circuits despite the many of them available. If it's a government and an elite whose aim was not to impoverish her own people so that they can be malleable they could have put facilities in place to hook into the circuits of tennis, golf, formula one and a lot of other sports that would boost tourism, local businesses and give the local talents a chance to shine on the global stage but no, why should they do that? So just like the buffalo which the lions separated from the herd so that they can feast on, a country like Nigeria is effectively cut off from such activities so that her predators can feast on her, unopposed, with no external help for her. A lot of you still think that this is just blind greed for money to build lavish houses, buy expensive foreign cars and high fashion by your ruling elites but this is a very clinical operation being executed right before your eyes, right under your noses and you're all oblivious to it. How long will you continue to drink, smoke and fuck yourselves to stupor ignoring the fact that you're being robbed and you're powerless to do anything about it? If you cannot face this thing and stop it in your generation it will be here waiting for your children.

Whatever stadiums that exist in Nigeria are in a run down and dilapidated state, no maintenance is done on them, the equipment are old, outdated, broken, vandalized or looted for cash like the equipment and books in the government schools. The roads leading to these facilities are terrible, power supply is not constant so who will buy and run generators for sporting events? The safety and security of event goers cannot even be guaranteed in these facilities so that tells you the general state and level of sports in the country. The back offices are just as terrible or even worse, there are ministries and bodies created to further the will and desires of the ruling class and they do a fantastic job of poisoning the waters to ensure that nothing survives their onslaught. It looks like the corruption in sporting bodies is world wide with what we saw exposed in FIFA some years ago, they were running that body like a democratic African nation and we could see the effects in the sport. The corruption is choking and there is no space to breathe; who can say that when we send out a team to represent the country we're sending out our very best at that moment? The corruption breeds its ugly heads in things like nepotism and ethnic race in team selections, godfatherism where some people are wards of powerful members of the political elites which ensures their continuous selection for national duty rather than on merit so that can also affect team performance. Who will survive these conditions? And you want me to be angry when some athletes are fortunate enough to escape these conditions to represent other countries? You want me to call them unpatriotic? How can I do such a thing? My conscience would not allow me because I am very familiar with what those athletes are running away from, I am aware that like me they love their country dearly but just cannot stay back. I am torn in the middle but I will not call them unpatriotic for not staying to work and care for a country that never cared for them all their lives.

Corruption is a terrible beast indeed, she sits atop the pinnacle of the pyramid of Nigerian sports roaring in every direction to announce her presence in broad daylight without fear or worry of being seen. She urinates down that pyramid on the heads of all within it marking her territory and letting everyone know that this belongs to her and she will not let go. In 2013 four teams in the Nigerian domestic football league played two matches that yielded 79 - 0 and 67 - 0 scorelines in a match fixing scandal for the ages which should say everything there is to say about corruption in Nigerian sports. So how does a country like this go on to host major sporting tournaments? You do not have the stadiums and facilities for it, you do not have the supporting infrastructures required for transportation, medical and nutritional purposes, you cannot even guarantee the safety of your visitors due to insecurity in the country. I imagine FIFA would use their bribe monies to pay kidnapping ransoms for years after that tournament. So when next you see that black athlete on the tracks or field getting ready to do what they have trained all their lives for and dreamed for and fought hard and terrible circumstances for, no matter the flag on their shirt, no matter the colours they represent, it doesn't matter if you like them personally or not just give them a second look and say a little prayer for them in your heart because now you at least know a little about the struggles that have shaped them.

THE ARTS

'The life of the arts, far from being an interruption, a distraction, in the life of the nation, is close to the centre of a nation's purpose - and is the test of the quality of a nation's civilisation'

- John F. Kennedy

Artists are gods because they create, a good and respected artist friend of mine once told me that: *a real artist knows he does not create but that he is being created through.* Art is life, art is expression, art is brilliance, true art is inspiring, art is perfection and imperfection, art is boundless, art is culture, art is therapeutic, art is liberating, art is an explosion... and in summation... art is everything. My father was a lover and a collector of art works, I grew up in a home filled with art pieces like paintings, metal works, mosaics, original ivory works, bead works, wood sculptures and many others. At a young age, I spent a lot of time after school wandering around the house staring, touching and marvelling at pieces of art works in his collection and they made quite an impression on me. The details of the craftsmanship were amazing, our mother always told us not to touch them for fear that we would break them but even though I was a good boy that listened to his parents I always looked around to make sure that no one was watching before I touched them. It was a big house and there were many diverse works, paintings that show village scenes from the past, they show our origin and who we really are from our small peaceful villages with a quiet and easy going lifestyle hung on the walls. One of my favourites was that of a fisherman and his son returning late from a day of fishing in his canoe, the darkened skyline on that one was the backdrop. Because of the interplay of the dying natural light of the setting sun on the horizon coupled with the settling darkness of dusk it created an interplay between the light and the darkness in frame presenting the fisherman, his son with him in his canoe and a flock of birds flying past at that exact moment in a kind of mesmerising silhouette which still managed to retain some details; such expert craftsmanship and they were all made in Nigeria.

I remember rubbing my palms on some of the paintings feeling the individual brush strokes of the artist in the dried paint on the canvas and the connection had been magical, it was like being transported back to that time. I could not speak to anyone about it until now and I think my mother will finally understand why I spent so much time with my father's paintings but when I touched them sometimes it had felt like I was there in person as in like I was in the painting itself. I could connect vividly with what the artist was trying to depict like I was there, I could smell the fresh air and feel the cool evening breeze on my face with the fading warmth of the sun, I could hear the flapping wings of the birds and the sounds they made as they flew away probably returning home to feed their chicks after a day spent looking for food, it was like I could also see the trees swaying gently to the cool breeze too. Like I said it was magical and I always felt that it was because our father took us constantly back to our village of origin for us to connect with our roots that's why I had those feelings when I rubbed on the paintings, maybe I was reliving those experiences through his paintings in the house.

When I speak about the arts in Nigeria I am lumping it all in with entertainment to cover not just tangible art works but entertainment like music and movies created by Nigerians in Nigeria. There is not much to say other than that the limitations of the society still affects the arts. A people locked in survival cannot fully unleash their creativity nor can they have the time to appreciate art, their attention and waking hours are geared towards surviving and satisfying the insatiable stomach god that every human carries. The music has been an escape for young Nigerians but the drawback to that is that a people who are trapped in the pit of poverty see it as their only way out. This has affected the quality of the finished product being put out as people lacking in the talent to create music who have no business being in the studio in the first place have all rushed into music making in the hopes that they can escape the confines of their immediate environment through the arts. It's not only in afro-beats made in west Africa, sadly hip-hop that has been a platform of expression for black people to get our stories and messages across has been overrun by these hustlers. The quality of the output has been low and the corruption in Nigeria has seen pirates illegally copy and duplicate the works of artists and sell them to make profits with no justice for the artists they are stealing from in the first place. The government has not done anything to help, the limitations of the environment has not stopped creatives from putting out their works to a global audience. The internet and new technology has opened the Nigerian arts to a wider global market and even though they say true art comes from a place of pain, I just wish to see our people create without the many shackles that hold them down and prevent them from immortality.

    I have been a recording artiste in Nigeria making music so I'm very familiar with the struggles involved. First of all you have to find a studio with the right equipment and personnel to create sounds with that you can afford, then you also have to deal with the incessant power outages sometimes while you are in the midst of creating and recording and that is no joke. I cannot recall how much I've spent to fuel generators in studios after I had paid for my recording session, the responsibility to provide power during the booked session falls on the artist so we have to carry our share of the inadequacies and inability of the Nigerian government to guarantee stable power supply for her citizens. All of this you have to cope with in one way or another and we were driven by our passion but the struggle was very much real to us. All these disruptions ate into our productive time and also were a source of distraction to us in an industry where focus was needed to produce so we were not spared from the Nigerian factor. Also the corruption in the industry to promote songs in radio and other forms of media is too tiring to expand on, it was walls and more walls to be broken down by the artist if they were ever able to advance and sadly, like the net that has been cast in Nigerian society in different forms a lot of talented people that would have lit up stages on a global scale had they been allowed to blossom and manifest got lost along the way.

    The Nigerian music industry is one of the most dynamic in the world currently. The movie industry called Nollywood is one of the largest in the world coming just behind Hollywood and Bollywood but the quality of movies put out still leaves a lot to be desired. In my opinion the music industry in Nigeria is currently ahead of the movie industry and will be for some years to come but there's still a lot of room to grow and develop for both. This has not stopped the creatives within the country to continue to find new technology and new ways to leverage on and share their talent with the world despite the great disadvantages they face. If with these limitations the artists are still able to break through to win the most prestigious awards on the planet one can only imagine what they can do with the right environment and the right support with funds available for them to truly share their creativity with the world. Piracy has not been eliminated from the industry because in the Nigerian set up the criminal elements have an important role they play on the masses on behalf of the ruling class which makes this system as it is in Nigeria to be possible in the first place. In conclusion I'd just like to say that with an estimated 200 million people Nigeria has the capability to create an internal market for her art products which can then be exported and properly monetized to a foreign global market which will in turn run and sustain an indigenous supply. There is no shortage of talents in the country in the different aspects of the art but sadly the Nigerian factor has eaten deep into the fabric of the nation rippling into every area of human existence within the territory. What we see today might seem good but can actually be better, the training and opportunities required for our artists to compete favourably with the rest of the world will only serve to create more opportunities for our creatives and boost the economy in the process leading to a better quality of life in general but this is not so and the reasons for that are known by now.

JOURNALISM AND THE NIGERIAN MEDIA

'The media is the most powerful entity on earth; they can make the innocent guilty and the guilty innocent.'

- Malcolm X

One thing I've always admired about the political ruling class in Nigeria is the soft but effective way they've carried out their operations in the country with as little sudden outward disruptions as possible to the everyday lives of the people. This strategy of theirs is why I used the boa constrictor and death by a thousand cuts analogies in my theories because the soft approach creates a false sense of normalcy, peace and quiet for the unsuspecting masses and puts them at ease taking their attention off the political ruling class as they introduce consistent little changes into the country that will ensure that their objectives are met over time and sustained in the country. This is subterfuge; the magician's gentle art of deflection and distraction used in a political manner over 200 million people that have still not been able to totally figure out what's being done to them. Generals know that in battle you're allowed to admire your adversaries without letting your admiration interfere with your duties, you can study them, learn lessons and techniques from them that you can incorporate into your own operations that will make you a better professional or operator depending on the situation but you cannot beat an opponent that you haven't studied to learn their ways and weaknesses. It is after you have studied their modus operandi and weaknesses that you can then formulate effective counteractions to combat them and to defeat them.

As a Nigerian you might dislike or even strongly hate the political ruling class, your emotion would be understandable to me and justified but to totally ignore the expertise they have displayed and the willingness that they've shown to adapt to changing conditions is where the Nigerian people and the Nigerian masses have committed mass suicide. For example as a group they have successfully moved away from the violent coups and counter coups of the 70s and 80s that threatened to destroy their way of life because they claimed lives and created bad blood within the elites. In doing that they have maintained the peace within their ranks and stayed focused as a group on their objectives which have never changed throughout the decades. Their deep knowledge of the Nigerian people has seen them avoid the mistake of unnecessary violence of their colonial predecessors because that would give the people an enemy to unite against and cause them to revolt at some point in time choosing instead to use violence sparingly to maintain their power and control during election cycles, to take out some prominent problematic elements that caused disruptions for them within the system and using it in proxy allowing other actors to do the dirty work and take the heat, blame and hate from the masses which creates total deniability for elites and distances them from the mess should the need ever arise.

One of the questions I meditated and pondered on a lot in 2012 was: how would the political ruling class react if the masses ever challenged their power? I thought of this question so much and it appeared on my first hand-written version of this book. That question was answered for me in the October 2020 Lekki tollgate massacre but that was an aberration and a disruptive occurrence in the Nigerian matrix as it's not the normal way the elites operate. By consistently projecting the image and the illusion of peace and quiet in the country they have carried out their operations and gone about their business undisturbed and unopposed. If any external observer was looking they would never suspect what was happening just as a lot of the masses within the country do not suspect what's happening to them, all the observer would see is a 'young' democratic country that's still in the 'developing' stage with a lot of problems that they are struggling to solve to provide a better life for their people. The situation will even evoke sympathy and help from the foreign observers but they like the people living in the country i.e the citizens would have been fooled again by master con men and women carrying out their operations in broad daylight. What has been the outcome of this their soft approach so far? It's seen in the success they've achieved in terms of their objectives, the duration of this their success and the fact that they've had as little disruptions and opposition from the people over the duration and it goes on.

We're supposed to be talking about journalism and the Nigerian mass media here so why have I taken the time and gone through the pains of this elaborate introduction and explanation? It's because we're going to briefly look at how a powerful entity like the media which is considered as the 4th estate of power in a democracy has been stripped down and rendered powerless, effectively turning what should have been a ferocious and fearful guard dog into an obedient and toothless pet that's constantly seeking for treats, pats and belly rubs. My opening text in this chapter by Malcolm X shows you the power of the media but a part of this that never gets talked about much is that: if they can make the innocent guilty and the guilty innocent what does that still say about those still wondering if humans as smart and intelligent beings can be controlled? And one more question for you while we're asking questions is that: if an entity has this much power to control humans what powers would the person that controls such an entity have? The Nigerian media as the other topics we've looked at so far is another metaphor for Nigeria as a country. It's an idea that has worked well in other places but crosses into the Nigerian space and gets acted upon by the Nigerian factor with a surgical soulectomy carried out on it that by the time it begins to operate in the country it retains only its name with all the other vital elements necessary for its effectiveness effectively stripped off.

Democracy is supposed to be a government of the people, by the people and for the people but Nigerian democracy exists in this form only theoretically in documents, pamphlets and the likes, in practical it operates in a very different manner as I've stated throughout this book where there are 2 distinct groups within the larger country. All the pillars of power in society are accumulated and congregated within the smaller political ruling class leaving nothing for the masses which creates the first foundational problem for the Nigerian masses which is the fact that they simply have no people power. Since this is so the Nigerian equation is imbalanced with power which is the ability to make things happen massively abundant with one party and non-existent with the other. Without the other pillars of power the masses could still have had some inherent power due to their sheer numbers but acute social fission and a lack of unity has ensured that their power share has been split up into many smaller interest groups who can do no significant damage individually against a united elite group. When these individual small groups try to go against the united elites, the elites are able to adsorb whatever force they exert creating a disequilibrium in the system with the scales massively tipping in the favour of the elites. The power of the media is derived from people power in that they seek out information and broadcast it to the masses influencing how they think and act in the process but when the masses have no people power the media is stripped of a great deal of their own powers and are left like the rest of the country to survive under the terms of and at the mercy of the political ruling class; this is the first death of the Nigerian mass media and its foundational problem that's beyond their control. They say information is power but information can also be powerless because what if I somehow get the plans to a nuclear bomb as I said earlier and give those plans to a people who don't even produce the cups and plates they use to eat daily in their homes how much power will that information I've given to them generate for them? Does it magically transform Nigeria into a nuclear power? You know the answer to that.

Among the two warring groups in the land, one of the main objectives of the ruling class is total control and absolute domination of the masses in the land which is a must if they're to carry out their exploitation agenda without resistance from the masses. This principle can be seen in the parable of the strongman as told by Jesus in the gospels (Matt 12:29, Mark 3:27 and Luke 11:21-22) where the protector has to first be overpowered and tied down before you can plunder his house and his resources. So when the protector is securely tied down and his trusty home security system sends him an alert that there could be possible intruders on his property what will he do in that situation? In fact the real question is: what can he do? The isolation strategy is when all means to call for outside help or automatically inform the police are disabled and the intruders go on about their business quietly leaving the lights as they are, even if the neighbours were to look at that house from the outside it would seem like a normal night in the neighbourhood making that house a closed system for the crime to be committed. The soft approach of the elites has seen them not rely on violence in their quest to control the media like have been seen in places like say Mexico where reporters have been violently executed by the cartels. This brings unwanted attention and could scupper the plans for the elites so they used other methods. The poverty they artificially created in the land worked in their favour as they also control the resources so it's like they start a war with only them having the ammunition, food and medical supplies... in such a situation the war becomes theirs to lose. Weaponised poverty became the second death for the Nigerian media because it made the members of the media vulnerable to compromise where they could no longer carry out their duties in an impartial manner due to low patronage from the impoverished masses who have no disposable income. This is where the infamous term known as 'brown envelope' journalism has become so popular in Nigeria today because the journalists in the different forms of media who are compromised already receive money in brown envelopes from the elites to write stories and for sure they would not write unbiased stories nor would they write against the source of the brown envelopes on which they depend for their own survival... another section of Nigerian society has been successfully soulectomized.

There are many other ripple effects of weaponised poverty on the Nigerian media in which it affects their operating level, output and the quality of the work they are able to do. When we say Nigeria is stuck in the past or actually regressing the weaponised poverty plays a huge part in this in all areas of Nigerian society. All of these factors are working together to create what you see as the reality in Nigeria today: without access to stable power supply, the latest technology and equipment, lack of proper transportation infrastructures, information and communication infrastructures, lack of proper training for the journalists and associated professionals you already know that the level of the output on the TV would not be able to compete with the developed countries of the world as it would come out in a substandard manner, this is the third death of the Nigerian media. So when you ask the question: why are all these 3rd world countries so bad at everything? Well there you have your answer and I know you're not going to ask why there are so many unemployed people in the country, right? All of these many shortcomings affect not only the local media coverage but also the area they can cover in terms of their reach and the speed with which they can cover the news and relay it back to the masses. Another key ripple effect of all this is that people now have access to cable and satellite TV so they are now addicted to foreign productions and publications which leads to a disconnect between the people and their society as they cannot be properly informed about the day to day happenings in the very society they live in. This ripples into ignorance of the masses and even though they say ignorance is bliss there's nothing blissful about this because the adversaries are able to carry out their evil deeds in silence and in secrecy without the knowledge or disruption of the people so even if you knew nothing about the tree that fell in the forest yesterday evening the fact remains that it fell and crushed whatever poor hiker or animal was unfortunate enough to be in its path when it fell.

The fourth death for the Nigerian news media comes in the form of control and their habitual soft approach is employed in this sector too. They shun all out censorship even though fines have been issued in the past to various outlets for going against the grain and the narrative but their master stroke was in using whatever government backed body or authority is responsible for approving licences for radio and TV stations to control which applications for licences they would approve through corruption. Do you see how these people move? Can you observe the intricacies and the multiple layers to their schemes? So in this way if they suspect that an applicant will not conform to their will their application could be under review indefinitely even after they have followed all the proper procedures mandated to apply and paid the necessary fees. Let me just add this as it's not limited to the media sector alone but another strategy they use through the boards and authorities is the money barricade where they astronomically increase the price for that government provided service overnight which the people cannot afford and stopping a significant percentage of them and discouraging others in the process. All of this should tell you by now that this Nigerian situation is not just about blind looting, corruption and greed, this is systemic and structural violence, irrefutable evidence of social engineering at work and I just had to mention that just in case you were still wondering at this point. The result of all this is that there are a few media outlets tying into the scarcity strategy that makes them easier to monitor and control by the ruling class. What are your local alternatives as a citizen? The state government owned media outlets are just as run down as everything else in the country so in this generation of social media and European football are you going to ask a Gen Z Nigerian why they do not follow their local news channels to be informed about the happenings in their state?

The death continues because when you do your research to find out that the owners of the 'private' media outlets are all politicians or politically affiliated individuals then you can see that the circuit has been firmly closed and we can all pack our bags to go home now as it's game over. This is how an effective system to manufacture the failure of a successful idea works because if you were a fresh graduate from a school for journalists in the country with a deep and burning desire to report the news and expose evil who employs you? What are your options if you will not compromise on your ethics, your morals and your professionalism? Where will you get employment? Do you see that your options are then to either leave the country to a place you can fulfill your dreams or to compromise? This is effective social engineering whereby through social architecture a system is designed and structured to carry out the work without daily supervision. They do not need to personally approach that fresh graduate with a burning desire for truth or any other like her in the country, through the system in place they have created a culture that she must conform to if she is to survive in this society and what else? It's self- propagating. The older ones already fully baptised in the way of the land induct the incoming ones on how things are done there. Who are the final losers in all this? It's the Nigerian masses. So if the narrative has been controlled via the media and is being fed to the masses what is the outcome? The outcome is success because the Nigerian educational system does not produce graduates that can think and solve problems, rather they produce good workers and employees so the outcome is that despite the level of education in the country the masses are vulnerable and susceptible to things like spin, media manipulation and propaganda which are all instruments of control and valuable arrows in the quiver of the political ruling class in its fight against the Nigerian people.

NATURAL RESOURCES

When the sad stories of black people are being told over time Nigeria will be one of the highlights of that story, and when the sad story of Nigeria is being told to the generations coming behind crude oil is going to be one of the highlights of that story but no matter who tells these stories or how they tell it, or what they choose to focus on in their own versions or renditions of these stories the eternal underlying patterns that have accompanied black people for centuries now will be there in one form or another and that has been the constant in the different stories within the stories of our people. No matter the location of the particular group you choose to tell their story, they could be in the motherland or in the diaspora, no matter their ethnic group or tribe, or the elements and actors involved in that particular group the patterns that have followed our people like a curse for centuries will be present there. Pain will be present there as well as suffering and loss, you will see unfulfilled promises and potentials either through violence or trickery, you will also see betrayal either from within or without or both, you will see waste of resources, talents, gifts or again of potentials and finally you will see things that were meant for our people to better our people, owned by us even always seemingly finding a way to end up in the hands of other people who use it to better themselves and use it against us. Over the centuries our people have sadly either through ignorance, generosity, stupidity, trying to be peaceful or multiple combinations of these factors developed a reputation as a people that you can take things from without much by way of resistance, repercussions or retaliation from them. This is something that we have to intentionally do away with and get rid of if we're to ever be our own in this world and with the current way the black race is going I have not seen anything to indicate to me that this is the case.

The parts and members of this world are constantly in competition with themselves, this is a world of forces and counter forces, tension is always in the air. When life pushes at you, you have to push back else you stand the risk of being pushed over, overpowered and controlled by the forces you did not push back. The story of Nigeria is a proper black story and as with black stories even though the actors and their modus operandi might differ, it is still a manifestation of those patterns in one form or the other; whether it is an excited King Mansa Musa who has taken the gold mined for him by his subjects in West Africa and freely given them out as gifts in North Africa and the Middle East, or the Colonisers that came for flesh and agricultural produce, you can trace the pattern down to the political elites of present day Nigeria who have taken our crude oil to be refined in faraway lands by people who have no crude oil of their own while our people queue for hours in the land of their birth just to get petrol to go about their normal day, these are the patterns I am talking about. With these patterns and others that you might have noticed going through the different aspects of Nigerian society with me up until this point you can see that it's pointless to really write an epistle on natural resources, you can trace out the similarities with the brain drain in every field of human resources and the end result is a loss and a deficit for the blacks. Resources are finite and that's all the more reason why they should be used carefully and wisely, surprisingly Africa which has been exploited for a long time now for her resources has somehow not been exhausted. I shudder to think of what would become of her people if her resources were ever to be exhausted and while my initial conclusions were grave and grim a part of my consciousness tells me that it could also be to her advantage as the world can finally turn their attention elsewhere and allow her people to develop in peace.

If you take the balloon theory into consideration it's clear to see that the people that designed and control Nigeria to this day did not design her to be successful, there is no way to go around this fact. What you see in her operations is political fraud and resource theft done in a systemic and organised manner under the surface but covered with chaos so as to throw her people off the scent trail, in that way they are kept in the dark about what is really going on in their country. You only have to look at other countries with resources and to see the way they have gone about it to benefit their people and then take a look at Nigeria to know that there is something terribly, terribly wrong going on here. You look at a place like Dubai and all that has been accomplished there then come to Nigeria and try to go to the communities that have the crude oil in a place like say Delta state and that is if they even have pliable roads to start with, that is when you will fully understand that under certain conditions man can be one of the most loving of all the creatures in the earth but without a doubt the human is the most terrible of them all. Nigeria did not need to be the best in the world in terms of the utilization of her resources to be in a good place as a country, she did not even need to operate at full capacity, just 50% efficiency and the difference would have been seen and felt in the society but what is going on is a terrible sight to behold.

Your schools were defunded from long ago to limit the quality of education they could give and that standard has dropped steadily over time except for the private schools. Unstable power supply and a harsh business climate has seen economic activities grind to a halt, systematically killing all avenues for indigenous production and increasing dependency on importation, your people have no manufacturing and production culture as part of their lives meaning they are ignorant in those fields. Intense poverty keeps them on survival mode with no time for anything else so when you bring in foreigners to construct refineries without a provision for technology transfer or a planned partnership for maintenance and repairs does it really come as a shock when those refineries shut down a short while later? Look I was born in Nigeria, so knowing the intensity of the corruption practised it would not surprise me if there was deliberate vandalism to cripple and shut down those refineries, it didn't make the news but that does not mean it could not have happened that way. So imagine your village was next to one of these facilities and you had lived your entire lives in poverty not even knowing what was going on in these heavily guarded facilities, that is an oil producing nation whose people have neither the knowledge or capabilities to drill and refine crude oil, it is the nation of the people who live next to the sea and are surrounded by rivers but cannot have drinking water supplied to their homes or have no modern ship building knowledge or capabilities and this list goes on and on and on and the fact is that Nigeria is a place filled with violent and questionable contradictions like these.

If the facilities and infrastructures that exist are from pre-independence times or just after independence then it tells you that true development stopped at those times despite the fact that technological advancements have taken place at a rapid rate around the world. Since then they've systematically killed off economic activities in the country under the guise of ignorance and ineptitude but it's all been parts of a grand plan and steps along the way to drag the country into the reality you see today. This is the reality of people who have oil wells that are owned by the federal government close to their farms but have to look at their children die of malaria right in front of their eyes because they have no money to buy drugs, this is the reality of a people who have to spend their nights in darkness in their rickety mud houses while they get feasted on by mosquitoes and kept awake all night by the noise from the generator in the local politician's mansion on the same street. This is the reality of a people whose children have to sit on the floors in classrooms without roofs, wearing tattered uniforms just to try to get an education while the children of the politicians are polishing their accents in posh London and New York schools. I cannot do anything but wonder, how long will these people continue to tolerate this rubbish?

We are talking about resources but there is no proper indigenous mining industry in the country with supporting industries that would have employed people and added to the economy but resource theft has illegal mining taking place with the products and harvests whisked out of the country, crude oil is illegally drilled and refined and what all these illegal operations do is steal from the pockets of the Nigerian people and destroy their environment in the process through pollution. The subsistence farmer in the village in the Niger Delta cannot go to the farm because the land is affected, the fisherman cannot go to fish in the stream because oil spills have killed all the fishes, there have been accidents in the past with explosions that have claimed lives and destroyed properties and all I can think of is: something that could have been done properly to benefit everybody is now incorrectly being done to benefit a few, punishing everybody else in the process. The corruption involved in these illegal operations goes all the way to the top but of course there would be plausible deniability, I would expect nothing less from these smooth operators. There has been violence in the past with the arrival of militant groups like MEND (Movement for the Emancipation of the Niger Delta) in 2004 but the quietness of that situation tells me that the lessons of the coups and counter coups of the 70s and 80s would have been applied because like the Boko Haram they certainly were not defeated militarily, these guys are smooth operators not fighters. This is one of the things that does my head in, if Nigeria was a country that was putting in her best effort but still coming up short I could have been able to live with that, you know, that she gave it her all but just was not able to cut it. But knowing what I know and seeing all these things happening makes the current situation a difficult pill to swallow.

The Nigerian government in an official capacity exports crude oil to be refined in foreign lands bringing back petrol, diesel and kerosene, they are characteristically deaf, dumb and blind about the many other by products of crude oil but the battle-weary masses are just happy to get enough of the magic juice for their cars and to keep their insatiable little beasts happy for a time and a season. Crude is the chief cash cow of the country, without it there's no party, as with the other areas there is a government body in control called the NNPC (Nigerian National Petroleum Corporation) which is the main body but there is also a ministry and many other sub-bodies that are involved. The NNPC is a different beast altogether when it comes to corruption as far as government bodies go. The end product of all the gymnastics and corruption is that the masses never get to benefit from something that's taken right from under their feet. This theme is consistent, there is a whole section dedicated to Nigerian gold in Dubai but how many Nigerians get to wear Nigerian gold on their necks? All the illegal mining does apart from make a few thieves very rich is that it does not allow a proper mining industry to develop along with a proper industry and culture of gold works that would be a trade to offer employment and can be passed on down through the generations imbibing modern technology along the way and world best practices but for a people who have been earmarked for poverty this is not the case. The sad tale of Nigeria goes on accompanied by a sad, slow tune in the background, what we've seen done by the elites in Nigeria over these past five decades in terms of the scale and magnitude of theft and waste of resources has never been recorded in history before now, all of my theories hold up to the light on this which is one of the main reasons no Nigerians will be making heaven.

NIGERIAN ECONOMY

'When Britain was the world's leading economic power, it used to be referred to as a nation of shopkeepers: but most of the goods in their shops were produced by themselves, and it was while grappling with the problems posed by production that their engineers came up with so many inventions. In Africa, trading groups could make no contributions to technological improvement because their role and pre-occupation took their minds and energies away from production'

- Walter Rodney
How Europe Underdeveloped Africa

Nigeria defies all textbook economic principles, theories and analysis, to try to use them to explain the Nigerian economic crisis is like trying to use your physics textbook to explain the tricks we see done in Indian Bollywood movies... you'll fail every time. My arguments have been very consistent from the start of this book, I did not take any detour nor did I ever once try to back track and retrace my steps, my vision of Nigeria and what I have determined to be the cause of her problems have been clear to me from the beginning and I have tried my best to present them in the simplest of ways to avoid misunderstanding. The thing that still causes me great amazement and is the great mystery is how they have taken a country that should be so obviously rich and well off and made her so obviously poor and miserable; this is the thing that has kept me awake for many nights, and you see, they did not just take her and make her average which is to say not good and not bad but in the middle, which would have been a bad enough situation because she could be so much more but they took her to the least possible position and kept her there. It was possible for them to embezzle from the country for all these years and still left her well off to fend for herself but what I do not fully yet understand is why her people had to be made to suffer so much in the process and why it had to be so wickedly done from the frying pan to the fire... this is Joseph the beloved son of a well to do patriarch finding himself in Potiphar's house and then straight to prison from there (Gen 37 and onwards). When he looked around to see his surroundings and the people with him in that prison for the first time I'm sure that one of the first thoughts to have crossed his mind would be that he did not belong in that place; this is what I think about when I think of Nigeria the country and the Nigerian economy.

When you look at the principles of wealth creation, retention and growing the economy in a simplified form you can see that the opposite has been done in every case in Nigeria. From the lack of infrastructures for entrepreneurs to leverage on for production and commerce, to the constant embezzling by politicians who move the money the country got paid for the crude oil they took far outside the country to be refined by others in the first place, back outside the country to be stashed so it's a double loss for the country. The opportunity to add value domestically to the crude and other raw resources for more profit is lost and then when basic raw materials price is paid for the crude and resources that money gets embezzled from the country's coffers leaving peanuts for the masses to barely survive on. What can you say about gross domestic product when your country has no domestic production in the first place and everything you consume as a people up to food items are being imported into the country as finished products from other countries by businessmen? The odds are stacked so high like a wall against the Nigerian people and even when they try to climb this wall new layers keep getting added to ensure that they never get to the top and over that limiting wall. When we talk about the war between the political ruling class and the masses it's not really a war at this point. Jesus said that a house divided against itself cannot stand but when the warring factions involve the poor masses versus people who have made chess moves to put themselves in a position where they hold all the power and authority in the country then the masses are doomed! It's not really a war at this stage anymore but a massacre.

When I think about the Nigerian economy I have come up with my own unique simplified way to understand it. I liken it to a human body with arteries and veins running through its length and breadth carrying life giving blood and nourishing nutrients to all parts of that body giving them life and keeping them strong and fresh. Wherever blood is not transported to in that body or say bad blood is transferred to begins to wither away and die affecting and weakening the whole body in the process but for as long as good blood is transported around to all the parts of the body with the waste excreted then the body is healthy. The physical locations of the body represent the locations of the country and the different aspects of the economy, the heart pumping the blood is the power, the arteries and the veins carrying the blood to all the different parts are the infrastructures needed for production and wealth generation, the life-giving blood being carried to and fro represents the resources necessary for production, capital for investment and profit gained from value added to the resources within that body. The brain and nervous system controlling and monitoring all these processes for smooth operations are the human resources which work the body and their leadership which acts as a regulator to ensure order within the body. This simplified model also ties in with the balloon theory in the sense that wherever the blood is pumped to remains turgid and alive while when the blood is sucked out of that part of the body it becomes flaccid and begins to die. The molecular theory of wealth creation is all of the operations, connections and interactions that keep that body functioning well.

The simplified rules for success of this body is to retain more than it loses in terms of resources, utilise its resources wisely, save its excesses, protect what it has and the people doing the work within it, do everything within its power to generate and produce more internally, and always seek to upgrade by seeking out and maintaining relations with other bodies better than itself. If it did this well enough it could be in a good enough position from where it could lend a helping hand and support to other bodies around it that are not doing too well but when it's struggling to survive it can't be bothered about trying to help others. Can you control an entire continent in the way that it's been done in Nigeria? The answer is yes because you do not need to catch everybody to gain control all you need is to get enough people and they will pull the others down. When you have a group of impoverished bodies side by side or a bunch of poor, troubled and vulnerable countries side by side why would this not be possible? I'm no expert on the economy but the simplified rules I outlined have been consistently avoided in Nigeria and made to look like it was due to mistakes or the ignorance of the people in charge but all the while the government was outlining medium to long term goals and putting out budget statements year after year so why were they not adhered to? When the consequences of a past action comes to prove that action as a mistake the right thing to do is to make adjustments to your strategy and try something different but when the so-called mistakes are repeated without repercussions or punishment to the elements officially in charge of that sector then it becomes hard to give that excuse as the reason why.

Look, we cannot waste our time here trying to give advice to the Nigerian government and Nigerian society on what they should do to become successful like they don't know it. The concept of wealth and prosperity for nations and for individuals is an old one with a long history of theory and practice, and the principles are widely known so if anything the study should be why a nation did not apply those principles in the first place. Nigerians often say that their society and their economy is a failure and I always disagree, they say that all the Nigerian society does is to consistently produce poverty for its citizens and I say if the society and the economy are doing exactly what they were designed to do and function exactly how the controlling forces want them to function can you really call them failures? You most definitely cannot. The failure of Nigeria as a country is not a failure of leadership as some may say, if anything it is a failure of the people for not being able to protect themselves or provide any kind of resistance to the operation being carried out on them.

> *'2% of Nigerians Own 90% of Banks Deposits in Nigeria'*
>
> *Alhaji Mohammed Umar, (2016)*
> *Director of Research and International Relations,*
> *Nigeria Deposit Insurance Corporation (NDIC)*

Take a close look at that statistic quoted there and spend some time to think on it so it can sink in and the implications of it can become clear to you. If 4 million people out of 200 million are responsible for 90% of all bank deposits what does that say about wealth distribution in the country? If a whopping 196 million Nigerians have just 10% of the deposits do you now see why she's called a poor country? If you're one of those unfortunate 196 million individuals what would you do? What can you even do? We have seen lots of people who were born poor in Nigeria and grew up poor in the country only to have the opportunity to travel to a different country and become millionaires the first month they spend in those countries so what can you say really changed for them? As long as this is the case the issue of brain drain which we cry about all the time because it takes the best human resources away from the country will never end because people want better. Most foreigners in the 1st world countries would look at the 3rd world countries and say secretly to themselves in their heart that they could do better but today I tell you to remove such deluded thoughts from your mind.

If it were you there would be nothing you can do differently and if you don't believe me you can ask Sir Richard Branson, a respected billionaire business man who has written books and has been successful everywhere else in the world he ever did business in, but lasted just 11 years in Nigeria when he had to do business with the political ruling class. If that billionaire in dollars who's one of your very best could only last 11 years doing business under the Nigerian economic factors then respectfully; who are you please? You can go and read up on what he had to say after he successfully cut business ties with the Nigerian government and made his hasty escape to give you more perspective. His situation should at least give you an inkling about the lives of the people who are born into this system, bred in it, and are somehow expected to survive the rest of their days in it.

Do you have big dreams? You want to do business in Nigeria as a Nigerian? Oh you want to be an entrepreneur? How sweet but do tell me please I ask of you; where would you get the capital to start from if you're not somehow connected to the political ruling class? Nigerian banks are not giving out loans but in the event that you do somehow manage to get a loan from a Nigerian bank the interest rates is in double figures do you know that? So what can you do with an interest rate of over 20% without you somehow ending up in debt and working for the bank? Banks are meant to drive economic growth but I never trusted any of these banks since I was young and don't trust them now that I'm older. The history of banking in Nigeria is one that is fraught with tragedies, admittedly it was worse in the past with some stability achieved in the Nigerian banking sector but I have never been able to overcome my bank-phobia. In the past new banks would be opened, they would receive deposits from Nigerians and then magically close up without any warning to their customers who are the poor masses that never get their money back. This scam was common in the 90s until structural changes were implemented into the banking sector. Who moves the moneys around for the politicians in the country? Who helps them to move those monies into foreign accounts to avoid international money laundering laws? You can make the excuse that they operate within the country and are just as subject to the powers that be in the country but the fact remains that they are not for the masses. Nigerian banks still charge you for every single transaction you do which is more money out of the pockets of the common folk but I don't want to make it a rant about banks and bankers. During my discussions with my friends about Nigerian issues over the years I have always told them that next to the politicians, the bankers are the ones I fear the most; those suit wearing, always smiling and soft speaking 'book boys' and 'book girls' because they are not innocent in all this. I maintain that the money guys should be watched closely, even Jesus Christ was betrayed by his accountant. If that does not tell you anything I don't know what else will.

Money is the key thing here, money makes the world go round as they say so you have to keep your eyes on the money at all times. If the leadership of the country wanted to develop any part of the economy they would have pumped money into that part to attract the attention of suitable people within the population who will make their livelihood from their performance, value and contribution in that area but when instead money is being constantly taken out of the system then the intentions are clear. Nigeria's problem has never been a lack of money; Nigeria's military head of state in the 70's, General Yakubu Gowon, who made the famous statement that 'money is not Nigeria's problem but how to spend it', fast forward to present times and the politicians of the day are trying to deflect and flip the narrative through the media to say that Nigeria is broke but I think we all know that that's not the case. This country has been one big heist from the start and that was never changed, she's being exploited as a business by those controlling her to borrow from the international bodies stacking debts for the future generations unborn all just to ensure that her yoke is never taken off. The reasons for the loans are infrastructures but can you please kindly point me to the infrastructures in Nigeria constructed with these many foreign loans? There are none because those projects never get executed. The borrowed money is embezzled and stolen to be shared amongst the political ruling class which is another case of double loss. Due to their practice of tokenism if any single thing gets done at all it comes overpriced with its budget padded beyond recognition, it's most likely sub-standard and is milked to the core by the handlers of the country such that by the time it is finished, it's presence is just a drop in the water and does not have any meaninful positive impact on the country or her economy. What do I mean by that? Well they say little drops of water can make a mighty ocean but if that ocean has large holes spread across its floor from which the water is being consistently sucked away into the ground, no matter how large that body of water is if you keep intermittently adding drops of water to it it's going to dry out in time despite the drops of water you're adding because it's losing way more water than you're adding to it, so this is why tokenism for me personally is frankly stupid and annoying but who can I blame? They know exactly what they are doing in the first place.

So there you have it, if you're looking for GDP, figures, KPIs and other indices then thank God for google as you can always get that information online but you can see that I avoided using figures in my analysis because the figures change drastically every few years in Nigeria, then the economists or analysts try to make sense of the new figures and just keep things moving without any recourse to the old ones. Not a lot of countries can survive what Nigeria has been through, just Covid a few years ago and the economies of some of your favorite 'developed' countries were shaking like leaves in the wind how much more they have to deal with the plight of Nigeria for just ten years? These self-proclaimed great countries, can you imagine what would become of them if they got a little taste? They would collapse or just simply implode but somehow Nigeria has still survived the torture and dysfunction for so long... please do not mistake this for praise. Every year Nigeria and South Africa compete for the biggest economy in Africa; Nigeria is Nigeria, a 3rd world country while South Africa is regarded as a 2nd world country but if the Nigeria that I've been describing for you up to this point and I didn't even put in the worst bits is competing with another powerful African nation which is more infrastructurally and technologically developed than her and who, I believe is doing everything within her powers to be a great nation in the world, then you can just imagine Nigeria operating at 40 or 50% of her original capacity, I put her currently at 10% and she is still constantly in the running for biggest economy in Africa. Please do not also mistake this for praise, if at all it is a cause for sadness and reflection and on this note I end my discourse on the Nigerian economy.

WRAP UP ON PART 1 - THE MASSES

'If the foundations be destroyed, what can the righteous do?'

- Psalms 11:3

I remember reading the expression *'to build castles in the air'* in my junior secondary school days when I was just getting introduced to literature. I must have taken it literally because I remember thinking deeply about it over and over again in my mind trying to resolve it because it occurred to me that something was off in that statement, and as I kept thinking on it I conjured up a picture in my mind's eye where a real life version of those Disney style castles we saw in the cartoons we watched as kids was just suspended in the air, I remember looking at that picture in my mind and thinking to myself how impossible it all was because there was nothing to support the castle and thinking back to that time now I think that was the moment that that expression took root in my mind and became real to me never to be forgotten again. Fast forward from that time to a little over a decade later and I was graduating from the university with a bachelor's degree in construction, well fast forward to the present times and I'm thinking about the expression and I think within myself that there was no way I could have known that I would end up studying construction but life can be unpredictable like that. I say all that to say, that from a young age in my life I've understood the importance of a strong foundation to a building and even today

I draw upon those experiences to help me make sense of the world around me that I am currently observing.

We're still in court and I am trying to present to you as much evidence as possible so that we can go through the motions of this case and have a ruling by the close of the day, don't worry about time because time works differently here in the soul realm. I know it feels like hours since we began proceedings but when you put the book away and check you'll see that it's only been minutes that have passed by in the real world. However, I do hope that in this short time I have been able to properly paint for you a picture of what it means to be an average Nigerian living in Nigeria, there are better and worse circumstances in her reality but I hope this account captures a balance in the country. There is no way to capture and document every single aspect of Nigerian society but between the theories and the aspects discussed already it gives an idea of the reality in whatever area was not explicitly outlined, to continue to list and elaborate would have put us at risk of too much repetition thereby boring you out.

I am curious to know what you make out of all this but I think whatever your disposition is we can all agree at the end of the day that the Nigerian masses simply do not have a foundation to build their country on and any house they try to build without a foundation or on weak soil will crumble on top of them (Matt 7:24 - 27). This is the crux of their malady, a workman cannot operate without his instruments or the right environment hence that great question that keeps ringing in my ears and just will not stop when I think about Nigeria: if the foundations be destroyed, what can the righteous do? The Nigeria of the 1960s is not the same as the one in the 2020s and between that time the foundations of the country have been slowly but surely vandalised, eroded and destroyed, chipped away bit by bit to make it what it is today. So subtly done was it that the masses were caught napping, they were not alert to what was happening because it was done so quietly and slowly that by the time they realised what was happening it was already too late for them. As the chains of the colonisers were taken off from their hands, feet and necks new chains were quietly slipped on them to replace their old ones and they not being privy to it jumped and danced away singing songs and making merry totally oblivious to the fact.

Ignorance, a lackadaisical attitude coupled with internal disharmony on the part of the masses contributed to the downfall of the masses. Their forefathers could not band together to protect their interests against their former colonisers for which they paid dearly and one would have taught that lessons would have been learnt and passed down through the generations but the descendants fell into the same trap and could not band together to protect their interests against their new colonisers and as it was before so it is today, they are currently paying for their inadequacies in anguish and great pain. Looking at the circumstances of the masses is only one part of the problem so we move on to the political ruling class and as we do so if I may just ask you for one last time: ***if the foundations be destroyed, what can the righteous do?***

PART 2: THE POLITICAL RULING CLASS.

'IN YOUR LIFE, IN ANY GIVEN MOMENT, THE STRONGEST DREAM IN THAT MOMENT WINS THAT MOMENT'

- Dave Chappelle
The Dreamer (2024).

INTRODUCTION:

This must be what heaven feels like, the Nigerian version of heaven at least and since we're just now coming from Nigerian hell it must be exciting to see the changes and the contrast between both locations. There was a country that was supposed to be, then things happened and that country did not become the country it was supposed to be but became the country that it is. Within the country that it is, exists another smaller country which we'll call the country that thrives within the country that it is; both are the different sides of the same Nigerian coin as we see it today. If chaos is both a pit and a ladder then we have just looked at the lives of the poor souls screaming their heads off because they are trapped in the pit and scrambling about trying to climb out of it, we're now about to look at those on the ladder kicking them back down to make sure that they stay put. One of the main differences between both of the countries trapped in the Nigerian chaos is that the ones in the pit desperately need Nigeria to change from how she currently is if they are to have any chance of living lives that bear any semblance whatsoever to normalcy while the ones on the ladder think she is fine the way that she currently is, they can't seem to understand what all the complaining is about and they would do anything to keep her in the state she currently is in.

In this second part we're going to look at the controlling forces of Nigeria, the power structure, the dynamics within this controlling cloud, and then feel out the relationships and interactions that exist between the controlling force, the Nigerian masses and the Nigerian society. Nigeria is a working mechanism made up of functioning systems and structures, and it is only when we have fully studied all of these components on both sides of the coin can we understand fully how she works and operates. To do this we have to look at the unique system of democracy practised in the country, how it has been able to stand the test of time being so successful and why it has been very difficult to change. The irrefutable fact at this point is that there is a conflict between 2 distinct groups and a lot of factors like preparation, ability, will power, strategy, skill set, ammunition, desire, mentality and many others depending on the type of conflict which play varying degrees of roles in determining the outcome of conflicts.

My opening text from legendary comedian Dave Chappelle's special titled '*The Dreamer* (2024)' captures this thought and this truth so simply and so beautifully that I forgot I was watching a comedy special for a minute because I did not expect to encounter this kind of depth. I was stunned and my mouth was wide open, all I could do was to press the pause button and stare blankly at the screen for minutes lost in my thoughts before replaying that portion a couple of times again to make sure I had heard right. People who have mastered what they do are always able to transcend the boundaries and limits of their profession to become something more and this is why Mr. Chappelle is widely regarded as one of the best comedians to ever walk the earth. You need to simply just replace 'dream' in that opening text with all the variables I listed as determinants to the outcome of conflicts and you have the answer as to why the political ruling class is currently winning the socioeconomic war in Nigeria against the masses and I tell you it's not even close. So let us go into the next phase and look at the political leadership dynamics in the country.

POLITICAL RULING CLASS: THE RISE AND RISE OF THE NIGERIAN MAFIA.

> *'The forest was shrinking but the trees kept voting for the axe, for the axe was clever and convinced the trees that because his handle was made of wood, he was one of them'*
>
> *- Old Turkish proverb*

The political ruling class is indeed the other side of the coin, it is the template and the true custodian of power in Nigeria. It is a sophisticated and very diverse group of individuals, and not everyone within this group is a politician but I termed them all as 'political' because of the method they use to collectively exert control and dominion over the masses which is through the accumulation, control and manipulation of political power in Nigeria. It is a clandestine organisation made up of wealthy men and women from every state and locality of Nigeria, every ethnic group, religion and whatever mode of classification you can think of, all bound together by common relationships, common bonds and common interests. These differences would normally be the cause of great squabbling, quarrels and disunity among the masses but that's poor people's problems; these ones are wise, focused and organised. They know that their strength lies in their unity, each member is strong on their own to an extent but they know that the times when the lion's pride is able to take down big prey is when they hunt together as a pride and right now they have set themselves up in strategic positions around the hapless and unfocused mixed herd masses scattered across the land, and they are in full control, free to feed as they wish. This group is like a secret society, when I hear people say that secret groups like the infamous Illuminati could never exist in real life I smile, shake my head and say nothing because not every argument is worth getting into. Besides, you know how obnoxious ordinary everyday people can be, especially hidden under the veil of internet anonymity; they like to speak authoritatively on things they know nothing about.

The diverse membership of this group includes but is not limited to top politicians, lawyers, doctors, fixers, bankers, engineers, power brokers, traditional rulers, religious figures, judges, civil service, business people, middle men, 'king makers', top military officials etc. This does not mean that it is every single person that falls into these categories that's a member of the political elites, that's not how life works: no matter how well a fisherman throws his net he can never catch all of the fish in that river, he just needs to catch enough to return home with a good harvest as compensation for his efforts for that day. So you can see that even though the wealth of Nigeria is accumulated within this group I did not just loosely classify them as all of the wealthy individuals in the land because there are still some outliers who have accumulated wealth outside of the power structure of this group. These types are not many because the way this group is set up, it's set up for total economic control of Nigeria so any noteworthy economic moves that must happen within this territory that they control cannot happen without the knowledge and involvement of members of the political ruling class in one way or the other but outliers exist who maybe have made their money internationally. If those outliers made their money locally they would have had to deal with this group at some point in time whereby they either get recruited into the group or come to some form of understanding with it. If it is an outlier that made their money internationally they try to recruit them too and if they resist being recruited they are left alone for the most part because this group is smart and operate the art of war so they follow the rule that says: choose your battles wisely. They don't go looking for unnecessary conflicts with powerful people because powerful people can also cause damage so why waste energy and resources, putting yourself, your organisation and everything it has built up in Nigeria over decades at the risk of harm in a battle that could have been avoided in the first place? Besides the meagre numbers of these outliers are never enough to cause any real change in the society in the grand scheme of things should their interests even conflict with those of the elites, so why bother?

I call this group the 2nd circle in Nigeria, let me explain what I mean by this. Think of 3 different sized concentric circles, the largest circle which is the 1st circle is the masses, within it is a far smaller circle which I call the 2nd circle and it represents the political ruling class, inside this 2nd circle is the smallest which is the 3rd circle and it represents the political government structure in Nigeria, in this way you will have a clearer picture of what is happening in the elites. The political government structure of all 3 levels in Nigeria i.e. the federal, state and local government structure is a child and a subset of the political ruling class, to this end you have 2 types of members of the political ruling class in Nigeria at all times, they are the governmental members and the non-governmental members. Since Nigeria operates as a democracy with 4-year terms for elected officials, the governmental members of the political ruling class are just members of the group that are occupying positions in the political government structure at that particular time while the non-governmental members are the general members of the group from which the political leaders are selected to fill the political positions and other key controlling positions in the country. Do not let these distinctions fool you for they are one and the same members of the same group, so in that sense the political ruling class is essentially a forest for the salad of the Nigerian political structure. In this way the political ruling class which mostly uses a soft power approach is able to indirectly exert its power and control over the masses through its subset which is the political government structure that it's in control of. The masses are mandated to obey and follow the rules and directives set by their political government as the highest authority in the land which is how modern political societies are set up so when you control that political government you essentially are in control of the masses and the resources in their lands.

Deception and subtlety are the bread and butter of the political elites, in their operations they try to be as secretive as possible, ruffle as few feathers as possible and create as few ripples as possible so as not to draw unnecessary attention to what they are doing or cause disruptions to the lives of the masses on whom they have put a heavy yoke with chains on their necks and are currently preoccupied with surviving survival mode. If they draw the attention of the masses to themselves to see how wealthy they are or how well off they are in the same country where the masses are suffering untold hardship there will be public outcry which threatens to disrupt the balance. To this end the political government structure goes through great pains to simulate a reality of normalcy for the masses, they have maintained the political government structures in place, they carry out elections every 4 years, put out regular information that a government would put out from time to time and play the part in words only so that to anybody that cares to look Nigeria is just a normal 3rd world country experiencing problems and trying her best to be better. This I think is done for different reasons like to lull the masses into a false sense of normalcy as they would seldom revolt if they felt things were normal and to continue to have legitimacy and acceptance in the eyes of the world so should they ever run into problems internally they could always cry to the powerful nations for military help and support to quell that uprising because those people who would be fighting for their survival would look like rebels trying to overthrow a legitimate democratic government to the foreigners... if only they knew.

This group is a ladder with a hierarchy of members operating at different levels of government and what do they do? What is their profession? Their business literally is Nigeria and business is booming for them because Nigeria is a high earning country they have created a pipeline through which they can legally siphon the wealth of the nation right from under the citizens living in it without the masses ever getting their hands on it. They are the ones that practise the prebendalism in Nigeria, theirs is a patronage and patrimonial kind of relationship where members on the lower rungs of the ladder have to consistently show their loyalty and allegiance to those on the higher rungs before they can be promoted step by step up the ladder. Promotion means that they are finally eligible for juicy positions within the political government structure of the country which guarantees more money, influence and prestige for them among other perks. These people have become extremely wealthy and for them Nigeria feels like a very different country to what the masses are experiencing. They and their families live in palatial mansions they have built for themselves, drive the expensive cars that are manufactured in the 1st world countries that you would normally see the wealthy people and celebrities in those countries driving, they wear expensive European high fashion brands, their children attend the top foreign schools in the world, they stash a lot of their ill-gotten wealth in foreign banks and offshore accounts, buy lots of properties in these developed countries boosting the economies and property markets of those countries while the masses in our country live in rickety mud houses and the list goes on and on and on but you get the picture already, all of this extravagance is maintained by the commonwealth of the Nigerian people by the way.

This is the life that they live in Nigeria and they get this free of charge because Nigeria is selling barrels of crude oil daily so the money flowing into the country is endless. All they have to do is just to wait for it to flow down through the normal budgeted and allocated channels to the different apparatus of the government and those atrocious ministries, boards and authorities that are supposedly in charge of infrastructures in different sections of Nigerian society but guess who's occupying all the official leadership top positions in the government and those bodies? Yep, you guessed right! It's the very members of the political ruling class who have been rewarded with those positions and one can even say tested because if they get those positions and occupy those offices without doing what they are supposed to do for the group that could spell the end of their political careers when their 4 year term is over or they could use other methods within the system to get them dropped from those positions so this keeps members in check so if you were wondering why their system is so durable, well this is part of it. So all they need to do is just wait for the money to flow down the political system and it is embezzled through corruption to be shared by the members of this group according to their positions on the ladder and who's the biggest loser in this scenario? Yep, right again! So you walk into this set up and say you want to do things the right way, can you begin to imagine the kind of resistance you'd be facing? So when the late great Gani Fawehinmi made the statement about 'it being criminal to be law abiding in a state of lawlessness' this is what he meant and those of us who have been subjected to this abuse all our lives knew exactly what he was talking about.

Well what about the law you might ask? Erm... I don't want to give too much away about that yet as we're still going to come to that properly in a little while but just know that members of this group are above the law because they ARE the law of the land and you can quote me anywhere on this. What we've been talking about so far in this section is on the non-governmental members so we will be moving on to the governmental members of this group in a bit. The Mafia was taken down by the government in the United States, they have faced stiff resistance from the government in their native Italy that has kept their activities in check, the Yakuza operates within the bounds that the government allows for them to do in Japan and the Chinese Triads have a similar style; all of these well-known organised crime organisations but none of them in their hundreds of years of operations or even thousands in some cases have ever come close to accomplishing what the unknown political ruling class in Nigeria have accomplished in under a century which is to OWN a country in its entirety and this is no mean feat. Please do not mistake this for praise, this is my country I am talking about after all and it happens to be a country I love and hate dearly for obvious reasons but the story still needs to be told and if it must be told then it must at least be told with a clear mind.

    I watched a documentary once about a parasite that attacks a snail and takes control of that snail, pulsating in its eyes and feelers to look like a worm. This parasite turns the snail into a zombie controlling it and moving it towards the light exposing it to predators so that when birds pluck out the snail's eyes mistaking them for worms, the parasite can breed in the belly of the birds to be propagated through the faeces of the birds when their excreta is eaten up by other snails and the whole time I watched it I could not stop thinking about the Nigerian situation. These parasites have taken over the country, maintained some semblance of her vital operations to fool the whole world where they have been rubbing shoulders with the leaders of the world in official capacities of the nation without being found out. They have the nation in a choke hold, they have the dragon in chains, it's a complete state capture and they have done this while remaining relatively unknown to the world except their victims who although know to an extent can do absolutely nothing about it. Viewing her through the lens of the political ruling class you can see that Nigeria is just a glorified contraption for organised resource theft so she cannot be a democracy as she repeatedly claims but is in truth, she's a kleptocracy. These kleptocrats are a criminal organisation systematically siphoning the entire wealth of the country leaving her citizens impoverished making the society's members some of the wealthiest individuals in the world today and they are still not widely known globally by any fancy names like the other examples I gave and I say that's a proper secret organisation. Well I don't think they would be much secret after this book is published so it's only right that they get a name to go with the part; to us in Nigeria they are the political ruling class but to the rest of the world - ladies and gentlemen I present to you the Nigerian Mafia!

POLITICAL LEADERSHIP: THE GOVERNMENTAL MEMBERS.

'Politicians as a class are dangerous, that people who are seeking power over us are not, by definition, our friends.'

- James Bovard.

Nigeria swears all the time that she's a democracy and tries to pass herself off as one but she is ruled exclusively by the wealthy who have gotten their wealth by robbing her blind which makes her a plutocracy not a democracy. So how is it, you might ask, that this same system of government successfully implemented by some of the top countries in the world today, how has it failed so spectacularly in Nigeria? And I'll tell you that it's not about the system because a system is only as good as the people in it. So if I can just bring to your remembrance our great coach of Social Engineering FC from before, if he chose a sweet attacking and free flowing 4-3-3 but say inherited a squad full of wing backs and central defenders who have been used to playing 3 at the back under their previous managers and he has no proper holding midfielder that can shield his defence then that coach would struggle. The coach has an idea and a system in mind which is free flowing attacking football, he has chosen a good structure to implement it which is the 4-3-3 formation, a formation that modern coaching greats like Don Carlo Ancelotti and Pep Guardiola live and die by and have had so much success with in the modern era. He did not choose a 4-1-1-4 or a 4-0-6 which frankly do not exist but would be imbalanced if they did because the team would have no midfield and would be overrun so with the 4-3-3 he has a good structure.

He has a good footballing philosophy and an idea of how he wants his team to play but if he doesn't have the right players that fit his methods then he can not be successful at SEFC. He has come to me as the club president to ask for players in the transfer market and I told him the cub has no funds because we had a bad finish on the standings last season which means not much revenue came in which is why we fired our previous coach and hired him in the first place. What's worse for the coach if those players are playing against their own team and playing poorly deliberately to lose matches so they can secretly get paid money under the table by big match fixers and betting companies? In this scenario you can see that the coach cannot be successful, despite his best plans and efforts his beautiful system and structure does not have functionality. Let me blow your mind and tell you that in the Nigerian reality of this analogy the new coach is in on the act too and is getting money under the table along with the president and the corrupt board so if you're a fan and supporter of that club you will not see that club successful in your lifetime despite having all the ingredients for success; this is the plight of the present day Nigerian masses.

The members of the Nigerian Mafia that currently occupy government positions within the political government structure are their governmental members. Nigeria operates a federal government system, everything that is not available to the masses is available to the government so these are highly coveted positions. The foundation upon which modern democracy is built on as explained by the Baron de Montesquieu in his phenomenal work *THE SPIRIT OF LAW* (1748) is the *trias politica* which is the tripartite separation of political power into the executive, legislature and judiciary. These 3 arms are to be separate, co-equal and independent of each other with each one having the power to limit the other 2 thus creating a balance of political power in the society, preventing a concentration of the said powers which will eventually lead to abuse; well someone should have told that to the Nigerian Mafia. All of this is social architecture and social engineering by the way dating back hundreds of years to where people tried to design a more effective system of government trying to use the different elements and variables to come up with a sustainable system that would better serve society. In Nigeria the mimicry continues and they are very dedicated to keeping up appearances, like the other democracies of the world Nigeria's is also split into the executive, legislature and the judiciary so once again if anybody checks it out everything seems to be as it should be; they get good official salaries and perks of their offices, for the elected positions they serve their four year terms and step aside for others when their time is up and put out regular information that most governments would put out so for the casual observers once again there seems to be almost nothing out of place but upon scrutiny this aesthetic starts to fall apart rather quickly and I'm here for it.

We will go on to look at these 3 institutions in Nigeria and how they function to try to find out the faults on why they have individually failed but there is no need to prolong matters for that, I will go ahead and tell you now. The first act of soulectomy that was carried out on the democratic idea and execution in Nigeria is that there is no true separation of powers between those institutions. Do not forget that the political government structure which encompasses these institutions and more is the 3rd circle in my previous analogy, and is a subset of the 2nd middle circle which is the political ruling class. Two, these bodies are one and the same and they are currently at war with the 1st circle which is the masses from which they were formed out of in the first place and continue to exist within like the parasites that they are. To this end I state here that without any doubts the executive, the legislature and the judiciary in Nigeria are one and the same thing, the only distinctions they bear are in names, offices and other outward showing designations which they have to keep up to continue to bamboozle the Nigerian masses and to string them along. This is deception at its finest, this is where the political fraud comes up again; I told you from the beginning to watch these people closely when they change the names of things, they change the name only to confuse and deceive the masses but the mandate and operations of the organisations never change along with the name change. So without further ado let us briefly look at the 3 arms of government in Nigeria and their operations.

THE EXECUTIVE

'When power is concentrated into fewer hands, wealth will be concentrated into fewer pockets'

- Will Spencer

These are the top dog positions in the Nigerian political government structure, they sit at the top of the hierarchy for their level and legally have the final say on issues within their area of influence making them the highest political authority in the land. As I earlier mentioned, their powers are not checked by any of the other 2 arms of government because these people are one and the same so they have an unhealthy amount of political power conferred on their office making them essentially mini-gods to the Nigerian masses, so with this broken system Nigeria is not really a democracy but a veiled form of systemic dictatorship. At the federal level you have the president, at the state levels you have the 36 state governors and at the local government levels you have the local government chairmen to rule over the Nigerian people and their lands but when you really think about it people who are lifelong members of a clandestine organisation with its own leadership structure and hierarchy cannot possibly be all powerful and autonomous in a position that they get to occupy for a minimum of 4 years and a maximum of 8 years, now, can they? Because before, during and after they occupy those positions within the political government structure they remain members of the political ruling class else they would not have been able to get anywhere near those offices in the first place so can their actions while in office really be said to fully be their own?

Surely, I think, you must see where I'm going with this, the only logical conclusion I can arrive at with this line of reasoning is that the executive as well as the entire 3rd circle in Nigeria are just projections by the 2ⁿᵈ circle to legitimately own, control and manipulate absolute political power in Nigeria and by extension the masses in the country who have to legally honour and respect their political leadership; the end of all this is of course resource control and theft. To put it plainly the members of the executive are just puppets but this does not absolve them from blame because don't forget that they remain trusted members of the political ruling class before, during and after their tenures as office holders within the political government structure. It's a never-ending process of rinse and repeat, the strings attached to the executive puppets can be traced all the way back to the political ruling class which remains concealed in the shadows, conveniently out of sight placing the members of the executives in the line of fire as the real culprits and architects of the problems in the country... this is just deflection, another trick from inside the big bag of political fraud being carried out on these poor masses. So for the 4 years or 8 years that these people stay in office they draw all the attention and ire of the masses, they get insulted, ridiculed and over analysed from sun up till sundown by frustrated Nigerians and while the attention is focused on them the masses and their country are quietly but consistently getting robbed and the booty shared within the group.

Catch yourself quickly if you start to feel sorry for them as it's not a thankless job, they get compensated heavily for their time in the sun and the ill will that comes with it that's why their wealth increases astronomically when they occupy these positions and when their time is done they get to quietly slither off back into the darkness from whence they came and into the loving arms of the political ruling class who welcome them with praises for a job well done. In the meantime an election has just been concluded, a new well-prepared puppet is taking the stage eager to show the Nigerian masses his own singing skills and dance moves to occupy them for the next 4 or 8 years depending on his performance to the political ruling class during his first term. Meanwhile the outgoing executive member disappears with all the wealth he acquired during his term back into obscurity, deep into the bosom of the political ruling class, very far away from the prying eyes and wandering thoughts of the Nigerian masses who have a new set of puppets on the stage to entertain them and keep them occupied, anyways so this is what I mean when I say that the whole process is rinse and repeat.

All of this reminds me of something that my father told me a long time ago when I was still a young boy that has stayed with me till this day. You see I was the son of a native man, a chief with a title, and I grew up in a native home where we ate native foods. One of those foods was alligator meat which was usually delivered to us live with a piece of stick in its mouth and its mouth tied shut along with the rest of its body down to the tail to restrain its movement and prevent it from injuring anybody while in captivity before it's killed. What caught my attention was that whenever an alligator was brought to us it was brought live, rarely had any injuries on its body but there was a piece of stick with the bark shaved off in its mouth but all the others save for some small fresh water fish came dead and smoked like the grasscutter, porcupine, antelope, monkey, freshwater stingray among others. So unable to contain my curiosity any longer after seeing live alligator after live alligator delivered without injuries over time I asked my father the question, how was this strong and formidable beast captured alive? What he told me not only blew my mind but also gave me a life lesson. He told me that the people that hunt this particular animal use an ancient technique where they first bait it with a hook inserted in a dead rat and firmly tied to a tree. After the alligator has taken the bait and struggled unsuccessfully to free itself the fisherman then approaches it. They take a strong piece of stick, shave off the bark, tie a strong rope to it then this piece of stick was then lowered into the water where the alligator is with the hook still in its mouth. They thrashed around the water with the stick to aggravate it so it either thinks it's a prey or it's being attacked then it bites down hard on the piece of stick. After it bites down hard they step on its head preventing it from opening its mouth and the rope is tied around its long tapered mouth taking away its most dangerous weapon before the hunters overpowered and tied it up securely.

Anybody can stay hidden, use a gun to blast down animals far away from their safe hiding spot and call it hunting but this type right here where you study the animal's characteristics and use them to take it down without a single shot fired or a machete wound for such a strong animal is impressive indeed. You have to study the trickery used from both the hunter and alligator's perspective to appreciate it; the hunter comes as an aggressor, gets the attention of the gator and when the gator is about to attack he presents the stick on a rope to it as a false target, the gator on the other hand does not know this. It sees the hunter as a threat or easy prey and strikes at him biting at what he thought is a part of the hunter and we all know that crocs and gators have powerful bite forces so it bites down hard and instinctively proceeds to do a death roll to disorient the attacker/prey and tear off huge chunks of meat from the victim but gets itself entangled in the process and becomes the victim. I will call this the 'alligator stick' lesson and when it was told to me I decided that for the rest of my life I will think things through and analyse them thoroughly before I act so I don't end up chomping down on an alligator stick. To link this to our subject matter you can see that the Nigerian people as a collective have not deciphered the system in place used to oppress them but instead attack different members of the executives tenure after tenure be it president or governors until their time expires and they fade into obscurity while a new alligator stick is presented to them with a new governor and the whole process repeats itself without any real change or development for the masses.

When I think about the gator stick I think about the word 'nigger' again and how it has come to be the global symbol of racism for black people and who can say it or who can't say it and all the while there's mass poverty, poor healthcare, police brutality, unfair financial opportunities, the fact that blacks as a people do not have a single country that's functioning for the interest of the collective among others which are far more devastating for black people but hey, don't say it or hell will break loose so for me I see it as a gator stick but I did not suit up for this particular fight today. As for the executive I think it's the main life source for the political ruling class because if they lose the executive their source of funding will be cut off and the negative balloon theory will take effect for their organisation so the political ruling class needs the power and influence they have over the executive to keep existing and to keep being this powerful so any plan of attack to dismantle them will have to include that but they are no fools, they have back up plans in place and we will see more of that as we go on. We talk about bad leadership, bad leadership and bad leadership all day but these are the root causes of it, you see the most powerful leadership offices in the country are not working for the interests of the masses instead working for their own personal interests and for those of their organisation essentially cutting off the masses who have no people power in the first place from the equation.

This I feel is the best way to go about this subject otherwise we could just write out a long list of names and the dates they held office coupled with the bad things we think they did to us as a people which would add another 100 pages or more to this book but most of these people are no longer actively engaged in politics and some of them are dead but the exact things we could blame them for are still happening so I say it is better to go after the hunter than to keep chomping on sticks. This is like the case of the biblical Israelites just getting out of Egypt as free people the first time, a band of recently freed slaves not the warrior nation they later became, so putting down names will get me powerful enemies that I'm not yet capable of handling in my current state. So there we have it, ladies and gentlemen, the executive arm of government remains the main weapon and the main pillar of the political ruling class, without it their powers are greatly diminished and they will slowly start to die off but this is not to say they do not have their hooks on the other arms but the executive is the main one because it has the highest seats of political power in the land. We do not need to go into the details on how they live, just think about everything we said about the masses and picture the extreme opposite of it, they always roll in convoys sometimes 30 or up to 50 cars deep with lots of security personnel, sirens blaring, and they could just be going to the corner store to get bread so it's a lavish life of abundance all at the expense of the masses. With this we can move on to the next arm.

THE LEGISLATURE: WHISPERS IN THE STREETS ABOUT THE BIG HALLS IN ABUJA.

> 'State is the name of the coldest of all cold monsters. Coldly it lies; and this lie slips from its mouth: 'I, the state, am the people'.
>
> - Friedrich Nietzsche

There has been a lot of whispers and murmurings floating around in the streets among the common folks, what could they possibly be whispering about amongst themselves? I put my ears to the ground and listen intently as I try to catch their words and I'll tell you what they said. The people say that there are some big beautiful halls in Abuja where wealthy politicians from all over the country come to gather every week in their self-importance to, as they keep telling themselves and others that care to listen, debate laws and bills that would help the citizens of this country and make life better for them. The common folks speak about the great wealth that resides in the great halls of the Nigerian legislature, there is also talk of the great power and influence belonging to its members among the ordinary ones in the streets as they go about their day, shuffling around the dirt under the hot sun looking for what scraps they can lay their hands on to eat so as to quell the pangs of their stomachs for that day until the next day comes along and the stomach-god asks for more; more and more it will require from you and you must give to it until the day you die, for what will the simple do? The lands all around these halls lay in ruins, death and destruction plagues these lands and the people in it but these halls have stood intact for long seemingly immune to all that is happening around it, the powerful men and the women inside those halls continue to hold their weekly meetings to discuss how they will improve the lives of the masses while the land is continuously ravaged, I have seen enough of the rubbish and can no longer stop myself from acting.

Behold, I look from the bushes and see all that is happening, I see the young men of the land, her strength, sitting down in front of huts confused and wasting away, some drinking palm wine and some staring aimlessly into space, jobless, some are fighting with machetes and killing each other off, fighting over nothing, blood is being spilled and lives are wasted, then I look at the village square and see the old men and women seated in their sense of self-importance and ceremony in their posh halls. Their well-guarded king is there too and a stained, torn, worn out flag of Nigeria rests behind his throne. It is the stain of shame, nepotism, corruption and foolishness that is associated with these people, they are having one of their numerous meetings or committees or whatever, meetings where nothing meaningful is ever discussed but everyone leaves with stashes of cowries tied safely in the wraps and folds of their traditional attires. I dodge the poverty, the decay and the dirt in the streets covering my nose as I do so because of the stench, then make my way to the village square; and when I get to the entrance of their hall I dance in and laugh maniacally. I dance into their midst with wild gesticulations and when I have their attention I point, first to their heavily guarded king and then to the rest of them. I can see the shock and surprise on their faces, 'such insolence' they say 'who gave this brat the right and the audacity?' they ask themselves in low whispers... I point to them and call them what they truly are, fools! And then I asked them these questions: when did you all betray yourselves? How do you live with yourselves seeing all the damage that you have done and the mess you have created for our people?

On paper Nigeria operates a bicameral legislative system made up of the House of Assembly and the House of Representatives which are supposedly the law makers and the representatives of the people. So when you look at the structure everything seems as it should be; elections for these positions are held every 4 years and there are people from every state and region in the country in those houses but it's when you start to look at the functionality and performance that the whole facade starts to fall apart and the right questions need to be asked; is the legislature independently pulling its own weight to create balance with the other bodies in the triarchic system? If not then who's the legislature really working for? We have house of assemblies in the federal and state levels but when was the last time any law that made any significant impact in the lives of Nigerians was passed in the country over the past 50 years? You can do your research and tell me, I'll listen. We have a federal house of representatives but how is the government so consistently deaf and oblivious to the plights of the Nigerian masses? Who are the people in these houses really representing? Are they there for themselves or are they there for the Nigerian people? These questions are getting a bit tiring for me, I feel like I should just go straight to my conclusions but I have to show my workings besides I feel like these questions will help those who are not too familiar with the situation and the subject matter to follow my logic to the conclusions for better understanding.

So let me give you some context at least; when you look at the members of the federal house of assembly for the past 15 years you'll see that it's made up of a lot of ex-governors and governors-in-waiting. The ex-governors are those governors that have done their 8 year terms in their states and see the senate as the next logical step in their political progression to cross over to the next level and climb another rung in their ladder while the governors-in-waiting are those that had to step aside for someone from their state who was just a little higher up the ladder of the political ruling class above them to be the governor of their state for the next 8 years while they try to keep busy and be part of the official government structure which will give them time/opportunity to embezzle and accumulate the funds they'll need when their time comes to make a push. Nigerians had a joke that the senate was a retirement home for governors. It's a good joke that got a few chuckles out of me but the real joke is on the Nigerians themselves because these ex-governors who were now senators with all the legal powers of the senate vested in them went ahead and speedily passed laws that gave hefty pensions and other lifetime benefits to guess who?? *drumroll* EX-GOVERNORS!! hahaha I couldn't help but still laugh because the craziness is just astonishing. Let's untangle it for a moment; so they were governors and got a lot of money legally and illegally through that position then they moved up to the senate to pass laws that will see them get paid hefty sums of money as pension for their time as governors while now receiving hefty sums as senators including perks like housing allowance, car allowance, security allowance, yearly furniture allowance, travel allowance, medical allowance, a robust home staff and sometimes over a hundred personal assistants and office staff all paid for by their rich sugar mama called Nigeria all at the expense of the Nigerian people while the masses live like rodents in their own country doomed to scurry along the hot sands day in and day out.

You can definitely see that it's just the political ruling class shuffling members between these positions but the crudeness of it all never fails to create shock or some type of response anytime you come face to face with it. We can try to look at the psychology and greed of the people that operate in this system but that will do us no good at this stage because that's a morality issue and preaching will have no effect on these people so the system they operate in has to be totally dismantled if you want to have an effect here. A Nigerian senator is entitled to a fat salary and all those many unnecessary perks multiplied for each and every single one of their 109 members but politicians do not step in front of the camera for a few seconds before telling the people just how broke the country is and how we all need to struggle together through it. Now you see why these positions are so highly coveted, they attend their weekly meetings to discuss a whole bunch of nothing which impacts no one but helps them pass time then they legally receive hefty payments and bonuses for doing absolutely nothing while the masses live in squalor. Can you see why I said the poverty for the masses in Nigeria is artificially crafted? There is no separation of powers here because the executive and the legislature are one and the same people with a common interest separated by name only.

> *'The way out of parliamentarism is not, of course, the abolition of representative institutions and the electoral principle, but the conversion of the representative institutions from talking shops into "working" bodies.*
>
> — *V.I LENIN*
>
> *The State and Revolution.*

You can switch out any of the houses under the legislature for 'parliamentarism' in that statement by Lenin and it holds true because for now they are just talking shops and very expensive talking shops at that. The Nigerian legislature which is also another metaphor for the Nigerian government is a very expensive body to run giving very little or nothing in return. If it was a machine it would be an inefficient one but it continues to run because of a combination of cowardice, ignorance, resilience and stupidity of the Nigerian people. The political ruling class have a choke hold in the legislature but you might ask why efforts have not been made by the masses to seize back this arm of government. First of all I must tell you that elections in Nigeria are an expensive affair that requires a lot of capital for candidates who are contesting to spread their names and buy influence. Anything in fact that you want to spread will require huge capital, if the politicians need lots of capital to do it I wonder why they expect the church to do it on prayers alone. Anyways the capital required is what a masses tied in poverty do not have access to and this is another reason why they are kept strongly in poverty as a people so should an outsider candidate or even a small number of them somehow make their way into any of the chambers they would find the going tough in a system that's based on numbers and majority rule. They would not be able to make any significant impact or change because they do not have the numbers and what they would be is a nuisance to the political ruling class who would use the time of their tenure to plot a proper expulsion for them in the next elections to get them expelled from their seat. Any smart tactician would leave a few outsiders in the mix though just to give false hope to observers that the system works but as I earlier said, as a far minority in the house they would make no impact, but these tacticians do not allow that because they know that a little leaven leaveneth the whole lump.

    The divide between the political class and the masses is too wide and this divide has been made possible by the money barricade; it is really a battle of the haves and the have nots. So efficient is this barricade that both classes hardly ever cross paths and their stories are wildly different from each other's even though they live in the same country. Their children do not attend the same schools, they do not use the same hospitals, they bank differently, they travel differently and it goes on, the only places both classes sometimes converge are in social events and places of worship without any proper interaction further highlighting the divide that exists between both classes. For democracy to work there has to be proper education of the electorate as to how the system truly works because the ignorance of the masses has been strongly used against them to take advantage of them to arrive at this juncture. The Nigerian masses on their own need to start taking politics the same way they take religion as the entrance of the knowledge will flood their minds with political light and knowledge is power. The Nigerian legislature at all levels leaves us with one more piece of brilliant magic by managing to exist in the country but simultaneously remain non-existent in the lives of the Nigerian masses as a working institution in our democracy, and all the while the whispers continue among the desolate ones in the dusty Nigerian streets about the big halls in Abuja where top of the line bulletproof cars come to weekly drop off and pick up dinosaurs expensively clad in native attires and escorted by an army of assistants and uniformed men The word on the streets is that they have all come to discuss ways that they can make life better for the dying and the suffering in Nigeria and all I can think of is one parable from my childhood that says: *'if the pesin wey hide something from you dey follow you to help you find am, forget! You no go ever see that tin'* meaning that 'if the person that has hidden a thing from you unknown to you has joined you to help you find that thing, forget about it! You will never find that thing that is lost'. How this translates to the situation is that the cause and sustainer of your poverty have said that they want to help you end it, will it ever happen?

THE JUDICIARY: CRIMINAL LAW AND THE JUSTICE SYSTEM IN NIGERIA.

'Written laws are like spider's webs, and will, like them, only entangle and hold the poor and weak, while the rich and powerful will easily break through them'.

- Anacharsis.

This quote by 6th century Scythian philosopher Anacharsis has been passed down for over 1,400 years with many different variations of it made over time but the original thought of the author and the truth they bear have remained intact through time and still hold strong in present times. My favourite out of all the variations is: *'the law, like the spider's webs, catch the fly and let the hawk go free'* and you can see that the soul of the author's words did not become corrupt through time. So who's the fly and who's the hawk if we liken it to the Nigerian situation? You guessed it right and the judiciary which is the 3rd arm of government in Nigeria does not offer anything different to the other 2 arms. How do I put it plainly enough to you? Okay let me go rhetorical since I'm the quester: what's a sunny beach to an eskimo? So in that same vein what is justice to the average Nigerian? They do not know her, justice does not stay in Nigeria but even if she came for a brief visit she'll walk past the Nigerian masses and elites without so much as a single person recognising her or asking her for pictures or even her autograph; that's the level we're talking about here.

The work of the judiciary is to interpret the laws of the land as laid down by the legislature but this is where the problem starts and ripple effect theory appears to land some more blows on the Nigerian set up because if there's no work done by the legislature to start with, where does that leave the judiciary? If there are no foundations laid on ground what can the righteous build on? It was Aristotle that said 'the law should govern' but the judiciary has also been heavily compromised and rendered toothless in Nigeria. One of the fallouts of a society where poverty has been so consistently prevalent is that everything becomes for sale and justice is for sale in Nigeria to the highest bidders. You can look through the history of all the parts of the world for clarity if in doubt, there is no single society where justice is perverted that has prospered significantly, not one! and looking at Nigeria it is clear that this land where we live in is a land of oppression where justice is continuously perverted day and night against the poor in the land. I will say it again for emphasis' sake, the lack of people power is the death of the Nigerian masses, even the current constitution that is in force was prepared under military regime but there was no referendum done to consult the people highlighting once again the disconnect between masses and leadership. Stitching these points together the conclusion is that as one of the arms of government the judiciary is not independent so does not provide the necessary balance and authority in the triumvirate system that we're supposed to be operating, and it cannot protect or uphold the rights of the citizens of the federal republic of Nigeria.

The fact that this arm of government does not have elected officials that are changed every 4 years like the other two must have been a challenge for the political ruling class in their quest to control it but as they say nothing is impossible if you set your mind to it. The legal profession was a profession that commanded respect when we were growing up, they went through the law school system and were referred to themselves as 'learned'. Before the legal sector was taken over by the political ruling class they were a constant voice of opposition standing against corruption in the country but that was then, today that body has also become a host for the parasite that's eating Nigeria from the inside out. The first attack on the authority of the legal sector was the political ruling class through the executive branch disobeying court orders over the decades so with no way to enforce its rulings their powers were greatly diminished because like the media when they risk their safety to publish stories to the masses after doing investigative journalism the masses had no people power then to act on the stories except gossip and to hurl curses at the politicians which was ineffective, matter of fact that's another alligator stick if I have not mentioned it before. Same with the judiciary when court orders that went against the wills of power in the land were openly flouted by powerful politicians, there was no people power on the part of the masses to stand by the legal sector thus they were isolated which prepped them for the next phase of occupation.

The next phase of occupation was money, the 3 arms of government cannot be truly independent when the salaries and all other costs to be used by the legal sector comprising the judiciary and the state criminal law apparatus are signed off by the current office holders of the executive. This great flaw allowed for the judiciary to be breached but that was not all, the handpicking of legal practitioners with dubious and questionable characters and allegiances for promotion into sensitive positions throughout the court hierarchy system in the country also allowed them over time to sow tares among the wheat of the legal sector. With this strategy you can see nepotism and the lack of meritocracy which is a common theme throughout all aspects of the country whereby in social engineering terms the best candidates do not end up in their best positions on the structure to allow it to function optimally, instead people were picked based on their loyalties, allegiances and susceptibility to compromise. This is a kind of corruption that affects true and hard work because the general body consisting of peers, colleagues and fellow professionals are watching and they know that such promotions based on ethnicity, religion, quota and allegiances are unmerited and dangerous to the health of the legal profession in the country. Do not forget that these people carry out active management through assessment of performance so if for instance a particular judge is refusing to play ball and give certain compromised rulings according to the will of the political ruling class they might find themselves suddenly transferred to a remote customary court in some village in the middle of nowhere within the Nigerian territory where electrical lines have not yet been connected to, you get the picture? Do you now understand how criminal it can be to be law abiding in a compromised and utterly corrupt system?

These things were and are done openly without regard, so all these years the legal sector and the legal profession in Nigeria also in line with the judiciary has become a big joke in Nigeria at all levels from the supreme court down to the customary courts scattered across the country. Nigeria has become a place where justice is not just frequently aborted but they have started utilizing condoms, IUDs, pull out methods and other methods to ensure that justice is not even conceived at all in the first place even if it means taking out her womb. Like the executive and the legislature that we talked about before it the once hallowed judiciary and the legal sector in Nigeria has just become a place where men and women play dress up in robes, ridiculous wigs and lace neckties looking like stage acts with bad costumes all just to pronounce pre-written judgments handed to them beforehand like they were programmed robots. All of these people or at least those that matter in that sector are anything but independent, they are stuck so deep in the pockets of the politicians like some kangaroo babies. Today when I look at the justices, judges, SANs, lawyers, attorneys or whatever fancy names they have given to themselves or bought for themselves in Nigeria all I see are a bunch of joeys peeking out of the corrupt cozy pouches of their political overlords, pitiful!

If you know the modus operandi of the political ruling class by now you'll know they work in layers with back up plans and back ups to their back up plans to catch as much as possible which is why they are so effective in Nigeria. The next layer of infiltration that they employ on the legal body in the country is even more sinister and is done through marriage. With this strategy you see aspiring, current and past members of the executive always married to legal practitioners who then magically speed up through the hierarchy of their profession either because of who they are married to or because they were the best legal students in their class that turned into the best legal practitioners. There is no middle ground here in this, it must either be one or the other and with their new high positions they are used to manipulate the law, to desecrate the judiciary, and the pervert justice in the country. Court rulings and judgments are no longer arrived at in the different court rooms in the country through evidence, jury debates and jurisprudence but are now settled late at night in between groans and poundings on squeaking matrimonial beds in resplendent mansions built with looted and embezzled funds of the country which is the very life blood of the Nigerian masses. More marriages like this are encouraged and more among their ranks are encouraged to study law as we find more and more politicians going to get law degrees today because you cannot break the law or even manipulate it if you don't know it.

> **'If you must break the law, do it to seize power: in all other cases observe it.'**
>
> - Julius Caesar.

How bad really is the corruption in Nigeria? Well on a scale of 1 to 10 it's 50 just to give you an idea of what's it's like and the courts who are supposed to check it are powerless in the face of this great beast because they have been compromised and infiltrated. Where they once stood tall and proud as beacons of light and justice they are now dens for thieves, places of slaughter, stages where third rate magicians sloppily perform tired tricks in full view without the advantage of a veil to cover their shame and a coven for demons that sow hopelessness and lawlessness into the land. You cannot even think of the millions of cases where ordinary Nigerians have been cheated and have seen justice aborted because someone with a little more money than them had paid the lawyers and judges money under the table to act in a certain way that's not in accordance with the demands of their profession. The pain and stench of those cases never go away and in the realm of the spirit they act as blemishes on the garment of the country by which accusations are laid against her night and day, and she is judged.

Have you seen lady justice in Nigeria? Have you really seen her or did you just not recognise her when she passed you by cat walking and humming a cheery tune? When you look at the symbol of mother justice in other countries she is a simple woman; she is modestly dressed and her eyes are blindfolded to signify that the law is blind to everyone and a respecter of no one. In her right hand she holds a double edged sword to signify punishment for those that go against the law regardless of who they are, and in her outstretched left hand she holds a perfectly balanced weighing scale to show that everybody is equal before the law but mother justice is different in Nigeria. Mother justice in Nigeria is not blindfolded, instead she has on dark designer sunglasses that were bought from one of the top fashion brands in Europe and gifted to her which tells you that she's not really blind to everyone but she sees some 'special' people only in the land through those dark shades, you know, the people who are able to buy her those type of expensive shades but all the others are insignificant to her. In her raised right arm she is holding a machete, the type that has one blunt edge and one cutting edge that farmers in the Nigerian villages make use of but the blunted edge of her machete is covered with foam, the poor masses get cut by the law, while the other people just get... how do you say?... a light tap on the wrist with the padded edge of the machete regardless of what they have done. The weight she is holding in her left hand is not balanced but pressed down to one side; the side pressed down has wads of cash on it while the lighter side has a few grams of sand and *garri* on it to show what the lives of poor Nigerians is really worth.

I always equated the lives of the poor Nigerian masses to grains of sand or more specifically 'earth' but most people did not get my analogy, they thought I was trying to say that the people are dirty.

No not that, when you look at the earth everybody just throws their stuff at it. Want to build a house? Foundation anchored to the earth, drill oil? earth, nuclear waste? oh no problem, earth, channel harmful electrical currents, earth, sewage and refuse disposal? Dump it there and so on and so forth and that is what the bulk of the Nigerian people weigh in the balance against the political ruling class. The *garri* on the other hand is a local food made from cassava and rich in carbohydrates but it has come to be the symbol of poverty and poor living to Nigerians. So have you seen our Nigerian mother justice? She is not modestly clad like the others from the nations but she's a lady of style, she has on a native attire tailor made from some fine imported fabrics with designer shoes and coral beads on her neck and wrists to match maybe that's why you Nigerians say you haven't seen mother justice in the streets because when she walked past you many of you did not recognise her and some of you even bowed in respect to greet her as she walked past humming her cheery tune under her breath. When she who was supposed to be a servant of the people becomes indiscernible to the oppressors then there's a big problem indeed.

In Nigeria when the really wealthy and connected people of the political ruling class get charged to court, I mean that's if their cases ever make it to court in the first place they come with a paid crowd of fans and supporters dancing, cheering and singing their praises blowing trumpets, beating drums and holding placards high with words of praise and support inscribed on them. I'm talking about the very members of the ordinary, poor, deprived and impoverished Nigerian masses escorting the very corrupt and wealthy politicians to court to answer for crimes against the same ordinary, poor, deprived and impoverished Nigerians, what do you make of that? This is another one of the many reasons why the masses have no people power and this is also one of the ways money is used to control the masses which is why poverty is very important to the success of this system. When a people living in poverty and locked in survival mode are given stipends they throw common sense and logic to the side doing anything to survive even to support the very people preying on them because they must survive one way or the other. This is also why I hate palliatives from politicians, why not create the right environment for these people to work and make something for themselves in dignity? The answer is because if they do so you will not be able to control them as they'll have a mind of their own but in this poor state just like my vision where few wads of cash are thrown into their midst to see them scrambling like animals for scraps, the dehumanization of the blacks has not stopped till this day.

    I got sidetracked but as I was saying, when the truly wealthy and corrupt make it to court to answer for their charges their cases have already been determined before that court appearance so the rulings would leave you speechless and questioning your sanity. When members of the political ruling class come face to face with mother justice in Nigerian courts they are greeted with warm smiles from her with inviting eyes, they are all one and the same after all. They put some more money on her already imbalanced scale and then proceed to bend her over in her attire, with the machete and scale in her hands, and then have doggy style sex with her right in front of the court house for everybody to see. By everybody I mean everyone present and those at home which includes the lawyers, the judges, the jury, the press, you, the orderlies, law enforcement officers, the onlookers and even the innocent birds flying by. When they are done, they put some extra money in her pockets as a tip right there and it's case closed! If they sex her good enough the crowd might even cheer, clap and hail them, 'Hey, what a performance!' they say to one another as they look on and that is justice for you in Nigeria if you're rich or more specifically the abortion of justice in broad daylight in Nigeria.

You see, mother justice in Nigeria is just a smart girl with a side hustle so the real criminals in the land have it easy, law enforcement cannot arrest them because the law enforcement are guards to these individuals. Whatever investigative journalists are in the land have long been compromised and converted from their original purpose turned instead into mouth pieces for the political ruling class and even the few that refuse to cave in to the pressure putting their lives and loved ones in danger in the process are too few to make any impact, and even when they expose the misdeeds of the land the system is too corrupt to take any action to right things or serve justice and the masses are too weak to affect things in any way and this is Nigeria for you. This ends my commentary on the judiciary as the 3rd arm of the political government structure in Nigeria and by extension the criminal justice system and as you can see there's nothing exciting to write home about here but at least you can see how the country came to be what it is today from a political leadership perspective. In its current state the judiciary just like the legislature has been absorbed by the executive so it does not and cannot exist as an independent arm of government capable of checking and balancing the powers of the executive in any way giving absolute monarchy-like powers to the executive. Knowing this Nigeria cannot be said to be a democracy but a veiled form of tyranny.

LAW ENFORCEMENT AND THE NIGERIAN PRISON SYSTEM.

*'The police are not here to create disorder,
they're here to preserve disorder'.*

- Richard Daley.

For me personally the police are a necessary evil in society, they are given the authority, the training and tools to maintain order but that authority and power can be abused and used to oppress the vulnerable in society. Usually not regarded in the best light even in the so called 'developed' and 'happy' countries you can only imagine what the police and policing is like in a place like Nigeria. Perhaps my bias may be because of the type of policing I have been exposed to growing up and I say this because I understand that the police like democracy is a system and depending on how that system functions and is executed it may be the best thing in the world for society or the worst nightmare and in this case it is a living nightmare. There is no easy way to go about this task because the individual stories about the Nigerian police are too numerous and too horrific to capture in such a small space as the one I have allocated for this topic. My interest in this topic as it relates to our subject matter is a look at the police as part of the criminal justice system but reading up to this point it should be pretty obvious that in the national chaos I have described so far the people who are supposed to be maintaining peace and order are definitely not doing their job if anything at all. The spiritual and physical realms that have free willed beings existing in them both have a justice system in place to punish those that abuse their free will; for the known parts of the spirit realm that relate to man's existence in the physical realm you have heaven and hell while man has developed a justice system to regulate the members of society in the physical earth realm.

Nigeria is one of the most corrupt countries in the world, there is no area of her being that has not been touched by corruption, the justice system is corrupt and the Nigerian police officers are some of the most corrupt in the world. Is this hyperbole as usual? Well, when police officers openly ask for bribes in the streets in full view of the public around the country what would you have me say? The culture of poverty in Nigeria which has seen corruption and compromise become a way of life as a means of survival essentially becoming the way things are done usurping justice, rights, law and truthfulness in the process then that is a twisted society with a twisted culture and this is Nigeria for you. Let me tell you a random fact; when you go to the police in Nigeria to report a case they ask you for money first before they begin their investigations, another random fact: after you report the case and they need to go to another location to make an arrest they ask you for money for petrol to do so. Are we done? Nah, we haven't even started to scratch the surface of the mess that is the Nigerian police. Here's another: if you're getting robbed in your house at night and you call the Nigerian police they won't come and if at all they do they always conveniently arrive just as the robbers have finished robbing and have made their escape but what was I expecting? Was I expecting too much from my country? The fact that Nigeria does not have a helpline for the police, ambulance or anything should have been a red flag if we wanted to go down this rabbit hole. The lack of a helpline shows you once again as with other signs that Nigeria as a country is not working because if the citizens have to provide electricity for themselves, drinking water among others and are left to fend for themselves and protect themselves without weapons I have to ask again: what exactly is the role of the Nigerian government in this relationship again? Or in the manner that the Gen Zs like to ask: what does the Nigerian government bring to the table?

I'm not so sure you really want to find out how dark things could get on this issue, I do not think you have the stomach or the balls for it and this is what the Nigerian masses are subjected to all the days of their lives. They are thrown into this hell with terrorists, kidnappers, robbers, rapists and all kinds of dangerous criminal elements without the means to protect themselves, we do not even have the right to bear arms like the citizens of the United States and you wonder where the insecurity comes from? By the time you start to think like me and see the Nigerian society the way I do you'll understand that anything allowed to thrive in Nigerian society is deliberate and is a tool for some desired effect under the principles of social engineering so insecurity being looked at as a tool, one only needs to reverse trace this to see it as a tool to spread fear into the hearts of the masses and to create chaos. The Nigerian police set up illegal roadblocks all around the country through which they harass and illegally extort money from motorists all day for the flimsiest of excuses and reasons, what if I told you that they have an organised system where the extorted funds are remitted to their higher ranked superiors in the force, would you believe me? If I wanted to take you into the true darkness of Nigerian society do you think you could stand and look it in the face without flinching? In a country where police officers in some states have their personal POS machines to extort money and bribes from the citizens what can I really say to you here about the Nigerian police? I will accept that it's not all the officers but tokenism will have 2 or 3 good officers who did not compromise their morals and duty to the Nigerian people just as the judiciary or legislature but those individual members and their deeds while commendable cannot make me judge the whole organisation as good so tokenism is a problem too in Nigeria because these few ones are sometimes used as examples for why the clearly broken system is working which is not true.

We have to take a different direction if we are to move forward, the stories are numerous, there are people that were wronged by the Nigerian police in the 80s who have died now, there were those in the 90s, the 2000s, the 2010s and so on and so forth so which of these stories would you now like me to tell here? Because if the system currently running in Nigeria persists and is not confronted and vanquished you can see that the stories of wrong doing by the police will persist into the 2050s, 2060s and so on, and if we follow the progression of things in Nigeria if nothing drastic happens to changer her course then those periods will be worse than whatever we are seeing happening today so my focus from here will be the role of the police force in the system, you'll just have to imagine how bad they are in your mind taking into account everything I have said up till now. Look at my logic closely and question it, if the Nigerian police exists in the Nigerian society to create order and protect the lives of the vulnerable masses but do not do this and are still funded, sustained and rewarded by the political ruling class then it means that the creation, existence and role of the Nigerian police force cannot be to safeguard the lives, rights and properties of the Nigerian masses. How can I explain this? Okay let's say you have a problem of rat infestation in your house and you buy a cat which is a natural predator of rats to deal with the problem of rats. Say after three months you notice that the rat population did not diminish but they have instead thrived in the presence of the cat while now your chocolates and other snacks you keep in the house which were untouched before even with the rats have started disappearing how would you view that cat and what will you call it? Would you call it a failed rat killer or just straight call it a chocolate thief?

So what is the Nigerian police to the Nigerian masses? Is it a failed law enforcement agency or is it something else? Remember what I've showed you about this Nigerian system that there are no failures in it, everything is working in it as intended to create the reality you see today. Tracing this vein of thought further you'll come to see that the Nigerian police is part of the last piece of this Nigerian puzzle, it alone is not the whole last piece of the puzzle but it is part of it. The last piece of the Nigerian puzzle is the physical backing of Nigerian authority, this physical backing consists of agencies and organisations comprising trained men and women armed with guns to form a force that backs the authority of the Nigerian political government structure. For example, a connected member of the political ruling class which is the 2nd circle can easily manufacture a court order through the court system in the 3rd circle at the snap of their fingers using money, connections or both against a poor member of the masses in the 1st circle. Now the court order is just a piece of paper from a judge whom that poor soul could beat to stupor in a fist fight including the person that initiated the whole process in the first place. This member of the masses can blow his nose into the paper of the court order, squeeze it into a ball and throw it at the face of whoever came to deliver it but because of an organised force comprising men and women with guns mandated to enforce that court order it becomes more than just a piece of paper. Same thing can be said about your politician occupying a political position within the government structure. He or she is a dinosaur and has corrupted that position to embezzle the commonwealth of the people, the masses know it but that office-holder is not standing on his or her own individual strength but the force of uniformed men and women with guns backing the office that they occupy.

This brings me to my last theory on the Nigerian situation that the system created by the political ruling class to exploit the masses is only made possible because of trained and armed men and women acting as a force to protect that system otherwise the system would be overrun and destroyed by the exploited and impoverished masses. The great disadvantage of the masses in this conflict is that this organised force have the right to bear arms while the masses do not and this becomes the deciding factor. This is why I like the American system where the citizens can carry arms, it levels the playing field to an extent and gives them a fighting chance at least in the case that they come into open conflict with their government which is a possibility. With this theory in mind it becomes clear that even though the police as a system was created to provide law and order, in this special scenario like we have in Nigeria the police is not here to protect the masses but to protect the political ruling class (combined 2nd and 3rd circle) from the wrath of the exploited masses (1st circle excluding the 2nd and 3rd circles). To carry out this function they do not need the extra specialized training that they would normally require to uphold the law and protect the citizens, whatever substandard training they have and rusty 1980s weapons they are given, as long as it serves the purpose of protecting the elites from the masses and keeping the masses in check then the police has served its purpose within this system and this is why you see no effort to upgrade them more than they are.

This method is what I call the changing fence; the fence does not need to be the best, it doesn't need to be the most secure or the most sophisticated but as long as it's able to keep the animals it was designed for in check it's the best or suitable fence for that scenario. So imagine you had a low fence to keep pigs in check in a pen, the fence is not tall neither does it have electricity or other deterrents to prevent the pigs from climbing it but pigs do not fly so that fence is adequate to keep them in check but if you had a cat or even a dog in that pen it would leap over that fence with ease. Same as the Nigerian police force and the entire Nigerian system, it is not a particularly sophisticated system but it's just sadly appropriate, adequate and effective for the people it was designed to hold. I call it the changing fence because whenever the authority that controls it sees that the people are getting smarter and are starting to climb that fence to escape they quickly add several layers to it until it becomes adequate again to keep them in check. This is my analysis of the Nigerian system and specifically the Nigerian police as a part of that system and why they are so bad and have been so bad for a long time now and why it seems that things are only consistently getting worse and harder for the masses under this system. If you took this same system and tried to copy and paste it in another country, say a 1st world country, it would fail because those dogs and cats would easily leap over it but for the impoverished and exploited ones it's effective. This is not to say that dogs and cats are all powerful because if you look closely at their own societies you'll see that they have fences designed for them too that are effective for holding them but that's not my problem to discuss.

I will tell you a brief story. For months I had been periodically having the gentle prodding in my heart that I told you about in the beginning of this book to write this book but I ignored them and in my manner I kept procrastinating until one day I was sent to do something in the police station in my hometown, I can't even remember exactly what it was I wanted to do at the station but I vividly remember what I saw that day. I remember walking through the gates of the police station in Sapele and standing for a moment taking everything in, to my left there was a big ebelebo tree and police officers sat under it with bottles of beer close by playing draft. There was a fat dark-skinned officer with his uniform unbuttoned exposing a dirty white singlet underneath playing against another officer and the whole place was just a scenario of unprofessionalism to behold. The female officer at the reception was rude and spoke badly to me and I could not believe it. Well I was young then and naive so the shock of that scene hit me hard, I looked around and asked myself: *WHAT IS THIS?!* that visit made such a strong impression on me that the next day I finally walked into a bookshop to buy the notebook and pen that I used to write down the first draft of this book because I did not have a laptop then. It was when my mother saw my seriousness and the work that I put in on that first handwritten draft that she finally gave me the money to buy the laptop I used to write all versions of this book which I have till this day despite the fact that others have been bought and discarded from that time.

As for the prison system I thought about it and decided that there was no need to do a whole chapter on it just to describe the poor living conditions that the prisoners in Nigeria are subjected to because think about it, if the 'free' masses are living like animals in subhuman conditions as full citizens of the country then what kind of conditions would the imprisoned members of society who have lost their freedom have? You'll have to use your imagination to conjure up pictures of what you think the prisons in a 3rd world country would be like and to help you in this I can tell you right now that it's as bad as you can think. These descriptions and stories distract from the system and my focus is to fully capture the system itself as best as I can. Now the terrorists that are killing, kidnapping and causing a rampage on the Nigerian masses around the country when they are captured by say a rogue security unit that's not been compromised and placed under the control of the 'system', that is to say they are doing what they were originally created and trained for, the government has a programme to 'rehabilitate', pardon and then free these terrorists back into society, no prison time no punishment. The mere existence of these programmes, their very existence itself is not only an insult on every Nigerian life taken by these terrorists but also an insult on the fathers, mothers, brothers, sisters, children and people who have lost loved ones to terrorist acts and kidnappings in the country. If your brain is working well then the mere existence of these programmes should tell you more about the controlling force of the country which is the political ruling class than I can ever get to say here but that's not all.

Follow me on this, the 'rehabilitation' programmes are the normal route for them. Now, if by some chance they have committed so much atrocities and find themselves in front of a judge who's not under the control of the Nigerian 'system' which means that justice would not be aborted that day and the due process will be followed, they are then sentenced and they end up in the Nigerian prisons. Now the state of the Nigerian prisons are very terrible but that is not even the gist here, it is the fact that the prisons which are designed to hold criminals are so unprotected that jail breaks are a common occurrence so the terrorists and hardened criminals that get sentenced to the Nigerian prisons find themselves back on the streets in no time so where is the justice in Nigeria then? This shows you the complete cycle of this rigged system as it pertains to punishment of criminals; first of all these people are poor and starving so how can they get the money to buy weapons to become terrorists? These people are poor and starving so how can they get bombs to blow up prison walls to attempt jail breaks to free criminals? These people are poor and starving so how can they fight against the Nigerian security forces in prisons during jail breaks but cannot fight against them to get their total freedom from this tyrannical political ruling class? Where is the justice here? Official statistics put out by the Nigerian Correctional Service for years now consistently show that more than a whopping 65% of all inmates in Nigerian prisons are awaiting trial, what does that say about the justice system in the country? Some statistics exist but I'm a story teller so rather than crunch numbers I prefer to tell stories. I love Nigeria as my country but there are many things about her that I genuinely despise from the bottom of my heart. When I was speaking about the judiciary and the justice system some might have said 'hyperbole' but the reality is there and those who know, know exactly what I'm talking about... a society without justice for its most vulnerable is simply one that cannot prosper!

JUNGLE JUSTICE IN NIGERIA

The people know that the justice system is corrupt, every day they are put in situations where they have to compromise themselves to survive but does that make them corrupt too? The natural laws of man all seem to agree that stealing is wrong but there are those who have stolen and those who are stealing but they seem to be on top so what message does that send? When 68% of all inmates in your prisons nationwide are mostly poor people who were wrongfully detained but were too poor and from poor families who could not afford a lawyer or bail to bribe the police since they have already been detained what does that say about the justice system in that country? All the while the rich thieves move around unbothered by it all, untouched by the justice system, given high positions in government and juicy contracts and it's like this system rewards thieves and criminals. In all this the people have no faith in their legal system and this is where jungle justice comes into the picture. Jungle justice is the situation where ordinary citizens take the law into their own hands via mob action beating or killing a person for committing a usually petty crime like theft. It can be said to be the act of members of such communities putting up a unified front against acts that are not acceptable and making the punishment as public as possible to pass the message so that other members can learn from it.

On the surface it sounds and looks good and noble until you're unfortunate enough to actually witness one of these acts of jungle justice to see these people flogged and beaten with big sticks, hit repeatedly on their heads until they are dazed and while yet alive tyres are put on their necks, the scarce petrol or kerosene is poured on them and they are set ablaze. The screams you hear from them while they are rolling on the ground helplessly before they finally die from the flames is gruesome. There is a large crowd of all ages witnessing these acts and in some cases the police stand by outnumbered and unable to stop these barbaric acts, there have been instances where some brave officers have with gunshots fired into the air been able to stop the mob before the culprits are killed but it varies and all for what? Because a petty thief was hungry and stole a loaf of bread to appease the stomach god for that day. These culprits are orphans and desolate people so jungle justice essentially is desolate people of the masses killing other desolate people of the masses. Now these are not lazy people who don't want to work, many are willing to work but there just was no opportunity for them to fend for themselves and they depart this world blanketed in flames and the screams of an angry and frustrated mob. I'll also admit that not all of the culprits are just petty thieves, some of them are hardened criminals that have terrorised the members of the community for some time through armed robbery, rape and property theft until they are caught and given jungle justice with the community choosing this route instead of the criminal justice system.

What all this says about the people is that they have a strong sense of justice, and of right and wrong, and that they are willing to go to great lengths or commit gruesome acts to uphold those values but when the politicians and members of the political ruling class make public appearances heavily guarded by armed uniform men these same upholders of justice throw themselves on the ground to worship these politicians. They beg for scraps and hail them and it is a shocking sight to behold because you see the desolate members of the masses worshipping the very people that created the conditions they are living in; poverty is powerful indeed and here we see that it has the power to induce insanity in its victims. Now where did all that strong sense of justice go to? Even the spider webs of jungle justice are useless against the biggest thieving hawks in the country and if anything this shows you the hypocrisy of humans in full display. At least this should add some balance to the thought that the masses are just innocent victims; there are different factors ranging from ignorance to stupidity to ethnicity and religion responsible for this stupid behaviour. So the little thieves get roasted like barbecue meat in the streets while the big thieves get worshipped like gods. What is the takeaway from this? Be smart, be a big thief not a little thief in Nigeria.

I have to appeal to the Nigerian people at this point even though it's been a while since we had a viral incident of jungle justice in the country. If only you showed this much dedication to ALL thieves then your communities and your whole country in general would be in a much better place than it is today but you continue to defend and show deference to the very people that are killing you in your own country. Your leaders serve as a mirror image of you, the masses, you love mediocrity too much as a people but love excellence as individuals which is another one of your many contradictions. Jungle justice itself is not a root cause of Nigeria's problems but a ripple effect pointing to deeper and underlying problems in the society and until Nigerians get to the point of: *'fiat justitia ruat caelum'* that is 'let justice be done though the heavens fall' for true justice I don't see any significant changes happening anytime soon.

CONCLUSION ON THE GOVERNMENTAL MEMBERS OF THE POLITICAL RULING CLASS.

For democracy to work the 3 arms of government have to be independent to balance political power and ensure that it does not get abused and regardless of the political system practised the most important thing too is the collective political will of the people that hold the political power in the land because if their will and desire is to better the lives of their people then they will find a way to do it so democracy is not the only way, if anything China exists as proof of this. The Nigerian political government structure does not have this separation because there would have been frictions between the different arms and there used to be but through evolution the political ruling class has achieved a unification of the powers in the land to form a strong bloc of power consolidated within a small group. You have to learn to read the signs in life, when you're playing a video game and for some reason the developers place a lot of supplies in a particular location along your journey then veterans know that a strong opponent is just around the corner so they start preparing themselves for the battle ahead. The ordinary Nigerians are not perceptive enough and do not know how to read the signs that's how they have ended up in this deep hole that was gradually excavated deeper and deeper for them by successive government regimes.

At the early stages of Nigeria's existence as a country there was more separation of powers and the signs of coups and counter coups is evident of that but now the military has gone quiet for a long time even though the politicians of today have done way worse than their predecessors so as a sign reader what should that say to you? I don't know about you but for me this tells me that an understanding and a common ground has been reached and everybody has agreed that to keep up appearances it is better to have a political government in the front while the military remains on the side and even though I don't have bank transfer receipts to show you I know that there are regular payments going from the political government to the military hierarchy to keep them mute and calm. The *Armsgate* scandal of 2020 if anything shows you that there is an understanding between the politicians and the military leadership because imagine it coming to light that politicians shared 100% of the money meant to buy arms for the military to fight terrorism while Nigerian soldiers were being slaughtered like livestock in the war against terrorism happening in northern Nigeria. If it was a regular military leadership concerned about the lives of their soldiers then that would have been a tipping point but there was silence on their part giving them away as far as I'm concerned. The *Armsgate* scandal is very well documented so you might want to read up on it. Scandals like that are few and far between but when they happen they give much needed insights into how a very secretive organisation like the political ruling class operates.

This is another way this secret organisation fools the whole world, if you were an observer from the 70s and 80s you would have seen that there is less friction between the judiciary and the executive today whereby in the past court rulings were flat out disobeyed and disregarded by the executive because it was contrary to them. This gave the health of Nigerian democracy a bad look on the international scene but in recent times this has become scarce and to the casual observer it might seem like the executive complies more with court orders in recent times showing growth in the democracy but they couldn't be wronger because the political ruling class simply played the long game and instead slowly and silently took over the judiciary by placing their people in strategic positions over time to make the judiciary the despicable toothless dog it is today. The absence of friction is a sign to tell you that the whole system is now streamlined, synergised and working smoothly, and I'll tell you here with a straight face that it's a living, breathing and dynamic system. What is the job of the political ruling class as a whole talking about the governmental and non-governmental members? I wrap it up by telling you that they are masters of waste, lack and poverty creation so much so that if they took control of the Atlantic ocean it would only be a matter of time and that ocean would run out of water and fishes, if you put them in charge of the Sahara desert then in a matter of time the Sahara desert would run out of sand and if you put these cursed individuals in charge of heaven located in another dimension where we're told that the streets are made of gold then in a matter of time these people would strip off all the gold from heaven and find a way to open a portal to transport all the gold in heaven back to earth. They will steal all the gold in heaven and bring them back to earth and somehow all that heaven's gold will tellingly end up in western Europe and north America, why? Well, I once heard a statement on National Geographic that says: every smart lion should have a pet cheetah to do their hunting for them. The Nigerian political elites are pet cheetahs.

As for the angels in heaven, those holy beings who are used to walking on gold will walk on the bare ground in heaven for the first time in eternity because the Nigerian political elites took charge in heaven for a short period. So woe unto you ye simple Nigerians, your legislature is the retirement house of your demonic past state governors who have looted their states dry and have then taken their trade, tricks and skills to the national level to continue hoping one day to become your president, woe indeed and a thousand more woes well packaged and delivered to you poor blessed and cursed Delta state as well as some of you other sister South-south states, your so-called representatives in the upper and lower houses have become so used to Abuja they do not even know the way back to their own father's house, among you in your towns and villages, they cannot point to it. Woe I say, where your senators and representative members of your legislature without fail periodically collect fat salaries and different allowances for representation continually making laws which speedily pass readings in both houses to secure this flow of cash into their own pockets legitimising it in the process but your poor and neglected teachers cannot even get their monthly stipend salaries for the work that they have done trying to educate the minds of your children. Woe unto the Nigerian masses who are starving because food remains very, very expensive in your lands above the reach of the common man who's just trying to serve the stomach god for him and his family. Woe unto you, desolate souls, your tormentors live among you and you cannot tell apart your judges and those who should be upholding the laws of your lands from your politicians, a thousand woes on top of another thousand on you all, you all will go to hell without fail, surely none of you Nigerian people will see heaven, I will stand at the door with a big sword to cut you all off if you try to advance. Gnash your teeth, roll yourselves on the floor and wail thou poor Nigerians, your lands are in ruins and your children will inherit these ruins after you.

THE NIGERIAN CIVIL SERVICE

'The bureaucracy and the standing army are a "parasite" on the body of bourgeois society – a parasite born of the internal contradictions which rend that society, but a parasite which "chokes" all its vital pores.'

- V. I. Lenin
The State and Revolution.

The Nigerian civil service is a menace to Nigerian society, they are an important and integral part of the power structure in the land, they are not the main body of the political government structure but they are a part of that body, they are its eyes, its hands and the legs through which the government body interacts and deals with the Nigerian people. Can you now remember all of those ministries, boards, authorities and other sub-agencies that I have mentioned over the course of this book while talking about different areas of the society? They are all parts of the civil service and there are many others I did not mention here but they are the same big cash consuming but low output and inefficient government organisations. The executive arm of the government is the alligator stick dangled in front of the Nigerian people, the executive occupies the minds of the ordinary Nigerians day in and day out but they only serve 4 year terms or 8 years when they serve 2 terms before someone else comes to continue the mandate but the civil service are parasitic government organisations filled with people that spend their entire lives and entire careers in them daily harming the society and in terms of importance I tell you that what the political ruling class is doing currently in Nigeria would not have been possible without the operations of the civil service. In a country of 200 million people where the government is the biggest employer of labour you have to ask yourself what exactly the business of that country is and the answer is pretty obvious, the government of that country is the biggest business and the biggest businessman in that country.

Please do not get me wrong, I'm not saying the executive is not important because even with the change of office-holders over the years the continuity in the mandate and its execution remains constant which is another proof of the political ruling class as a blanketing body to the political government structure but the civil service remains doing its dirty and destructive work far away from the observant eyes of Nigerians. We have to properly look at the civil service, through it the government is able to maintain a strong control over very vital aspects of Nigerian society like health, education, agriculture, oil, natural resources, power, housing, sports, transportation, media, the economy and so much more under the guise of *the people cannot do it for themselves* or *the people are not ready to handle these things* but they hold control over these sectors and do it very, very poorly holding the entire country back in the process. How do they do it? The agencies, bodies and ministries in charge of these sectors have their original system, structures and functions from the beginning, the same corruption that was carried out in the executive was also done in the civil service but it has its own unique characteristics that separates it from the political government. Whatever you do, do not forget that keeping up appearances means a lot to the political ruling class so they have kept these different parts of the civil service intact and created more over time but it's in how they are used and made to function that's where the sweet science of corruption, embezzlement and exploitation was implemented.

The political ruling class has different types of members; they reward lieutenants from among their ranks who were instrumental in say an election cycle by providing money and support to the candidates by giving them positions atop the hierarchy of these bodies. Some of these heads, directors and the likes can have as much as 200 staff comprising friends, family members and the likes all plugged into the system and receiving salary every month, they do not even need to show up for work to get paid and this is how we have 'ghost' workers in Nigeria but that is still another racket. These different bodies of the civil service gets a monthly budget to pay staff and fund their operations. Let's say the ministry of housing is supposed to construct cheap and affordable houses for Nigerians and the body in charge of power is supposed to provide infrastructures for electricity which is a whole lot of money in the first place but when these moneys are paid and approved, to these bodies, they are never used for the intended work instead the money finds its way into private accounts through different means. This is one of the major ways in which the country is being bled. Lenin expounding on the raw thoughts and ideologies of Karl Marx and Frederick Engels wrote the words I used as my opening text for this chapter which calls the 'bureaucracy' which is the civil service in this case a parasite to society and they were not all wrong. These bodies under the civil service have government backing, and we already explained who the government is in the first place, they are mandated by that backing to provide services to the people on behalf of the government so let's say Nigeria does not manufacture her own cars so in the case of importation of cars into the country the clearing costs can be doubled by whatever civil service agency is in charge of importation which automatically increases the cost of the used vehicles imported into the country. You already know the implication of that in an already poor society, many people will not be able to afford the new rates so in this way the government has little pumps, valves and taps in the system which they are able to turn on and off to regulate the level of suffering that they dish out to the masses and this is in every major important aspect and sector of the society, you name it and there is a government authority backed to be in charge of it and to control it.

With such control in place the people will never be able to provide those services for themselves or escape the poverty net that has been prepared for them so the chain of command continues, the executive regulates the civil service and the civil service quietly does the dirty job for them. By increasing the price, like in the example I gave on car import duty they are able to extort the average Nigerians and raise more money for the civil service which climbs all the way up through the hierarchy back to the political ruling class so you can see that Nigeria is not really a country but just one big business clean-up operation in progress. These people would rather die than see this very profitable business venture taken away from them. The ones in the lower levels of the civil service are not particularly rich people, they are members of the masses because they are just as poor as the masses but they do not identify as members of the masses because through affiliation with these bodies under the civil service they have been given authority over the masses and they have some form of relationship with the executive which is the true seat of power. Where this benefits them is that they are able to have access to things the ordinary members of the masses cannot have access to within the government and are able to get things done within their organisation and even with other sister organisations under the civil service umbrella based on solidarity. I see them as native doctors because while you see them as poor due to the fact that their salaries don't get paid to them regularly, they are able to make money through many other corrupt practices like deals under the table. For example Nigeria is a very corrupt country so people that want a government provided service like a Nigerian passport will pay almost twice or thrice the official government listed prices for that passport because the members of the civil service in that area which is the immigration have made the official means for this simple service so laborious, time consuming and impossible that you have no choice but to pay the unofficial amount. Now multiply this for the thousands of people across the different centres daily who come for this service and you get an inkling of an idea as to the kind of money these people are able to generate for themselves by fleecing and milking the hapless masses.

This is why I called the masses earth, they are like farm animals trapped within the country whose sole aim is to be exploited from all angles through different ways. Now if an external body was to take a casual look at the passport process they would find an official process with an official rate listed on the website but if you try to follow that process you might wait a year and not get that passport. So this is another reason why we say that the country is not working. By killing such services and processes in the country they make life harder for the masses and I've come to learn through time that every time I see a service not properly provided in Nigeria I know that people are making money from the already poor masses through that block on the road that's why the service was made deliberately bad in the first place. The people in Nigeria are just like animals being farmed for the wool, for their meat and for their young, it's an endless process of exploitation and do you still wonder why they are poor? I promise you I did not show you the worst here in this book, all of these are just random examples to give you an idea. Every time I've paid for a passport in Nigeria I have always paid above the official rate and that's for every passport I've ever owned so maybe that makes me an enabler, maybe that makes me just as corrupt as the rest of my countrymen and women but I ask you, oh great righteous one, how else was I supposed to get my passport made to escape from the country? I knew that the situation was dire when a friend of mine who paid such unofficial rates sometime back to secure a driver's licence was given a fake driver's licence right from the office of the issuing body by members of that issuing body themselves who had taken his money!

These low level members of the civil service are loyal to their organisations because they are addicted to the illicit money they get from their shady deals, the authority by affiliation as they are a part of the system, connections and the relationships through other sister organisations but even though they do not identify as part of the masses they are part of the poor starving masses still getting played by the system like the rest of us. Take for example the police that spends his day guarding the system and political government, he will not leave that position because of the power his uniform gives him over his brothers and sisters and even though the political structure didn't give him world class training or does not pay his salary regularly he still knows that he and his colleagues could set up an illegal road block to harass and extort Nigerians going about their day and they would still make money for that day's collection after they share their booty so if everyone abuses the masses even the masses themselves who would want to be an ordinary member of the masses? Another thing that gives them hope is that the political ruling class views the civil service as a training ground for new members. A Nigerian proverb says: *'na many road naim lead to market o'* which translates to say *'there are many roads that leads to the market'*, there are other variations even in English like *'there are many ways to kill a rat'* which all mean the same thing, to say that there are different ways of gaining membership into the big leagues which is the dream of most Nigerians and the civil service is one of those ways for those who are trying to get into the political ruling class and the benefits it offers all at the expense of the Nigerian masses.

I told you from the very beginning that the purpose of the whole system is exploitation of the Nigerian masses and Nigeria as a country, and I promised that I would show you before the book ends just how this is done, I'm usually a man of my word so I hope I have delivered in this case too? The government is the biggest employer of labour in Nigeria so the members of the political ruling class and existing members of the civil service determine employment in these government bodies. They put friends, family members, girlfriends and the likes in these offices so already you can see that it's not about meritocracy. Actually a lot of the theories like dinosaur status, ethnic race, Nigerian factor, corruption etc. can be seen within the civil service. These 'ordinary people' are also part of the web, their brothers and sisters within the executive embezzle money from the system and if those moneys don't end up in Europe or North America, they buy choice properties in the country using the names of these family members and friends, they also have them open accounts in banks for this purpose and in some cases they keep huge amounts of cash in large safes in these properties scattered all over which is drug dealer modus operandi. We know this because some of them have been busted over time and you can check to verify should you doubt it and my argument continues as to why in my eyes, Nigeria and most of these sub-Saharan African countries are not really countries in the true sense of the word.

It is a tradition in the country, it is a culture and a way of life, it is a must that these civil service bodies are always poorly run. That's the only way money can be stolen, Nigeria is supposed to produce world class athletes but proper stadiums are not built, proper equipment is not supplied, proper medical care does not exist for the athletes and they are not properly paid if at all but when you check a body is in charge of that work and money has been made available for that work on paper and in the budget so where did it go? Same for housing, same for roads and then tomorrow we come and say Nigeria does not have good roads, well why is that? Is it because road technology is still a new and imperfect technology? you know the answer to that question. Whatever they do in the civil service they make sure that they are very poor at keeping records, they collectively become deaf, blind, dumb and stupid when it comes to keeping records so that their deeds are never discovered and even when they do this there are still enough traces to implicate them because the level of the theft that they have done is too big to hide so civil service buildings have been set on fire especially the records department to destroy everything and these are old buildings without proper fire protection in place and even if the Nigerian fire services exist you can tell what state it's in judging with all the other services provided in the country. They have been known to show up to scenes of fire without water in their tank in the past so this is the country, who can survive these conditions? Many records have been destroyed by these mysterious fires always starting in the records department which is a mafia tactic and they are all classified as 'accidents' so there really is no extent these people will not go to, to achieve their objectives. If the Nigerian masses had this same dedication and determination they would have changed the country for the better by now.

In the past when I still thought that the Nigerian government was trying its best to help the masses like many people I always wondered why they had such control over key areas of the society; why did they not allow the public take over some areas freeing them and their resources up to focus on the key areas like the economy and others? How stupid I was back then because it looked like too much stress and an ineffective way to run the government. I thought it was a bad design that the government had so much control over these key areas which translates to too much work for it until I came to understand that that was the plan all along. You cannot determine what you do not control and you cannot control these people if you do not control these key areas of their lives in the first place. So we're presented with a superman government that's in charge of all these areas; toiling, huffing and puffing to carry them all along but it's all a farce, that superman government has their people strategically placed to choke the lives out of those areas keeping the masses poor and docile in the process. The system and the structure that they have built is too strong, young ones are employed and after a short time they are baptised into the ways of the civil service, those that cannot cope will have to leave or find a way to coexist but they must know that they cannot get far up the ladder in that system if they refuse to participate. In a society where poverty is very strong and opportunities are scarce how many people can walk away from a paying job? In a society where people pay money to be given jobs, parents and family members contribute money so that their family members can be given job positions who would really walk away from a job? In this way the cycle is propagated, it's a self-propagating and recycling system as the civil service remains one of the main reasons how the Nigeria we know today came to be in the first place and why she has remained that way till now even getting worse. These are the people that Sir Richard Branson tried to do business with and he ran away for his life so I ask you this question again: what is your Ivy league certificate in the face of this ferocious beast called Nigerian corruption?

THE ARMED FORCES

'The bureaucracy and the standing army are a "parasite" on the body of bourgeois society – a parasite born of the internal contradictions which rend that society, but a parasite which "chokes" all its vital pores.'

- V. I. Lenin
The State and Revolution.

In Mark 3:25 Jesus said *'And if a house be divided against itself, that house cannot stand'*, I highlighted the acute social fission in the society and its effects as seen in the skilful compartmentalisation of Nigerians at the base versus their consolidation at the top and the clash of the different interests of these groups even the ones at the splintered base as the root cause of the problems in the country. I will use the term 'armed forces' or 'army' as a blanket term for the army, navy, air force, the police and every other uniformed group licensed to carry arms in the country because the aim of this work is not to pick at these groups to castigate them but to unravel and unveil the very hidden dynamics by which the country operates and these groups all play a part in said dynamics in one way or the other. I would first like to pay homage to the men and women of our armed forces that have laid down their lives to serve and to protect us, that said my main interest in this topic is to split the nation into those that are legally mandated to bear arms and those that do not bear arms. Now hold on a minute, I know that you might not like this approach I'm taking right now on this topic and might argue that this mode of distinction is too vague but when you consider the picture that I've painted for you up to this point and the society that I've described so far where the masses have no rights and are continually exploited, it becomes pertinent to ask how this system has been sustained over such a long period of time without the chaos in the country tearing her apart and this is where this blanket body of the armed forces comes into focus.

When I spoke on the police I called them a part of the final piece of the puzzle, well the armed forces is the whole final piece of that puzzle because they hold the whole system together. Now let us follow the progression of things like this: the official role of the armed forces is to protect the rights, lives and properties of the collective Nigerian people as a whole, now keep in mind all of the different groups and their interests as I explained with the 3 circles that make up the whole country. The authority of the armed forces is backed by government authority, their salaries are paid by the government which means that they are also sustained by the government and we have already looked at the break down of the government so in this system that I have been describing, where do you think the loyalty of the armed forces lie? Now you can see why in this scenario I separated the people with guns from those without guns and because the guns give the holders power and as a collective makes them a force that can make things happen in the country it becomes important to clarify their loyalty and their function within the system and I say it here again that it 'does not' really align with those of the masses. You have to look at the history from the time of slavery with the treatment of blacks by outsiders, and the treatment of blacks by the blacks themselves down to the time of colonisation and after colonisation to see that whoever the abuser was or is, the pattern of abuse of blacks in some form or the other has never stopped until this present day and it continues. So when a defeated peoples with a long running and established culture of abuse tracing back centuries have all these political and civil systems built around them over time, how can they then fight for their rights and privileges in the midst of these systems that are clearly not functioning for their benefit and their advantage? This is one of the big questions that life throws at every disadvantaged member of the Nigerian masses as soon as they are born into this world.

You see that all of the political ruling class, the political government structure, the civil service, the armed forces and all the other groups are born members of the masses sharing ethnic groups, foods, dress style, traditions, religion, languages, hometowns, villages and other deep ties with the members of the general masses but the mysterious change occurs when they are transformed into these different groups operating together to form the system of repression and exploitation at work in Nigeria against the very masses they came out of! Now understand that the masses are a mixed multitude, like every other population in the world they are made up of right thinking people, foolish people, uneducated and educated people so there are definitely individuals within the group that are capable of critical thinking even though herd mentality prevails most of the time so when these people come back as brothers and sisters with like skin colour, dressing the same as them, speaking the same languages and seemingly worshipping under the same religious roofs with the masses they seem to get confused and are thrown off course. So any casual observer observing what was happening in the country from afar will see a black country, filled with black people and governed by black people. Without the knowledge of the different interests, systems and forces at play within the country, they can never understand why Nigeria and others like her have come to be the way that they are today and this is why I am taking the time to break things down the way I am doing right now. Their assumption would be that an all black country should be functioning for back interests which is not the case.

So like the civil service the different agencies of the armed forces are made up of individuals from the masses that have been elevated above the masses by reason of the authority and backing of the government bestowed on them and in the Nigerian case knowing who controls the government gives you a clear explanation of where they lean towards because they know what side their bread is buttered on. You have to understand that the masses are totally exempt from this arrangement, in a society where members of the armed forces can beat up a member of society without repercussions over minor provocation that they have to be hospitalised with people walking past unbothered or too afraid of getting attacked too to intervene, what rights do these people really have? And what does this say about the judiciary and other components of justice in the land if we say that the law should govern? The post-colonial culture of abuse coupled with years past of military regimes ushered by coups and counter-coups have created a culture of deep fear of the army and the armed forces in the hearts of Nigerians passed on from parents to children and repeatedly reinforced by open brutality on the streets. Dear reader, after all of my observations and study of the subject matter I am convinced that it's not shared beliefs, identity, religion or ethnicity that holds Nigeria together as a country but this very fear of the armed forces highlighting again the distinction between those with guns and those without guns in the land. I reiterate that it's not the kangaroo political structure that holds this country together on its own because were it so I doubt that a bunch of mostly old men and women with their young converts can prevent these impoverished people from fighting for their freedom but rather it is the organised legal guns that they have at their disposal that barely keeps this chaotic train on its tracks all at the expense of the exploited masses. Putting it simply: in this battle between the political ruling class vs. the masses, the government has a monopoly on violence giving the political ruling class a key advantage over the masses that they cannot overcome.

What then is the function of the armed forces? If the function of the police is to police the nation and some police stations across the nation are closing early at 6pm for security reasons then what is their purpose? If the job of the military is to protect the territorial integrity of our country and we have places in Nigeria where the green white green of our flag does not fly but the black flags of terrorists then what is the purpose of the military? If the role of customs and immigration is to protect the borders yet terrorists flood into the country unchecked through the North and weapons flow in through the ports and borders of the South under their watch while they work hand in hand with smugglers then what is their function? We can go on but that's not the focus in this, my question is that if these government funded agencies are failing so much at their primary duties but still get funding and support from the government what then is their real purpose? Is it the case of a bad rat catcher cat or a straight chocolate thief? We try more to press for the answer. I always make a case for the human resources in Nigeria and say that these organisations under the armed forces have the potential to operate at their best but the Nigerian factor at work in them manifesting through different means has effectively seen to it that this is not the case.

One of the main ways used to attack, pollute, colonise, corrupt and reprogramme a body in Nigeria is through its leadership. Zechariah 13:7b quoted by Jesus in Matthew 26:31b says that **'I will smite the shepherd and the sheep of the flock shall be scattered abroad'** highlighting again the importance of leadership. They do not bother with the wider body but focus on the leadership so when they attack and successfully take control of the leadership the wider body has been overpowered and has to comply. We see this happen in the general country itself with the political leadership and we see it also happen in other sub-groups across the country which is why I said these people have a curse of bad leadership on them. So when they take over the leadership, they can then use the authority of that leadership over the body to implement their agenda with little to no resistance from the rest of the body. So when you look at the armed forces ethnic race plays a very strong role with people from the core Hausa and Fulani ethnic groups in the North being favoured over the other ethnic groups in the country in terms of recruitment and promotion into leadership positions regardless of competence, meritocracy or suitability for the roles. The focus and aim of all this is power and control over other ethnic groups in the country in this ethnic race battle that is somewhat separate from the other economic battle going on but still has its effects on the society and the overall system. There is a dinosaur status in the leadership that ensures that people are recruited not because they have a burning desire to serve or that they are capable but because they fit the ethnic profile and religious requirements so they are plugged into these positions in the system to control it and also for government payroll through these agencies where they rise quickly through the ranks (ethnic race, nepotism, corruption etc.). Then the Nigerian factor comprising of the culture in the country will not see them get the best training for their roles or be issued the best equipment to help them carry out their duties so when you add this all up coupled with the leadership direction of these separate bodies you can already see that these agencies of the armed forces just cannot perform their officially intended duties to their best.

So take for example the Nigerian army that gets a monster sized budget year in and year out but could not win a single fight on Nigerian soil, they could not defeat tiny Biafra in a straight fight until they cut off their ammunition and food supply to starve them and even though you might say all is fair in love and war I will not argue further, they could not defeat the militant group MEND in the South-south in a straight fire fight until their daddies, the politicians intervened and came with truckloads of cash to bribe and disperse MEND to stop that conflict. They could not also defeat the Islamic terrorists in a straight fire fight and we still have areas in Nigeria where the flags of terrorists hang high and blow proudly in the sky but Nigeria has a government. Look at the air force, they recruit people in secret and buy old war planes from western countries but the terrorists in the North are regularly supplied ammunition and food with helicopters deep in Nigerian land and they seem to be powerless to stop this trend. Look at the Nigerian Navy that converted a revenue generating facility like a port in the South to a naval college and they receive their large chunk of the national cake too but oil theft occurs daily from the southern coasts of the country into the Atlantic ocean that they are powerless to stop too and recent whispers and scandals allege that they are even part of this racket which being a Nigerian is not even difficult for me to believe without hard proof so what is the true function of these bodies? In my visions of the politicians in the beautiful house to explain the Nigerian situation that house was guarded by men with uniforms holding guns to keep the masses at bay and that's the only conclusion I can get to because if all these bodies are so poor at their official duties they should all be useless but as far as they can keep the masses in line and in check while exploitation takes place that's their real role in the Nigerian ecosystem. It is a double-edged role where they keep the masses in check and protect the extended political ruling class and don't forget that the uniforms also offer perks to the wearers - connections and relationships within the civil service and the larger Nigerian systems for the wearers.

During the October 2020 nationwide **ENDSARS** protests people in Lekki tollgate were shot and killed, all because they dared to demand better from their government and if anything this buttresses my point on this matter that the collective armed forces is the last piece of the puzzle effectively answering a question that I asked myself as far back as in 2012 when I first put pen to paper to write this book. The question is: how far will the Nigerian leadership go to retain their power over the people? And that loaded question contains other questions within it like: how can the political ruling class continue to loot and exploit the country without proper resistance from the masses? And the answer is that the armed forces is there to provide protection for the political ruling class with the understanding that the political ruling class will take care of them in return in a mutually benefitting relationship at the expense of the masses. Nigeria has no expansionist agenda else she will keep her military in a top shape, top level and carry out regular drills to prepare herself. All the other agencies are poorly run and poorly equipped but in this their poor state they are still strong enough to prevail should a fight ever arise in the country between those with guns and those without guns so for the masses living in this system the fear of the uniform is the beginning of wisdom.

TOUTS AS NON-STATE ACTORS.

I am done with the general work of painting this picture for your consideration, anything beyond this point is just putting final touches with my brush strokes to get a perfect finish. The political ruling class through the political government structure are slaves to appearances. They project an air of normalcy in the country while in reality they have the whole country in a choke-hold which makes Nigeria essentially an open prison for the masses, make no mistakes about this, the masses are not willing collaborators in this system and that is why force is needed to keep them in line. The collective armed forces are the state actors that bring the force of the political government structure to bear on the masses so when they act they are basically acting under the authority and control of the government which also means that when they act they are acting on behalf of the government but this poses a challenge in delicate situations of conflict between the government and the masses where the government wants to act with force to keep the masses in line as always and enforce their will on them but does not want to be seen as to be acting with force on the people and this is where the non-state actors of force come into play.

We humans are so alike and yet so different in our individual mental and physical attributes, society has its members performing different functions that benefits the whole to make them survive and thrive. The old villages and human settlements had their members divided into farmers, fishermen, hunters and warriors according to their suitability but modern societies are not so different from this arrangement just that things have become more stratified and more organised. In a country like Nigeria where poverty is predominant there are undesirable elements within who would have been warriors in the old world but did not make it to the armed forces in this new world so they are left hanging. Others could have been artists or even singers in the old world but the harshness of this new world comprising of the poverty, the hunger, the lack of love of a stable home and other such factors have forced their survival instincts into overdrive metamorphosing them into the touts that we see today. They are known locally by different names like *area boys, agberos, street boys* and others which are a sub-element in society of people forced to grow in painful and harsh conditions, harder even than the ones the Nigerian masses are experiencing which has hardened and toughened this sub-element up and filled their hearts with hatred for the masses of society not knowing that they and the masses they hate are all victims of the same system and soldiers of the same struggle.

I do not want to paint a whole group with one brush as some of these people are just genuinely trying to survive and climb out of the hole they found themselves in a society that just does not care and cannot care but all the social sciences tell us that this is the sub-elements from which criminals that terrorize society are mostly made from. They have chosen a different path in society choosing to make their living off the masses themselves through various ways and for various reasons chief among which is the fact that not being educated they cannot compete for scarce job opportunities with the rest of society so succumb to vice on the dark side or labour intensive jobs on the other side and there is an army of people like this spread across the country. This army is what the political ruling class taps into to use as a force against the masses in delicate situations where they cannot use the armed forces. It is said that when rats in a population due to stress and hunger start to feed on other rats they become a different kind of rat entirely and cannot easily stop this. These are people that have proven their ruthlessness and notoriety in society over time and have shown their willingness to hurt members to please their masters in the political ruling class.

They are used to threaten members of certain ethnic groups whom they perceive to be rivals not to come out to vote or face violence in the very country they were born in before elections which affects the outcome of elections, when that does not work they employ direct means by using these touts to steal ballot boxes while the security officials look the other way, they are used to beat up and harass voters who have come to quietly perform their civic duty which is to vote and have a say in who their next leader should be and I can even go as far as to accuse and say that they have been used to eliminate political rivals in the country. They are used to violently beat up and disperse protesters in the country who are only demanding better from their government and in true infiltration strategy they are sometimes sown into the protesters to cause dissent, loot shops and commit other violent acts that can then be blamed on the protesters 'forcing' the government to deploy the state actors. If you observe closely a system always reveals itself in a moment of chaos and panic, during the **ENDSARS** protests of 2020 we saw the armed forces and touts working hand in hand to corral protesters like a pack of sheep dogs, some of the touts were even carried to the scene of the protests with official government vehicles caught on camera. The things we have witnessed in Nigeria as Nigerians cannot all be documented and they keep getting worse. Where we have earlier thought that the state actors cannot abuse their uniforms we saw uniformed men of the Nigerian police and military stealing ballot boxes in the 2022/23 elections so maybe now we can say that we have finally seen it all.

These touts are rewarded with cash gifts after the elections and given an elevated status in society which they then impose on the masses in the form of levies and taxes which are extorted from them daily so who suffers the consequences again? It's the masses which I called earth, anything you want to dump just dump it on the earth and it will be fine. In certain areas they impose daily taxes and levies on poor transporters who have come out to look for their daily bread and all this while the government and security forces conveniently look the other way and you can imagine how much is being daily raised with these national rackets on the people. In poor parts of Lagos there are shabbily constructed pedestrian bridges where touts stay daily collecting money from anybody who will pass that bridge, there are certain places you cannot pass without paying money. In Delta state and other states for example you cannot build a house without first paying money to touts, you cannot have building materials delivered to the building sites without paying money to touts who claim that they are the owners of the land. So a prospective home owner buys the land, pays for it, pays the surveyor charges and other governmental charges involved then still has to come up with money to pay touts so you see that the cost of development in Nigeria is very high. You pay the touts, you pay the government so who's the real authority in the land? All these monies meanwhile are daily siphoned out of the pockets of the Nigerian masses so they remain a poor people. I need to mention here that the rich ones among these touts rise to become members of the political ruling class, as I told you there are different ways to gain membership and from there you know what's next, they are cleaned up and will one day find themselves in political government positions standing in front of the masses, above the masses. I'm not against men and women rising in life but it's in the manner in which they rise and what they become that I have a problem with. In conclusion, the state actors and the non-state actors are the effective tool of force in the hands of the political ruling class to defeat and dominate the masses in Nigeria.

THE DYNAMICS OF NIGERIAN POLITICS: GAME OF LIES!

'We know they are lying,
They know they are lying,
They know we know they are lying,
We know they know we know they are lying,
But still they are lying'.

- Aleksandr Solzhenitsyn.

In a classic case of brood parasitism the cuckoo bird perches on the tree then looks to the left and to the right, seeing no one watching because they have all gone out to look for food for the day she quickly swoops in, lays her single egg among the other eggs in the crow's nest and flies away. The eggs are the same colour and even though the cuckoo's single egg is slightly bigger than the others the mother crow does not notice when she comes back home from her day's search so she sits on all the eggs in her nest, incubating them all but the cuckoo's hatches first before the others and she not being able to tell the difference between the foster chick and hers begins to feed it and so one of nature's great injustices is carried out. By the time the crow's biological chicks start to hatch the cuckoo chick already has a size advantage over them so every time mother crow goes out to look for food the seemingly innocent cuckoo chick carries one of her foster sibling-chicks with her in the nest on her back and pushes it over the side of the nest tumbling to its death. In this way it ruthlessly eliminates competition for food in the nest simultaneously increasing its own chances of survival in the process. Chick after chick this ravenous little murderer tosses off all the competition until it's left alone in the nest to eat all the food from mother crow until she grows bigger than mother crow because she was all a different bird from the start, her feathers taking on their true colours which is significantly different from those of the crow and being now strong and able, it flies away after having fed off the strength, care and resources of the unsuspecting mother crow, wasting her time, killing her chicks and leaving her with nothing but grief. Every time I think about Nigeria these are the kinds of things I think about, fraud in progress.

It's important to me for you to see that what's happening in this country is a sham that's why I called it a political fraud perpetuated on a naive, ignorant, trusting, confused, unfocused, unsuspecting and sadly foolish masses, yes, they have played the role of enablers and are not innocent in all this. The void between the political ruling class and the masses is vast, and the disenfranchisement of the masses from the power and resources in the land is real. What is called politics in Nigeria are the rumblings and striving within this little group that ripples out into masses, and politics is political will so what should originally have been the political will of the masses to decide for the collective body has now been corrupted to be the will of the political ruling class imposed on the masses hence the mess that we see today. Pseudo systems and structures were then created around this imposed aggregated will to serve it and to give it false legitimacy with which like the cuckoo's egg she can then insert herself in the midst of other democracies and parade herself as one of them but she is not, so what do we call her? Is she just a deficient democracy or has she always been something else masquerading as a deficient democracy? I'd like to know your answer on that. Historically the first political parties in Nigeria (NPC, AG and NCNC) were not built on ideology but rather to further ethnic interests with a subtext of religion by the prominent individuals that created and spearheaded them. In fairness the people were just coming out of colonization so what did they know? If it was a strong, united and educated people then this party system might not have worked, and if the true wills of these strong and prominent individuals was the betterment of the collective rather than ethnic superiority then with the authority and resources of the nation at their disposal they could have forged a strong and blended nation but the ethnic race runs deep, so deep it runs that in Nigeria today, ordinary people still think that members of the other tribes and ethnic groups are their enemies.

This kind of mindset and mentality leaves them open to propaganda and manipulation and this has been the case to a great damage over the years so even when the military took over you have to note that these are still individuals belonging to the different ethnic groups. So the sentiments persisted but with authoritarian military rule true democratic roots and foundations could not be laid in the hearts and cultures of these peoples. In my opinion both the military and civilian rules in Nigeria have been exploitative, the only difference is that the military used strong power on the masses while the civilians exercise soft and sheathed power. So after the military rule the new crop of parties that came up like the PDP, ACN, APGA, LP, NPC, DPP and others still retained a little of their ethnic foundations but focus had started to shift to the strong individuals inside of them that were merely using them as vehicles to attain power for themselves. Like I asked you at the beginning: which of these political parties ever really won election under an ethnic banner and exclusively focused on the development of an ethnic group over the past 25 years? None! So when you look at it an evolution had already occurred where the shift was on the individuals themselves within the parties and that's why they were able to switch countless times between different parties with no consequences to their conscience because it was all a game of power and they merely moved into the next party they felt gave them the best chance to grab that power. A person who has served his or her own purpose all their lives and wins election into office in this way cannot be suddenly expected to serve anything or any person other than themselves.

Male lions in the wild rarely fight themselves to the death, they fight for intimidation and dominance then the loser has to run away. This is because both know that they are strong and they know the level of damage they can inflict on themselves so why go all out? Same thing you have seen between the United States and Russia over the decades that they can never engage in open warfare with each other because both of them possess the capability to end this planet as we know it so instead they fight proxy wars using small countries that are stupid enough to allow themselves to be used as a pawn in their conflict. The African proverb says *'when elephants fight it is the grass that suffers'*. Likewise the heavy weights within these new crop of parties realised that they are strong and it would do them no good to fight among themselves and that's where the consolidation really took place so everything politically since that time in the country has just been different consolidated interests of strong people warring against each other. So without a firm foundation the democracy is just skin deep, the politicians ignore the people for 3 years after assuming office then a year to elections they start to distribute food items branded with their faces printed on the packaging and other household items to the masses. The poor masses are gathered in stadiums across the country and other rally points where branded t-shirts are given to them to wear to listen to some candidate halfheartedly drone on a speech that was written for them by paid assistants, then some stipend is paid to gathered masses at the end of the day for their troubles and brown envelope journalists cover these gatherings and this is what election campaign is in the country as it involves the people.

The political parties print banners with their candidates on them and tie them to electric poles in the streets that do not supply electricity and on roads that cars cannot comfortably drive on, and Nigeria, this is what you call democracy? Stop playing with the patience of the serious people in this world. Inside the parties, serious bribing is taking place between the delegates and other shareholders as meetings are held to determine the fate of the candidates and this is where the real selection takes place but the political system in Nigeria is a slave to appearances as I must have said a million times by now so they have to show the people that they are legit and that the process is real because it is better to have the people on board this way than to do it solely by force, it's soft power people, don't forget. So the elections are held and winners announced and then the politicians disintegrate into thin air right in front of the masses only for them to return in 3 years with a new banner to tie on the electric poles in that same street with the candidate promising the people who have lived from childhood to adulthood on that street that they will fix that road for them if they give them support... this is a brief description of what democracy in Nigeria looks like.

INEC AND THE VALUE OF A GOOD SELECTION PROCESS.

> *'I consider it completely unimportant who in the party will vote, or how; but what is extraordinarily important is this - who will count the votes and how'.*
>
> *- Joseph Stalin.*

Depending on what side of the divide you're on the system does not work, if you're on the side of the masses then it definitely does not work but if you're on the side of the ruling elites then it's a perfect system that does not need changing about it, so what then can you do with a system that doesn't work for you? These people are thorough in their operations and leave nothing to chance, they heap layers and layers of strategies to ensure that the odds end in their favour. What is it they say about gambling casinos again? The house always wins? Yes that's it. So when the masses brave past all the threats to their freedom and right to vote along with the violence that comes with elections in the country they have the final boss of the electoral process sitting back with a calm assured smile on its face just watching the masses scramble around. That final boss is the electoral commission tasked by the government to handle elections in the country, it has a bored look on its face as it watches on. *What will you, poor masses, do with me?* It asks in derision, and the poor people of Nigeria have no answers for its questions. The Independent National Electoral Commission or INEC for short pronounced as eye-neck is your typical government body that has gone through several name changes over the years and as the typical criminal organisation who are slaves to appearances and always hunting for legitimacy that they are, they quickly snuck in 'Independent' into its latest name change as if anybody needed reminding that this particular body is supposed to be independent in the first place. Gosh! These people are so smart, so what next will they come up with? Drivable cars? Breakfast bread? Livable house? Sitting couch? I wonder *raises palms and looks up dramatically to the skies*. Surprisingly, the witty Nigerians have not yet come up with their own names for INEC like they did for PHCN and NEPA, maybe they'll see this and get inspired to do so.

    Well whatever names in this world you choose to call this body you just cannot call it a body that has ever conducted free and fair elections in Nigeria since her inception. There's nothing much to say about INEC that hasn't already been said in the section for the civil service, the one thought I'll leave you with is that: in a body where the leadership is picked, appointed, approved, signed off on and paid by the executive or their brothers in arms so how 'independent' and impartial can that body really be? When you capture the head the rest of the body becomes easy work. Stalin and other cynical greats before him called it right, they knew that in the democratic system the masses could come out to vote all they want but the people that counted the votes and announced the winners are the true deciding factor here. Now if in your country you have somehow perfected this system to be free and fair then kudos to you, that is not to say that this system and its processes cannot be tampered with. Democracy like other forms of government have their flaws which makes the collective will of the people behind the different systems very important to the point that the desired destination is greatness but there existing different roads to reach it. The Nigerian system knows very well how to make a mockery of the high things in this world, you see renowned professors who have published papers in different international journals all of a sudden cannot properly do simple addition and subtraction of numbers on national TV when they are brought on as election officials all because their stoves ran out of gas while they're trying to cook the election numbers. Still they are paid handsomely for their contributions to the cause and this is why I'll ask again just for the last time if you will permit me: remind me again what good is an Ivy league certificate in the face of this great Nigerian corruption?

The violence associated with Nigeria elections have been well documented over the decades so no need to stretch things out here. Electoral officers who do not want to co-operate have been held at gun point over the years by state and non-state actors to change the results in favour of a preferred candidate which is why I say it's a selection process. The winners have already been selected and determined by the political ruling class behind the scenes then the charade of an election is put on show to try to legitimise those decisions. The masses are not all innocent in the process, the lower hierarchy of INEC and her field agents are made up of people who are just as poor and desolate as the very masses they are being used to cheat and disenfranchise but they carry out their assignments with vigour and gusto. They see election cycles as periods to make a little extra money for themselves by selling their souls and their conscience but post-election clarity hits quickly when they see that whatever stipend or booty they think they made during the elections cannot serve them for 4 years until the next election cycles. The voting masses who already know from experience that they are disenfranchised from the whole process have resigned themselves to their fate so that mixed with the poverty they are fighting in their daily lives they go to polling units on election day and sell their votes for stipends right there in the polling units to vote for particular candidates. How do they achieve this? Low level members of the political ruling class protected by non-state actors can be seen with wads of open cash close to the polling units paying members of the masses stipends on the spot immediately they cast their votes and can show that they voted for a particular candidate and candidates of the party they represent but just like Esau immediately he ate the last spoon of pottage (Gen 25:29-34) the reality of what they have done hits them pretty quickly especially as the money they received to sell their votes finishes in that day or the next day in the highly inflated economy and they realise that they have to suffer another 4 years of bad governance because they have taken their dividends of democracy on that day and it was an unfair exchange. These are mostly poor and ignorant people, they are not really bad people but they are just poor and hungry and in their survival mode reasoning they think that instead of waiting hopelessly for the government that might not work in their favour it's better to take whatever they can on the spot, a grave mistake indeed and this is one of the key things that the artificial and enforced poverty on the masses was meant to create in the first place; compromise, control and vulnerability for the system to work. In my heart I'm not even angry at them, I just truly pity them because what a sad waste indeed! As for the political oppositions, some of them are really just members of the political ruling class who are there to create the illusion of choice in the minds of the masses, they will be rewarded with cash, choice positions where they will make a lot of money in the new government, award of contracts and other perks but for those true opposition who are not a part of the system what can they really do? If they try to protest the results of the sham elections that INEC just announced they have the state and non-state actors to contend with so it essentially becomes a battle of men with guns against men without guns and in all the many writings in this book this is the true final hurdle of the Nigerian people. They are not ready to fight this unfair battle where they will take losses and pay the true price for their liberty so in bondage they must remain. The other remaining option available to the true opposition is to take their grievances to court and right in front of the courtroom mother justice awaits twerking joyously with an inviting look on her face so dear opposition: what will you do in this situation? Or more appropriately: what can you truly do?

ECONOMIC AND FINANCIAL CRIMES COMMISSION AND INSECTICIDES.

'Even a superb hawk will not catch game until it is loosed'

- Old proverb.

I will tell you a quick story and a true one at that. We once had this neighbour years ago who had this dog that he loved so much and didn't put on a leash. For whatever reason that dog did not like me and always barked at me and showed aggression when I walked past so I always told him to secure his dog but he paid me no mind until one day the dog chased me while I was walking past his place and scratched or bit me, I couldn't tell for sure but I was injured from the encounter and I shouted curses at him as he was trying to get the dog back into his house. He was one of those weird types of pet owners who somehow thought that the life of their beloved pet somehow equated to human life so he shouted curses back at me and I told him bluntly and calmly that I will execute his dog and walked away. Well he must have thought hard about what I said to him because he came later to apologize and make peace with me. By that time I had gotten home, looked at the wound which was not as great as I thought so my anger had somewhat subsided and I let the issue slide but a part of me was still angry because I had told him to secure his dog several times before this incident. When I slept that night, I dreamt that there was a farm where dogs were taken to have their teeth removed, and when I saw all those toothless dogs I just thought about the EFCC. I don't know why but right then in that dream and when I woke up I thought about the EFCC.

Another government agency? You might ask me, and yes we almost have one for every citizen in the country at this stage and they are plugged right into the budget with a specially selected hierarchy put in place to oversee that new pipeline. So what do you do if you're a corrupt country that likes to masquerade herself as a legitimate country and the international community accuses you of not being hard enough on corruption? You quickly create a government body tasked with fighting corruption and financial crimes and this is what former president Olusegun Obasanjo did when he created the EFCC in 2003. Now, whatever his intentions were at the time he created this body I'm sure that they must have been noble and well-intended but by now you already know what the Nigerian system through the Nigerian factor and corruption does to great ideas introduced into it; it does not outrightly kill them but renders them ineffective by carrying out soulectomy on them, leaving them to parade themselves around society like ridiculous caricatures of their original selves. As at the time of its inception and the times immediately following it the EFCC caused ripples throughout the political stratosphere. It was the new boy on the block with new moves that no one had seen before so Nigerians did not really know what to expect from it. The elected officials within the 3rd circle all have immunity so the EFCC went after immediate past governors who had looted their states dry during their tenures and were unfortunate enough not to get immediate admission into the federal legislature.

Ordinary Nigerians were happy as a new corruption-killer weapon had been deployed in the country, they dared to be hopeful as is their manner asking questions among themselves. *'Is this the new weapon that will finally rid us of their yokes and burdens?'* they asked themselves. *'Will we finally be free from our seemingly never-ending bondage?'* they wondered but time which is that ruthless eternal snitch would tell them all they needed to know.

The neophytes within the 2nd circle did not know how to counter the new boy's moves in the beginning so some of them got hit with different combos but the veterans among them calmly sat back and watched the new boy closely, carefully observing his kung-fu moves for openings and weaknesses that they could exploit for their counter attack and it did not take long before the initial ripples created by the EFCC after its creation started to die down. In my opinion one of the greatest weaknesses of the EFCC was that the core of its officers were pulled from the Nigerian police force which we have already covered in this work, so those core officers with few from the secret police and other agencies were used to form this new anti-corruption and financial crimes commission. Before long there were already accusations that the EFCC was now a weapon in the hands of powerful political figures who used it to shoot at their political opposition and rivals, and that they were also used to keep those climbing the chaos ladder in line, the ripples in the political stratosphere had all but disappeared by this time.

The EFCC was no longer going after politicians at this time, they had found a new hobby and easy targets who could not afford the robust and experienced legal teams that the politicians have in seemingly affluent youths of the masses whom they suspected were surprisingly still doing well despite the harsh economic reality in the country so they were labelled as fraudsters, after which they were daily harassed, chased around and extorted. The emblem of the EFCC has an eagle on it but by 2018 the EFCC would perform one more miracle in front of the Nigerian people by instantly transforming that eagle to an owl the way they turned their necks 200 degrees to look away when members of the 2nd and 3rd circles who had been caught red handed stealing money claimed that it was a big snake and a big monkey in another separate incident that had come into their offices to steal huge sums of money amounting to millions of naira. That was money that was meant for the masses and the society but you know what usually happens to money meant for the Nigerian people. These days we don't hear much from the EFCC chasing crime, I think they finally realised that they're just comedians so their official handle can be seen on social media making witty remarks and jokes to their followers. Well maybe they employed a new social media team to become influencers, I heard from friends that that line of work pays handsomely through clicks and engagement, so who knows? Do anything to raise extra money to fight crime right?

I do not have much else to say about this government body that I haven't already said about the others before it so I'll leave you with an analogy to close this topic. Another one again? Well, yes, this is the last one I promise, I know we have spent much time here in court and some of you are itching for this session to end but the seriousness of the issues at hand and the subject matter warranted this type of attention. I do not claim to be an expert on security or crime so like the observer that I am I will try to explain to you the way I see it. Imagine if you had a room full of female mosquitoes in Africa who are known to suck the blood of their human victims to fertilize their eggs. This is a natural process except that the mosquitoes can be a disturbance to much needed sleep and vectors that carry diseases like the much dreaded malaria. Well, the mosquitoes are the perpetrators of financial crimes in Nigeria in this scenario so you do the normal thing by buying insecticide to spray in the room to kill the mosquitoes bugging your life and giving you malaria, this insecticide is the EFCC. Still in the spirit of imagination, the insecticide that the manufacturers and the marketers promised in their adverts would kill all mosquitoes was sprayed into the room and instead of killing them the mosquitoes got stronger and bigger now, almost able as a group of 4 or 5, to lift you up from the bed while they are sucking your blood as you sleep; what does that say about the company that makes the insecticide? Or the material from which the insecticide was made? What does this say about the insecticide itself? Your answer to these questions is what I have to say about the EFCC as far as Nigeria is concerned, perhaps that must be why I immediately thought of the EFCC in that dream that I had seeing toothless dogs. These are the shortcomings in full display of a system operating without sufficient internal or external mechanisms in place to regulate itself... moving on.

NATIONAL YOUTH SERVICE CORP (NYSC)

The NYSC is one of those seemingly brilliant government ideas that suffered soulectomy and got lost somewhere in time and implementation. It was initiated to further strengthen unity within the country after the civil war in 1970 but these days it has become a burden and a necessary evil that graduates from the tertiary institutions must pass through before they can continue with their lives of survival in the country without jobs. I did my NYSC in 2012 and I hated the exercise not because of the ideals it represented but because of the way it was implemented (**functionality**). I just want to drop off a few points about it as an example of how government programmes become problematic and do not get their desired results.

1. Partakers of this exercise are required to go through a three-week concentration... oops sorry for that, it's actually orientation, yes, orientation camp before the service starts, and the living conditions of the camps are a nightmare for the fainthearted like most other government facilities across the country. The buildings and utilities are not ever serviced, maintained and upgraded in the off season when they are not in use and this tells you what the government and those responsible for this programme think about the citizens of this country. The overcrowded rooms, bad pit toilets, limited water supply and bad food are just some of the highlights. To relieve themselves some people got creative with polythene bags and newspapers which they threw around the

living area to avoid using the toilets so you can imagine living in such conditions for three weeks.

2. Simple operations like data collation were transformed into time wasting activities as we normally experience in Nigerian banks when their servers are 'down'. The NYSC still stores most of its information on paper in this computer age and I can only imagine the number of trees that get whacked down to fuel such stupidity. Dinosaur status has seen that modern techniques like biometric technology cannot be utilized to effectively manage the growing numbers of graduates that are mandated by law to go through the programme.

3. The overly bad-tempered officials found in a country where customer service is either dead or has always been non-existent from the start are on hand to shell out bad treatment and insults that are characteristic of government agencies in this dysfunctional democratic environment. The air of self-importance that the officials portrayed was not lost on me... I was tempted to smack a few across the face but the presence of soldiers with guns kept my wilder tendencies in check. This air of self- importance shows the lack of discipline and open impunity of the NYSC staff and by extension the Nigerian civil service all derived from the governmental and non-governmental members of the political ruling class. It is the culture of a people that know that they are secure in their position and the masses present no threat to them, classism too if you will.

4. Insecurity in various parts of the country has seen to the deaths of corpers in the past years. Some of them were kidnapped, raped and then killed right under the nose of a government that has failed to protect its people. The manner of the response by the government to such issues and cases has only served to add salt to so sensitive an injury but I told you that the value of a Nigerian life is a handful of sand or garri (not that garri is useless, Nigerians would tell you that it was garri that filled their stomachs in the '80s '90s and 2000s when they were visited by

poverty due to the acts of their leaders). A Nigerian life has no value and this is sadly reinforced into the minds of the masses on a daily basis. I sympathise with parents, family members and friends of those who have lost their lives in this pointless cause. It's not like money will bring back the dead but if we do a thorough check we will see that most of the parents who had to go through untold hardship in this dungeon of a country to send their children through school were not compensated for their loss in any way... it is just sad.

5. Logistics and planning for the movement of corpers to the different locations is just poor, the corpers transport themselves which is not unusual for that age range but considering that they are strangers in parts of the country with different cultures and violence due to insecurity special plans should have been put in place to ensure their safety. In most cases there are accidents due to bad driving, faulty cars, bad roads, you know... the usual suspects which lead to injuries and even deaths. In life accidents happen but avoidable accidents are the most painful ones.

I don't want to personalise the issue because statistics show that no less than 400,000 graduates pass through this programme every year. You can literally build this house with blocks and pieces I have already supplied in this work but I just want to show you the patterns of government run organisations and initiatives. You can take a brilliant idea, toss it into the pot of the Nigerian system, mix it up and it always comes out different from what you put in and I mean different in a bad way. Everything the government touches dies, everything! The NYSC experience was hellish for me. With some bright spots, I think I could have enjoyed it more like some of the other graduates that went through the process with me but I was already actively observing at that point so it was very easy to point out many things that could easily be fixed but were ignored. I would have said that whenever or if ever a proper audit of the NYSC and other initiatives like it are ever carried out the bones from that excavation would shake the country to its foundations but scandals are a regular occurrence in the country by this time so the people have lost their sensitivity to them. If that audit were to ever be possible you have to wonder how many of their records departments and buildings have not been razed down by then. The Nigerian people, always ready to make a joke out of every situation renamed the NYSC to mean: Now Your Suffer Continues which is quite funny I might add. I must admit I got a few chuckles out of that one but I sadly could not fully share their light sentiments on this issue. You might be tempted to call me a downer at this stage because it might seem like all I've done since the start of this book is complain and complain to you, I apologize but this is not my true intention. Some of my friends say that I complain about everything like the weather, for example, they say I complain that it's too hot or too cold but never say it's good or perfect so maybe the extended period of observing has taken its toll on me. It was Nigerian great Wole Soyinka who said that 'humans are born crying, live complaining and die disappointed' so I might only be human after all.

No matter your stand on whether I complain too much or not, the fact is, I wrote my first entry about my NYSC experience in 2014

complaining about the conditions of the NYSC camp I attended in Ekiti state and it took 10 years for nothing to be done about it only for me to look at the news in 2024 and see that some buildings in that camp collapsed on people and some of them had to be hospitalised so there goes that *shrugs* luckily, no one lost their lives if that newspaper article is to be entirely believed.

TITLES vs. VALUE

'The greatest threat to freedom is the absence of criticism... But the trouble with most of us is that we would rather be ruined by praise than saved by criticism.'

- Wole Soyinka.

In my life I have been greatly impacted by the environment I grew up in so when I observe the people of this world first in Nigeria, then around the world, for me there exists a battle between the titles they hold and the actual value they impart to the people around them, their immediate community and the world at large. Titles like professor, commander, Your Royal Highness, *oga*, pastor, engineer, madam, general, doctor, chief, specialist, barrister, Excellency, your honour etc. are representations of respect bestowed on the bearers and the value they hold to society such that when you meet them and they are introduced you already know who you were meeting and what they were capable of assuming. Also that they must have had to work hard to earn it but when you grow up in a society where these titles can be bought, bestowed at will or wrong people always get pushed into positions that warrant titles then you can understand my scepticism and general distrust of people and the titles that they bear. Whenever I am introduced or I hear a person addressed with titles I look at the person and ask myself questions like: what has this person done to earn this title? What value do they carry within themselves for their world? What systems did they go through to ensure that the people that come out of the other side of it have earned the right to be called that title? Growing up in a society where ill-gotten wealth or connections to friends in high places can get you anything has made me not to take anything at face value, so I question everything.

Money is important in the whole world and for the places with high poverty rates, understandably money becomes importanter. I usually argue that money is not everything but it is something, and to the man that has nothing, it is better to at least have something than to have nothing at all but some people are so poor that all they have is money. In Nigeria we see people who should have led quiet lives or gained mastery in some other field to be of service to society being shoehorned into positions doing things they would never have thought they were capable of to their own people and given titles just to 'belong' and hang with a certain crowd to make money, this is a survival tactic. Everybody talks about the crabs in the barrel pulling each other down but no one stopped to think that maybe these crabs were not some wicked crabs who don't want their friends to escape, maybe they were just scared in that dark barrel waving their claws around trying to grab anything they can get a hold of. Humans are not crabs and this is not to absolve anyone but no one asked the most important question of them all: what are crab who are supposed to be roaming the lands and waters of this world freely doing cramped up in a dark barrel, who put them in that barrel in the first place? When a structured system has too many people that have lied and forged their way to their top, occupying positions they cannot handle because they lack the capacity then that system cannot flourish or even stand, it will come tumbling down like a pack of cards. These elements do not care because the titles and lies and everything else is just to get wealth at the end of the day and money is the ultimate in Nigerian society.

It absolves them of all and gives them legitimacy, with money they can finally be anything they want to be. Oh, you want to tell the world that you're a learned scholar who graduated from some prestigious school in London many years ago despite the fact that you never saw the 4 walls of a school in your whole life? No problem, money will accomplish that for you. You want to present yourself as some seasoned professional who worked for top companies in foreign lands and have gained experience in that field but have just come back home to help your people? Hmm, do you have money? If yes then... done! Do you want to erase your glaring criminal past and present yourself to Nigerians as some good and upstanding citizen all your life? Ill-gotten wealth embezzled from Nigerians will cover your sins and absolve you of all. Confucius says that 'it is *a shame to be rich or wealthy in a dysfunctional society*' because he knew that in such a society you couldn't have come by your wealth through virtuous means. It's the same for me with titles - when I meet people I try look into their souls to gauge them as persons not the titles or fancy alphabets they have at the end of their names because I grew up in a circus with a lot of ring masters and because I cannot vouch for the system that conferred the titles on such individuals or their worth and value to society, I question everything.

REPUTATION AND FOREIGN RELATIONS

'When Jesus came into the coasts of Caesarea Philippi, he asked his disciples, saying, whom do men say that I the Son of man am?'

- Matthew 16:13

We cannot live our whole lives wondering what people think about us or what they have to say about us but every sane and self-aware person must at some point in their life contemplate the impression and the effect they have on people and the world around them because we do not exist in isolation. Thinking about my country and all that's happening in it, some I have said already in this book and a lot more was not mentioned, I always wonder, when the committee of nations gather themselves together what do they think and say about Nigeria? Remember we cannot let ourselves be shackled to the thoughts and approvals of others but Ecclesiastes 7:1a says that *'A good name is better than precious ointment.'* and Proverbs 22:1a which is also like it says *'A good name is to be chosen rather than great riches'*. The good name here does not refer to the nice native names with beautiful meanings that you give to your children to be called all the days of their lives except they change it, the good name refers to reputation. Knowing this I can now ask: what is the reputation of Nigeria in the world today? The reputation is not good, the world has known for a long time that ours is a country with many problems but as to the nature of our problems they might not be aware. In the past I tried to put myself in their shoes but now that I've had the opportunity to travel out of the country I have directly asked the people around me what they thought of Nigeria and the impression I got was that Nigeria and the other sub-Saharan countries like her were nations made up of black people who just could not get their things in order. Fair enough, you need a lot of maturity in yourself to be able to discuss mature topics with different people in a mature way, and if you cover everything under a blanket of racism then you'll miss out on some knowledge.

It is collectivism over individualism as far as countries are involved no matter your individual attributes, the thing is that we're all members or citizens of the country and are affected by her reputation. A Nigerian proverb says that: *'red palm oil on one finger easily spreads and stains the others'* so we're all affected. Our fathers before us faced the problems of this reputation when they went around the world, those problems were not handled so we are now facing them too and if we do not defeat them once and for all then the patterns will continue and our children born into the world will have to contend with these long running problems waiting for them when they arrive. These problems manifest in different ways like the treatment we get from foreigners outside the country and restriction of our movement in the world as it pertains to approval of visa applications for Nigerians. Other nationalities have it easy when they want to come here, that is if they want to come but it becomes a herculean task for a Nigerian trying to visit other countries; these restrictions somehow do not affect the rate at which top talents from Nigeria find their way into these countries. I cannot lie, the brain drain is one thing that hurts my heart deeply because it can be a dream killer; you have our young engineers, doctors and lawyers in these countries trading their dreams and their lives away tending to their aged and mentally disturbed so that the people of those countries can go for vacations and live their lives free of this burden. A country that cannot protect the rights of her citizens outside the country will leave them vulnerable to abuse and attacks in places where the people did not have good intentions in their hearts to begin with. If we're being brutally honest here and I am an honest man, Nigeria does not even protect the rights and sanctity of her citizens within Nigeria to begin with, how much more of those that have left her shores? My conclusion is that the bad reputation of Nigeria has also negatively impacted the people of the country and the country's ability to build productive bonds with other countries of the world.

PART 3: CLOSING SUMMARY: MAD COUNTRY.

'THE LIMITS OF TYRANTS ARE PRESCRIBED BY THE ENDURANCE OF THOSE WHOM THEY OPPRESS.'

- Frederick Douglass

WHAT REALLY IS A COUNTRY?

I bought a big map of the world and hung it over my bed, I wanted to see the countries of the world and how they are arranged. I take a look at this map from time to time and I speak words to it, but all this while a question has been stuck in my mind that robs me of my sleep on some nights, that question is: what is a country? Or more specifically what makes a country a country? Is it just the land space on a continent? Or the apportioning of an area within the land to make it a territory? Is it the fact that there are people to occupy that territory? Or that they have leaders to rule over them? What is a country? Is it the flag they have beautifully designed to be hung around their territory and the national anthem written for them to sing to? What really is a country? My answer to these questions is that it's people that make a country so if we go by these criteria then that means the countries of sub-Saharan Africa make the cut but is that all? No, I was not convinced, that is not all it takes to make a country because without some form of claim or part ownership by everybody in the country then the people are nothing but just a commodity in the territory they live in. Not just a commodity they are also just occupiers of the land for the time they are alive but then I thought to myself that we're all just occupiers the earth whether political ruling class or masses because we will all die at the end of the day plus we brought nothing with us to this plane and will leave with nothing but still… crossing over is into a different plane with different laws, our focus is here on the physical plane.

What is a country? How do you say a country is a country or when does a country become a country? Is it just when a beautiful coat of arms with symbols on it is designed for her? Or when a constitution is written and signed? I ask because Nigeria has every one of those things to show you upon asking so does that mean she automatically becomes a country? My answer is no because there can be no country without part ownership, contributions and benefits for every member of that country. In this scenario a country is then like a big company where the citizens are the staff of that company and the leadership of that country is high level management. In this company everybody including the staff, the cleaners, middle and high level management, all have an equal amount of shares in that company split among them and their positions within the company is not for a higher ownership of shares, more than the other members of that company but for functionality and to effectively oversee the operations of the company for the collective good of the company and everyone in it. The shares here are the rights of the people so equal shares means equal rights for all; anything short of this is political fraud. Everything important has previously been discussed in these pages so I don't want to prolong matters with multiple repetitions but the Nigerian situation is peculiar, it was not a bunch of well informed, intentional free men and women that came together to form a country based on their shared values and ideals but a broken and conquered, mixed multitude of people who had lost their freedom to outsiders a long time ago and had successive generations born into this dangerous situation, adapting to it over the years and with each new generation born, the pain of what was lost becomes less and the present conditions become accepted as normal and you know how the saying goes: you cannot miss what you've never had.

> *'A people without the knowledge of their past history, origin and culture is like a tree without roots.'*
>
> - Marcus Garvey.

Nigeria was forged in the harsh flames of colonialism by external authority from England, it was a group of people who they and their fathers that birthed them and the fathers that birthed their fathers and so on were all born into a condition of abuse and exploitation that had become normal to them because of how long it has existed. Their forebears had long lost their freedom so their offspring never knew what freedom was, for the sake of survival they accepted their fate and tried to make the best of whatever life threw at them with the eternal hope that they or their progeny will one day see the sun shine again on them. These new Nigerian peoples as at the time of her creation did not have the authority to form their own country, they did not have the relationships or the power and resources to rope all these many different tribes together to form a country, it was a powerful external force that had earlier abused and exploited them without mercy for centuries until it had even gotten tired and said enough, that forged this country and handed over the reins to people from within the country and when they received it what did they do with it? Did they speedily go about trying to heal a heavily wounded and broken people? No, did they speedily move to try to restore their ravaged lands and give new hope to a people with low morale? No, for a people that had been left far behind in the global race for development and were a couple of hundred years behind did they try to build them back up to make them competitive and to try to catch up to the rest of the world? No, they would not have any of that but instead proceeded to take the exploitation of their own peoples and their own lands from whence they were conceived into new heights or new lows, depending, of further exploitation and suffering over the decades since she was formed, and all for what?

The odds were always stacked against this country from the start but they were not insurmountable odds that could not be overcome if they were faced, not even in the slightest, and this fact adds more pain to the reality of the situation. The mixed multitudes of tribes of people with different cultures who reasoned differently and wanted different things for themselves and the country posed a challenge, Amos 3:3a says *'can two walk together, except they be agreed?'*, but even the ethnic differences of the Nigerian people have been exploited to make a mountain out of a molehill by people that mean to profit from their fault lines, cracks and conflicts. If man can put together crafts that escape the atmosphere of the earth to land in Mars, is it little ethnic squabbles that cannot be sorted out for the benefit of the whole? It is a sad thing when a people love mediocrity for themselves and have accepted it to be the norm in their lives, they no longer strive for excellence neither does anything bad happening in their communities worry their hearts anymore. They have been hit down hard for so long that they no longer know which way is up so even when the hits have stopped they can no longer lift their heads perhaps for fear of provoking more hits. It was always a sad mix from the start, you had ethnic groups who saw in themselves that they could dominate the world and wanted to follow in that path, you had others who just wanted to roam around with their animals and run around bare feet all day with no ambition other than to dominate the other ethnic groups. You also had other ethnic groups who neither wanted to dominate the world or run around with animals but just did not want to see the ones who would like to dominate the world do it and there are others of which you could not even decipher their true intentions or desires all trapped together in a country and playing games of superiority among themselves. I consider myself to be a good writer but I don't think that even I could have written up such a script of a people doomed for disaster if I had tried.

I would like to briefly speak to my black brothers and sisters around the world for a minute; it seems to me that you have all forgotten the pains our people endured and that we still carry to this day, perhaps the pains of the present has made you to let go of the pains of the past. A lot of you do not know the sacrifice that was made for the freedom you enjoy today, you did not know the amount of black blood the earth drank up nor at what cost of pain and anguish it came, you did not pay the price so you do not know what it cost to those that paid that price for you, a lot of you do not know that not everything can be walked away from in this life, a lot of you look at the chains on the ground that those before you were forced to wear but do not see their scars on your wrists and feet, a lot of you have become distracted by the beautiful singing birds on the trees that you have strayed far into the forest and far from the sure bush path that takes you back to the safety of the village. You children of antelopes have somehow come to the conclusion that the lions that hunted down your parents have somehow lost their appetite for sweet antelope meat, a lot of you look back at the chains lying on the ground and do not think to contemplate on what they were used for, some don't even bother to look back which is irrelevant because many of you do not know that shackles come in different forms, that's right, a lot of you do not know that you're not all yet free but you carry on, recklessly you carry on but you forget that those before you paid a price for you to be here today and in that same way you must do your part to pay the price of today for them that will come after you. I do not ask you all for much, all I ask of you is that you open your eyes well and carefully look at the world around you; if you see anything different when you do, good, and if you do not then no worries, we will all at some point go the way of all flesh at the end of the day.

What is the reward of those who have betrayed and continue to betray their brothers and sisters? What's their portion in all this? They get shiny cars imported for themselves, they get some fancy high fashion clothes and build big mansions for themselves to live out their days. What is their exceedingly great reward? They get to flaunt their ill-gotten wealth over a hurting and a dying nation, they get to eat choice meals but how much can one man or woman really eat before it starts to endanger your own health? You send your children to schools abroad while the schools in your home lay in ruins so what next? They finish those schools and become ordinary black people in those foreign countries. What is your reward in this system? The police and the other men in uniforms illegally extort and harass the people on the streets from sun up to sundown taking a curse upon their heads and their generation without knowing and I have never seen an old retired policeman in the country who is living well, they mostly all die in pains of mysterious illnesses and they seldom die rich. What will happen to past leaders when they die? A big feast will be organised and soldiers would shoot bullets into the air, people will make merry but no matter how long and how big the feast it will come to an end and people will have to go about their business, and I know because my father was buried with 15 days of merrymaking as he was a great chief in his time but the music stopped at some point, the canopies and tents were dismantled and the echoes of the shots that rang in the air had long vanished so in the end you are inevitably put in the ground and that's it, all vanity. When you take the time to consider this word you will see that there is truly nothing in it, time passes and everything changes and that's it really.

This is a mad country, one existing in a state of continuous chaos by all means unsustainable so what will be her end? The people in charge of this Nigerian exploitation operation all know that this will not and cannot continue in perpetuity and that's one of the reasons why they stash their loot abroad because in their minds the day the whole system crashes they want to have something to live the rest of their lives with, and so said the climbers on mount Everest to themselves but suddenly the avalanche came crashing down on them and they were buried in its icy embrace. This system will be tested as the people get tired of it more and more and at some point. The only way it can be held up will be by direct force so all that soft power strategy will have to be put aside. The runners had all taken their positions on the tracks, patiently waiting and ready, then the whistle was blown and they shot off, all of them but one who waited back watching. The crowd were cheering and screaming to urge the runners on but that one waited, watching as the gap got wider and wider. The clock was ticking and people stared in disbelief at this lone runner still crouched waiting at the starting blocks then the whispers started to filter about the crowds in the stands, perhaps he has a plan they said, perhaps he' a master and has faith in his ability to catch up to the other runners because he's faster, or maybe they'll all witness something wonderful today as that last runner is superman and will magically fly to catch up to the others, overtake them and win the race they said among themselves. The lone runner calmly watched the other runners disappear around the bend then he took a deep breath and made ready to start running. The whole crowd drew its breath and gasped at the same time, the phenom was about to take off, what will happen next they wondered, what is he going to do? The rippling muscles on the body of this lone runner twitched, the sweat dripping down his dark skin and finely toned muscles made it seem like he glowed under the sun and the crowd was on its feet, expectant, were they about to witness something great? The runner stood up, faced the other direction away from the runners and started sauntering along the tracks running his own race, all hell broke loose in the stands, what did I tell you? Mad country indeed.

So *'Dear mother Nigeria, why dost thou feed on thine own seeds?'*, this question no longer troubles my mind as it once did, it has a new prison now or better still a new home. Finally I've been able to exorcise it, pulling it out of my head and trapping it forever in black and white. My head was like a prison for it because all the time it was running around and hitting on the inner walls of my skull demanding to be let out and I obliged. I trapped it in black and white simultaneously letting it loose onto the world in the process but my quest has ended and I achieved my purpose. I now know not only why mother Nigeria feeds on her seeds but also how and you should know by now too if you had taken this journey with me step by step all the way. She feeds on her seeds not because she likes to or because she wants to but because she's sick, mother Nigeria has a sickness nestled within her, controlling her and pushing her to do the horrible things she does to her own children and every sickness has a cure, every single one and if you wanted to argue to the contrary just remember that at one time malaria was considered as a death sentence too. Anyways I feel a freeness within me from deep inside like something has given way, like a block in a pipe has just been cleared and it's welling up and flowing around my entire being. I'm calm now when I look at her with a knowing look, I now know, so when she rattles her chains and screams out her garbled nonsense at me my question to myself in that moment is: how do I still feel about her within me? Would I be able to love her still or would I pull away from her in resentment? Dreading the very feel of her touch on my skin, what would I do? What would I feel? Well enough of all the questions already, let me rather hold on to the peace I feel in this moment, the peace in just knowing, knowing that for sure ours is not a sane country but without a single doubt ours is a mad country.

VERDICT

'From the beginning of creation, there's been a lot of tribulation,
Understand where am coming from,
And you will see that this world that we live in is one big mighty prison,
We're all on death row,
We're just passing like a journey to wherever we go,
Why don't we make that place heaven and that heaven is this very very place that we are living in so...'

TuFace Idibia
(One Love, Grass to Grace Album, 2006)

Alas! We're back to court on the streets, the sun is still up as it was in the beginning when we started, actually the sun never sets here but it's okay, things work differently here anyways. There is no respect for purchased titles and stolen wealth here in this court, I see Nigerian lady justice standing in the corner just waking up from her nap, good of you to join us ma'am. She's looking directly at me but I can't tell her expression because I still cannot see her eyes from behind the dark designer shades she has on but I know she can see me, she has ditched her machete and scale because like the rest of us she wants to hear the verdict.

I have provided all of my evidence to you all, and you can check them out from start to finish to verify them should you need to do so. Nigeria, you stand accused, your streets are filled with the tears and pains from the souls of your tormented children, the earth stands as a witness against you because it is tired of receiving the blood and the remains of your children, the air and the atmosphere around your lands is choked up with the many cries and complaints of your many children rising daily to heaven. Those of your children who have managed to escape your cold grasp hate you for what you are and for the diverse pains you have caused them, those of your children who manage to grow into old age curse you with their very last breath as they depart this world because in you they knew nothing but pain and suffering. You owe a great debt to God just for the way you have wasted the resources He has given to you and He is not happy with you, He will also ask for the many great destinies of your children that had been exchanged for pain from the dark parts of the cosmos where the light does not shine. The souls and destinies of other children from neighbouring lands who were tied to your rising are now stuck in limbo because your great fall interfered with already carefully laid out plans. These souls sigh and groan all day as they await a different plan for their manifestation, how do you plead, mother Nigeria? The accusations laid against you are much and we haven't even been through them all.

Dear mother Nigeria, why do you continue to feed on your seeds? Why is the only way of your existence for them to suffer so much and go through much hardship? Why have you shut your ears to their screams and pleas for mercy? It is a joyful thing when children properly say their long goodbyes to their parents at a ripe old age but why have your lands become a place where parents constantly bury their children? Everyone born into this world carries a destiny and a purpose but why do your children always die so young before they are ever able to fulfil their destiny? Thieves, killers and chronic oppressors of the people walk freely and tall in your lands where they always seem to thrive while the righteous ones are forced to pick their food from the ground like destitutes, your daughters have no covering or protection so they must now kill their souls to exchange their bodies for survival, why is evil and perversion so comfortable in your midst? You, who was so richly blessed with many gifts and adorned with precious stones, you were the envy of the nations all around you, they could see the abundance of your riches so how come you have been made so poor and untidy? You sit on the floor in the dirt daily gorging on your seeds, you who was supposed to sit at the mountain tops how have you been brought so low to the valley and cast aside like an orange peel? Your spiritual energy is low and the fire no longer burns in your eyes, the virus within you that you refused to rip out while it was yet like a mustard seed has grown and spread to your vitals threatening to choke the very life out of you but still you do nothing, you take no decisive actions to restore the balance and the natural order of things.

Your citizens have no rights within your borders and are nothing more than modern day slaves without the physical chains to show it, your villages are poverty and your cities are mausoleums, there is no perfume in this world to overpower the strong stench of death and decay that hangs over your lands. You never bothered to build back up the walls of your cities so outsiders and passersby still cross into your territory and your lands to steal what is meant for your children yet you do nothing, you sit down, eat your seeds and do nothing, do you want to die? If you have lost your taste should you not just be tossed out into the streets like bad salt so that men may trample on you and you perish once and for all? But I know our God is gracious, God is full of mercies and will spare you even if He finds one righteous within your walls but you have not done anything worthwhile to help your position or to plead your case. You have blatantly refused to take proper medication for the sickness that is eating you from the inside. I ask again, do you want to die? Should you be allowed to die like that? Violence has a place in this world for if it did not then the nations of this world would have no need for their military but yours sadly is a nation of cowards.

Everything about you is out of course; you corrupt the laws of man and have defiled everything held sacred, perversion thrives within you so you have become a land of opposites where good is bad and bad becomes good. Your charges read like a phone book and I think everyone is just about ready to hear the verdict so we can wrap this bitter case up.

All that said it is time for my verdict as judge, as the prosecution I have extensively laid out my charges against mother Nigeria and given you, the jury, enough evidence to back them up... ponder on these things for a little, let them ruminate. I am still standing on the same pile of bones as from the beginning so I pull out a long piece from the pile, could be a femur or a tibia by the looks of it but I'm not sure neither do I have the time to verify *quickly glances at watch*, we have serious business to take care of here so I pick it up because as the judge I need a hammer, then I use the skull of one poor dead fellow as makeshift gavel, sorry about this poor fellow, this will not take long and you're playing your part in this historic case. I beat on the skull furiously with the make shift hammer as I spit out my verdict with no apologies on my part but with resigned sureness to all of you: By my own authority as a Nigerian and as a man standing on my two feet, aided by the forebears who have gone ahead, I pronounce it that based on what I have observed about the past and what I see happening today in the country, it is certain that No Nigerian will make Heaven! Yes... NO NIGERIAN WILL MAKE HEAVEN!!! *throws down the hammer* court rise!!!

But then in my heart I know that I am not God because only God has the power and the authority to pass a judgement of that magnitude on anybody let alone a whole nation. As a Christian I have my personal salvation race to run to make heaven, how much more determining where the next man would end when his time here is done? But then we have to think figuratively if not literally, it's no secret at this point that Nigeria has been made a living hell for her people, a place where their souls are tormented night and day and where they are buffeted on every side by many ills so when you think

about it you can see that in this living hell that she is now the people who are living in it and those that will be born into it, unless they are changed cannot create a heaven for themselves. That heaven is not the heaven which is a location in the spirit realm but a heaven on earth which is to have a working country where the rights of her citizens are respected and they can work, provide for themselves and their families, be rewarded for their hard work and to live out their days in relative peace, joy and harmony without poverty. So when you think of it like that you can see that the verdict still stands when I say that no Nigerian will make heaven because they cannot yet make Nigeria a heaven and a haven for themselves! And if you're a Nigerian and have been able to escape to other havens prepared by the hard work of other people I applaud your efforts, and while I understand perfectly your motives I would just tell you that what you see in those countries is proof that it can be done back home and no matter how far you run or how long you run away your home is waiting for you.

But weep not! This does not have to be the end for all Nigerians, there is usually a chance at redemption in such cases of condemnation. For the heavens in the spirit realm Jesus Christ presents the way back to redemption and re-connection to the Source where all we have to do is to believe in Him and confess our beliefs to receive the Holy Spirit in us. While for the heaven of the new Nigeria the road to redemption is not a mapped out road per se, rather it's a thinking, enlightened and well-structured society made of the different tribes properly united together with common interests and are capable of making the best possible choices for the group and following it up with actions according to the conditions of the particular time. And so, with all that said let me just take the time to thank you so very much for following me into the rabbit hole and taking this journey with me, I hope you had some good take outs from all this, erm... my name is Peter Aghogho Omuvwie, it was nice for me but I have to go now so I guess I'll see you when I see you then eh? Bye *smiles*.

ALTAR CALL

However you look at it, life at the end of the day is spiritual. It is fashionable in these modern times to insult religions and the religious but whatever your thoughts on organised religion let me just say that no one has ever called for a stop to air travel because of plane crashes that claim many lives and bring so much grief. The world moves along the path of its agenda but through it all the voice of the Spirit continues to call out to men and women, and tug at the heart strings. If you heed His call and want to make Jesus Christ the Lord of your life today then all you need do is say this simple prayer with me:

'O Lord God, I believe with all my heart in Jesus Christ, Son of the living God. I believe He died for me and God raised Him from the dead. I believe He's alive today. I confess with my mouth that Jesus Christ is the Lord of my life from this day. Through Him and in His name, I have eternal life; I'm born again. Thank you Lord, for saving my soul! I'm now a child of God. Hallelujah!'

Congratulations! You're now a child of God. To grow as a Christian you have to find a bible believing church close to you and start attending regularly to fellowship with other believers and experience the fullness of your new reality. Jesus is Lord!

www.ingramcontent.com/pod-product-compliance
Lightning Source LLC
Chambersburg PA
CBHW070456120526
44590CB00013B/665